Due Process in Special Education:

On Going to a Hearing

Milton Budoff
and
Alan Orenstein

and
Carol Kervick

THE WARE PRESS

CAMBRIDGE, MASS.

Library of Congress Cataloging in Publication Data

Budoff, Milton, 1929–
    Due process in special education.

    Bibliography: p.
    1. Handicapped children—Education—Law and legisla-
tion—United States.   2. Administrative procedure—
United States.   I. Orenstein, Alan.   II. Kervick, Carol.
III. Title.
KF4210.B83   1982   344.73'0791   82-21930
ISBN 0-938552-51-1   347.304791

Printed in the United States of America at Braun-Brumfield, Inc.

The Ware Press, Inc.
28 Hurlbut Street
Cambridge, Mass. 02138

Dedication

To Sam and Nathan—who make it all worthwhile.

To the memory of Mrs. Ceil Orenstein.

Acknowledgements

This work would not have been possible without the support of Grant #GOO7502322 from the Field Initiated Studies Branch, Division of Innovation and Development, Office of Special Education Programs, Department of Education. The opinions expressed in this work are those of the authors, not the federal government. The major staff who worked on this project: Sibyl Mitchell, Lydia Sinclair, Sue Litzinger and Sharon Weissboch. Robert Audette and Carol Kervick of the Massachusetts Department of Special Education, encouraged and supported our efforts. Most especially to Rachel Kranz, whose editorial efforts went far to increasing the readability of this volume.

Most of all, we must thank our informants—parents, hearing officers, mediators, and school administrators who shared their honest concerns about the system.

Table of Contents

Section V. Evaluating the Due Process Reform.

Section I.

An Introduction to
Due Process

1

Introduction:
The Significance of
Due Process Reform

One of the most significant changes accomplished by the quiet revolution in special education is the application of due process safeguards to procedures of identifying and programming for special needs children. These safeguards legitimate for the first time in American educational history parents' right to be fully involved in determining their child's educational program.

Due process in special education began in the 1960's, when parents' approval of proposed programs for academically backward poor children was made a precondition of federal funding. Under Title I, schools had to organize parent advisory councils, which were required to agree in writing to the programs proposed for their children before federal funds could be received.

In the 1970's, Massachusetts' Chapter 766 and the federal act, P.L. 94-142 involved parents directly in the education of their handicapped child. These laws require parents' informed consent in writing at the time their child is referred for special assistance, before any tests or other evaluations can be administered. Parents must be included in the evaluation as a primary data source; they must be included in the development of their child's educational plan; and they must accept the plan, in writing, before it can be implemented. If parents judge the educational plan to be unacceptable, they can contest it, first before an impartial hearing examiner and, ultimately, in a court. The parents' position is thus radically different from what it was before the reform.

3

Special Education Before the Reform

Traditionally, "slow" children had been somehow identified, usually by teachers, as possibly mentally retarded. Once referred, they were given an "IQ" test, and if their scores were below some arbitrary cutoff, they were placed in a special class for the mentally retarded, usually without the parents' knowledge. While the placement was ostensibly to address academic backwardness, the children referred were likely to be serious behavior management problems for the teacher.

The emotionally disturbed child also got short shrift. Before the 1960's, classes for such children were rare, and the criteria for that type of eligibility were much looser than for the retarded. Those determinations were therefore usually based largely on the opinions of school personnel or consultants, without formal testing. Emotionally disturbed children were often placed in the same classes with retarded children, though their IQs might be much higher.

Parents of either type of child would frequently not discover any change in their child's educational placement unless they visited the school and saw the child in class. Often, when told, they naively thought the special class would provide their child with all the extra help s/he required. Then they watched their child's response to school deteriorate as s/he came home unhappy, was unwilling to go to school each day, and told of being called "dummy." Mostly, the child seemed not to be improving. The children assigned to the "dummy" special classes became the targets of verbal abuse and prejudice expressed by peers and the school staff. Once placed, they were often not re-evaluated for many years because the myth of the IQ decreed, erroneously, that an intelligence test measured a constant and thus the score would not change. This soon became a self-fulfilling prophecy: once children were assumed to be "dumb" they were undereducated in the special classes and were rarely able to return to the regular grades. These children's considerable unhappiness and their lack of improvement in academic skills became abundantly clear to parents, who gradually began to fight for reform.

Abuses were particularly striking in the case of poor, minority, or non-English-speaking children presumed to be mildly mentally retarded. Research has shown that these children operate differently in problem solving than the school expects. Cultural and language difficulties may depress these children's IQ scores and academic performances, yet they do manage successfully outside school in their communities. These children are not mentally retarded, though they are often seriously academically backward. Traditionally, they were disproportionately placed in segregated classrooms for the retarded.

The plight of these children was dramatized by court decisions which recognized the cultural bias in IQ tests and acknowledged the need for testing and instruction in the language of the child's home. The evils associated with the disproportionate placement of children from these backgrounds into segregated classes for the mentally retarded became a major force propelling special education reform. This disproportionate classification continues to be of concern to state departments of education, the federal government, advocacy groups, and professionals concerned with school psychology.

Many other public school practices, which had been seen by professionals as routine, also came to be viewed by parents as ultimately detrimental to their children's education. These outmoded practices affected not only the poor but also handicapped children from more privileged strata. Once handicapped children's programs had been identified as a legitimate target for change, these affluent parents joined the protests of the poor, accelerating the pace of reform. For example, a long-standing practice excluded from school all children below the age of seven who were not toilet trained. In addition, many states held that mentally retarded children below age 7 did not have to be admitted to school, regardless of their toilet training. Yet early intervention for these children was coming to be seen as critical to their later ability to learn. Similarly, there was little or no understanding of what has come to be the burgeoning field of learning disabilities, addressing the needs of children with idiosyncratic problems in learning, for whom public school-based programming was meager, at best. In fact, most of the disputes reported in this study concern the lack of appropriate public school programming for bright children who were nonetheless having trouble in the regular classroom.

The most difficult group of children, and one of major concern to special education reformers, consisted of children whose multiple handicaps required varied, complex, expensive, and often interdisciplinary programs. Such children had often been routinely excluded from public education and presumed to be the province of another agency, for example, the state mental health or anti-delinquency agency. When they were placed in public school programs, these tended to be custodial, with a very narrow range of supporting services. These children fell between the cracks of the splintered human services system, and even after the reform of the 1970's, they posed difficult problems because of the inability of human service agencies to work together.

Even children who did receive services before the reform often did not receive them in a coordinated way. For example, physically handicapped children requiring physical or occupational therapy could not get it in school during school hours but had to go to a clinic—always assuming their parents knew enough to request such a service. Under the reform, schools had to give parents a comprehensive assessment of the child's needs, and either deliver the required services themselves or assure their delivery by others.

The Movement for Reform

The struggle for equal rights for handicapped children in Massachusetts began during the 1960's as part of a general struggle for equality by low-income and minority persons. With the war on poverty, and the concomitant concern with human rights, the needs and rights of handicapped persons became a new source of concern. Parents became emboldened to seek more appropriate services for their special needs children when local, state, and national advocacy organizations publicly criticized school and human services practices. Parents who had once wholly trusted the school professional's judgment came to realize that schools had difficulty programming for children who required services beyond those provided to regular students.

Middle- and upper-income parents were concerned when their bright child was not learning to read and was unhappy in school, or when no services were available to their seriously handicapped child who was therefore excluded from school. These parents joined with those agitating for services for poor and minority children, pushing for a more responsive system of special education. In many cases, intervening for their child forced parents to become better informed about their child's needs and consequently still more frustrated when school professionals refused to recognize increased parental understanding. Radicalized by their experiences, these parents sought remedies through court suits, exposes, and legislation.

In Massachusetts, change came in the form of a 1972 law called Chapter 766, which prescribed an omnibus reform of the philosophy, structure, and practice of special education services. The law calls for comprehensive evaluation of the special needs of the child; individualized and educationally effective programming; frequent re-evaluations; strong parental involvement; an explicit due process system by which parents can appeal decisions; and advisory commissions of parents and professionals to monitor activity in each school district. All children between the ages of three and twenty-one, regardless of degree of handicap, are entitled to an adequate educational program in a setting that is appropriate to their particular needs.

The main philosophical underpinning of this law is "mainstreaming," also known as placing the handicapped child in the "least restrictive" setting. This has been interpreted to mean that the handicapped child should be placed in regular classrooms whenever possible. Segregated classrooms must have space and instructional materials equivalent to regular classrooms; moreover, educational facilities and opportunities in separate institutions for special needs children must be as similar as possible to those offered in regular schools.

Chapter 766 specifically abjures the use of categorical labels that stigmatize children. In the past, such labels were all the diagnostic process yielded. The new regulations require that a multi-discipline *Child Evaluation Team* assess each child's special needs and then prepare an appropriate *Individual Educational Plan* with long-term goals. These goals must be in the form of specific, measurable objectives stated in behavioral terms, so attainment can be evaluated by both professionals and parents. Along with instructional services, such as tutoring in reading, a plan may include physical or occupational therapy for the child or psychotherapy for the child or family. Ideally, children are not labeled, only provided with program options.

With the emphasis on labeling removed, Chapter 766 opened the way for a dramatic expansion of eligibility for special services. The law takes the radical step of considering all children to be in actual or potential educational risk. For example, if a child is in danger at midyear of not being promoted, or indeed fails, s/he can be referred for services. In effect, any child who is not progressing at an adequate pace in regular programming is considered to be eligible for a special education evaluation.

Chapter 766 also prescribes an active role for parents. Parents must consent to the initial decision to evaluate their child, they contribute data for the evaluation, and they participate in the conference to draw up the individual educational plan. If they do not agree with the plan, they must be given a prompt hearing, followed, if necessary, by an appeal at the state administrative level or in a court of law. Once it has been agreed upon, the plan must be monitored. If the evaluation team decides a child cannot yet be mainstreamed, it must specify to the parents what the child must attain before s/he can enter a regular classroom. The school must give parents quarterly reports on the child and annual reviews of the plan. Finally, parents advise on policy formulation, since they hold half the seats on the regional and state advisory councils.

As significant as these new procedures are, the single most important principle established by the law is that the local school district is responsible for the education of all handicapped children of community residents, regardless of the degree of handicap. Districts are required to seek out all children aged three to twenty-one, evaluate their special needs, and provide suitable and educationally effective programs for them. The same legal responsibility covers the education, care, and treatment of all institutionalized children from a community. Prior to Chapter 766, the more severe and complex the child's handicap, the more likely it was that parents would be shunted from agency to agency with a high likelihood the child would not receive services. Parents now have the legal right to demand that schools arrange an appropriate and coordinated program of services for their children. Further, in a virtual revolution for human services delivery, schools were given the responsibility of assuring the delivery of all appropriate programs to each special needs child. Schools had not only to provide education, but also to coordinate the provision of other health and social services from the relevant state agencies, although there has been little attempt to meet this requirement in practice beyond a few arrangements with state agencies to share the costs of some children.

In its initial period, the reform in special education led parents to expect that for the first time they could participate as full partners in planning programs for their child. Their ability to appeal a school's decision via the hearing system insured this participatory right. Because the hearing system gave them the legal mechanism to contest the program proposed by school personnel, parents thought this right to appeal would give them the power to counter the schools if they were dissatisfied with their child's program.

But there were early indications that the hearing system was not functioning as intended. Using information drawn from the first two and one-half years of the new law in Massachusetts as its data base, this report will document the difficulties inherent in structuring a formal administrative hearing system, and the consequences—many of them unanticipated—of special education's rather naive plunge into legal proceedings.

The Reform in Massachusetts

Chapter 766 was passed in the Massachusetts legislature with the active lobbying of a large consumer and parent advocacy constituency, which received support from state legislators and the governor. Budoff (1975) describes the events in the state which led to its passage.

This citizen involvement created high parental expectations that the schools would expand the diversity and quality of their services. Despite these expectations, which were expressed quite concretely by the steadily increasing number of parents referring their children for evaluation, the schools made few preparations during the period between passage of the legislation in July, 1972 and its effective date two years later. Although preliminary drafts of the regulations to implement the law were widely available by October, 1973, many schools postponed taking any action until the regulations were officially adopted in June, 1974, just as schools were closing for the summer and their staffs going on vacation.

Thus it should not have been surprising that parent requests for evaluations of their child during the spring, summer and fall of 1974 did not elicit the expected response from the schools until well into the 1974-75 school year. This lack of response tended to confirm the worst fears of the parents requesting educational plans, who had often had prior negative experiences with their schools. These parents had eagerly awaited the new, more appropriate programs which they thought the new legislation would provide.

But the schools clearly did not know how to respond to the new legislation. They had particular difficulty dealing with parents' expectations of a prompt and timely response, with informed parental consent, and with allowing parents to participate in the educational planning process. A school's initial response to requests for an evaluation was often seriously delayed. A child's assessment might not be offered for several months, yet when the educational plans finally were developed, they tended to restrict parental participation to only minimal or token involvement and failed to specify sufficiently educational goals for the child and the services the school proposed. Parents felt the schools were offering them the same old services which had already failed to prove effective in earlier years. They quickly became bitter, but still hoped that a hearing might rectify the situation. Many parents went so far as to register their child in a local private special needs school when the public schools did not respond to their request for an evaluation. At the same time, they initiated hearings to request reimbursement for private school costs, claiming that the removal of their child from public school had been necessitated by the school's failure to act in a timely manner.

This cycle of expectation and disillusionment resulted in a huge number of educational plan rejections, with subsequent appeals by parents. During the first year of implementation of Chapter 766, 160 appeals were filed; in the second year, 522; and in the third year, 688 cases were put on the books, for a three-year total of nearly 1,500 cases (*Appeal News*, 1977). This total probably exceeds the number of appeals in the other 49 states combined following adoption of the federal statute, P.L. 94-142, which had similar provisions, and this rate of appeal has continued in subsequent years. Clearly, Massachusetts has been a crucial arena for use of the special education appeals provisions.

Evaluating the Due Process Reform

We have used Massachusetts as the laboratory in which to study the operation of the special education appeals system, looking at the hearings system during the first two and one-half years of its operation. This report focuses on two themes: the formal structure of a state-managed hearing system, and the experiences of the parents, school personnel, and hearing officers involved in these proceedings.

This is the first comprehensive study of the effects of applying due process safeguards to special education. The special education reform assumed that procedural fairness would lead to substantive fairness—that a fair procedure by which parents could appeal school decisions would ultimately insure the fair treatment of handicapped students by the schools. Thus we begin with a brief look at the legal basis of these procedural safeguards and how they came to be applied to special education. The rest of the book examines the extent to which these safeguards in fact achieved their intended goal: the protection of handicapped students' rights to free and appropriate public education.

One way to measure the success of the reform is to examine the experiences of the parents who used the hearing system. Did this system resolve their disputes with the schools to their satisfaction? We report in considerable detail on the disagreements which initially led parents to reject their educational plan, on the hearings which resulted, and on the subsequent events over the next four years. We have based our reports on three interviews: one within weeks of the parents' hearing; a second about 20 months later; and a third about 42 months after the initial hearing. Our main concern was to understand whether the hearing in fact resolved the disagreements between parents and schools over appropriate programming for the special needs child. Our conclusion, as this book abundantly documents, is that it did not. This failure has been a source of continuing dismay to all who are concerned with special education in the public schools.

An Overview of This Book

The first section of this book introduces the legal background of parents' rights (Chapter 2), and details the process of referral, evaluation, and appeal in Massachusetts during the study period (Chapter 3). The second section presents parents' experiences, beginning with characteristics of the parents and their handicapped children, and the concerns being contested (Chapter 4). Succeeding chapters recount parent encounters with school personnel in the course of developing their child's educational plan. We focus first on the issues which precipitated the plan's rejection (Chapter 5), then follow parents through their hearings (Chapter 6), and through the two-year period afterward (Chapter 7). Finally, we return for a follow-up four years after the hearing, and describe the subsequent educational careers of children involved in the most frequent type of appeals dispute, placement in private school (Chapter 8).

We have presented parent experiences in great anecdotal detail to help the reader see the sources of conflict between parents and schools. To understand why so many parents feel that the hearing system failed, we must first see what parents sought for their child, how school staff reacted, how they might have reacted, and what disagreements triggered the conflict. Thus we often present long excerpts from the interviews, trying to confront the reader not merely with the "objective" facts of these disputes, but with some of their subtleties, particularly with the anguish and frustration of parents who have become disillusioned by the promises of special education reform. At a time when parents are being encouraged to become involved in their child's educational program and to assert their rights on behalf of their handicapped child, we must become more sensitively attuned to the factors that can either engender or destroy a collegial relationship between parents and school personnel. Presumably, the more the home is able to support the school's efforts, the better for the handicapped child.

To understand parent concerns about public school programming for the learning-disabled, who have traditionally been the least well served by public schools, we present parents' comparisons of public programming with the services they found in a select group of private special needs schools. This comparison suggests some of the important changes which public schools must make if they are to retain the trust of parents increasingly well educated about learning-disabled programming. (Chapter 9).

The much briefer interviews with school personnel discussed in Section III were originally intended to elicit information on particular cases. However, half of the administrators involved in these specific cases were no longer working in the same school district within one year following the hearing. We were astounded by the extremely high turnover among these administrators. The interviews we did hold indicated a wide range of opinions, from those who supported the appeals process as the legitimate expression of parents' rights, to those who felt the schools were being "ripped off" by sick or greedy parents. The one thing on which everyone could agree was that rejection of an educational plan and consequent attendance at a hearing is traumatic, confusing, and demoralizing to school personnel. Like many parents, school staff initially expected hearings to be a kind of working group convened to resolve differences. Instead, the hearings turned out to be bitter adversarial legal battles which caused serious morale problems among school staff and required significant expenses in the form of preparation time and legal fees. School personnel unanimously saw hearings as proceedings to avoid. If they could not avoid them, administrators became increasingly concerned with beating "unreasonable" parents.

Both our attendance at hearings and our subsequent interviews made it strikingly evident to us how traumatic the hearing had been for parents and school personnel alike, but we feel parents are in a particularly difficult position. Assertion of one's rights can be a painful experience. It is hard to feel comfortable in the adversarial setting of the administrative appeals hearing. Parents who dared to contest the school's plan found the psychic and economic costs to be high, often far higher than they could have anticipated. This report testifies to the parents' bravery, even when they had considerable help from attorneys and independent professionals.

Section IV describes the conduct and content of hearings and hearing officers' views of how they should be conducted. Chapter 12 focuses on the nature of an administrative hearing, including both Massachusetts' rules for hearings and a discussion of the problems which those rules present.

We also asked hearing officers for their views on the nature and purposes of hearings, their conception of their role, and their suggestions for improving the hearing process. Chapter 13 reveals that though these officers had worked closely together as a full-time state-employed cadre, they held widely varying opinions about hearings and the appropriate procedures for conducting them, a range of views quite different from those of parents and administrators. Chapter 14 presents our analysis of the decisions written during the first two and one-half years of the hearing system, both to expose some of the procedure's shortcomings and to propose a model for writing decisions.

The last section of this book summarizes the findings of the study and proposes areas for further action and investigation. Our final chapters present strategies schools might employ to minimize disputes (Chapter 16), as well as strategies by which parents might minimize their disputes, and offer tips on preparing for their hearing (Chapter 17). We are particularly concerned with developing procedures to flag potentially difficult cases early, before the dispute can escalate. The final chapter and an epilogue indicates how the special education appeals system has developed during the past three years in Massachusetts.

The Need for Change

Parent-school communication.

The dissatisfaction of both parents and school personnel reported in this study suggests that profound changes in the appeals system are needed. The predominant impression we retained at the conclusion of our work was of the extreme difficulty professionals have in establishing responsive and respectful communications with parents. This is not to absolve all parents, some of whom pursue agendas of their own, often not to the benefit of their handicapped child. An abundant literature describes the difficulties parents have in accepting and cultivating their handicapped child's potential for learning and personal growth. For precisely this reason, it should come as no shock to teachers and school assessment personnel that some parents have serious difficulties in learning to live with their child's handicap. Yet these insights are not usually incorporated into the working style of public school professionals who deal with parents.

As professionals, we have come to develop a conflicted relationship with parents. On the one hand, we resent their intrusiveness, their inquisitiveness, and their assertive concern to ensure their child's progress. We would like them to remember to "keep their place" and be properly respectful of our professional knowledge. We forget that these parents must live with their child every day and every night and must deal with their own reactions to having a handicapped child. On the other hand, we want them to become more involved, and we decry their detachment. But we want their involvement only in situations that we, as professionals, can control.

The seeds of many disputes are found in this failure of school-based professionals to honor parents as partners, while still trying to help them cope with the sometimes terrible shock of discovery or confirmation of their child's handicap. It is a difficult line to pursue without falling into the "power trip" that human service professionals so easily adopt. Most parents told us that they tried to communicate with the school staff but were prevented by what they variously described as lies, evasions, or inconsistencies. When their concern about their child's lack of progress was rebutted with vague inaccuracies ("Johnny *is* making progress"), or with accusations that the child's continuing difficulties were due to "home" or "family" problems, parents became justifiably upset. This type of interaction also reduced the credibility of the educational plan offered to parents, reducing their confidence in the future efforts of school staff. For many parents, it was these alienating contacts with school staff (usually other than the child's special education teachers) which led them to an appeal.

The school-based clinician must navigate within a complex set of roles. Some school staff are now so wholly focused on parents' rights and their possible resort to appeal that they feel intimidated. We also know that many parents do have personal difficulties in understanding and accepting their child. School-based clinicians seem to have considerable difficulty in combining a vision of "parent as advocate for the child" with "parent needing to be helped to deal with the child's difficulties." The building of partnerships on behalf of the handicapped child, which was the original rationale for the legislation granting parents' rights, has been impeded by this confusion in the schools' perceptions of parents.

Poor school-parent communication was not simply due to staff's bad attitudes, however. In some cases, a single staff member was charged with arranging and conducting the evaluations, running the evaluation meetings, writing the educational plan, and negotiating with parents. Often this staff member had little support in the system if the parent contested the proposed plan. On occasion, these isolated staff members were unaware of special services appropriate for the child in the same system. In other cases, evaluations were conducted by a central evaluation team so overwhelmed by a backlog that they did not have the time to develop working relationships with the staff closest to the parents, let alone with the parents themselves. The defensive reactions of staff may be best explained by their sense of being exposed and in a fragile situation because of the organizational arrangements within which they worked.

In any case, good school-parent communication is not enough. As the following chapters will amply document, the "bottom line" for special needs parents is their child's continued improvement. Parents in Massachusetts told us and tell each other that their child makes considerable progress academically and in developing a more positive self-image in certain private schools. Even when the public school has tried its best to offer programming and to maintain a positive dialogue with parents, parents may come to feel their child can progress more quickly outside the public schools. While responsive and respectful parent-school communication will minimize appeals, an overriding critical factor for parents has been their sense that the different style of special education programming offered by certain private schools is more effective than the public school programs. Not only do private schools offer an easily visible alternative for disgruntled parents, but also many private schools actually encouraged parents to use the hearing system, hoping to pressure public schools into offering better programs. Parents' growing disillusionment with public special needs programs must be addressed by public school personnel. Some suggestions for what this might involve may be found in the last section.

Procedural versus substantive fairness.

This book is concerned with the conditions that assure procedural fairness— that is, insuring that the families of handicapped children have a fair and effective means of obtaining appropriate public education for their child. We have briefly outlined the legal history of this concept in Chapter 2 because this is the context in which the idea of "fairness" must be considered. But fairness is not just a matter of the letter of the law. We are concerned with the social as well as the legal obstacles to procedural fairness, with the practice as well as the theory of families exercising their rights to an individualized program appropriate to their handicapped child. Thus, in succeeding chapters we will consider not only the legal requirements of the hearing system, but what actually happens at a hearing and the actual consequences of participating in the hearings system. Our focus will be on the social, political, and personal factors which shaped those events.

Significantly, schools have often seen the very existence of procedural safeguards as an indication of bias against them. We contend that the safeguards are necessary precisely because of schools' long-standing difficulty in allowing parents to help determine the programs appropriate to their child. Parents often find themselves at odds with educational and human service bureaucracies for which political and fiscal constraints are more pressing than the needs of the clientele they were created to serve. These conflicts are at the heart of the disputes which hearings were designed to address and with which the succeeding chapters of this book are concerned.

At the time of this study, hearings were the primary formal expression of parents' rejection of their child's educational plan. However, administrative hearings may be the worst possible way to resolve special education disputes since by definition they are adversarial proceedings: one party must "win" and the other "lose." Both parents and schools have deplored the adversarial posture they must adopt, which can have only a negative influence on the long-term relationships among parents, children, and schools. An adversarial posture is particularly destructive in educational matters, since there is only one school system. Thus, after the conclusion of a bitter hearing, parents and schools must return to working together. After such a pitched battle, it is understandably difficult for parents to trust the school system to meet properly the needs of the child, or for schools to respect the requests of the parent. Later parent-school communication becomes exceedingly difficult, as the chapters in Section II indicate.

The primary concern of this book, then, is not with explaining the niceties of the legal rights accorded to parents. Rather, we want to identify procedures to assure that due process safeguards in fact enable parents and school personnel to develop collegial, sharing, mutually supportive relationships on behalf of the handicapped child. Little systematic attention has been paid to the question of fair treatment in education, which, for the most part, has been addressed by advocacy groups lacking adequate empirical data. The question of how to insure that ascribed legal rights are addressed by the relevant institutions has attracted substantial social-science interest in some areas, such as desegregation, but not in the case of handicapped children and the public schools.

Who Can Use This Book?

This volume is for the variety of audiences who want to understand the practical implications of parents' rights in special education. We hope to aid parents trying to obtain programming for their child, school staff faced with a traumatic hearing, policymakers and administrators who run the system, and lawyers and advocates whose clients are preparing appeals.

Parents unfamiliar with their rights, for example, may want to look at Chapter 3, a step-by-step outline of the evaluation and referral process. Anyone attending a hearing for the first time will be interested in Chapter 12, a detailed description of what happens at a hearing, what kinds of evidence are accepted, and the rules by which the proceeding is conducted. Those who must prepare a case should examine Chapter 13, in which hearing officers discuss the basis for their decisions, and Chapter 14, in which we analyze the content and structure of decisions written during the first two and one-half years of the hearing system. Finally, parents may gain insight into the attitudes of the schools they oppose by looking at Section III on the schools' role.

First and foremost, however, we hope this book will help school staff understand the position of the parents they must deal with every day. In the end, they are the ones who must convince parents that the schools are trying to help them and their child to cope more effectively. We believe this increased understanding by school staff will lead to a true partnership between schools and parents, which will ultimately support the teachers' efforts to help special needs children. Such a sense of mutual support will surely minimize the occurrence of appeals disputes. Anecdotal evidence supports this thesis, and further documentation of it would be a valuable contribution, since it might convince school personnel of the benefits of better communication with parents. This sense of alliance is critical to assuring the ultimate success of the special education reform.

2

A Brief Legal Joust with Due Process

The Meaning of Due Process

The constitutional concept of due process is the legal basis for the special education reform considered in this book. The procedures laid out in the hearing system are derived from traditional due process safeguards. The theory behind including them in Chapter 766 was that *procedural* safeguards would achieve a *substantive* result—that is, a fair hearing procedure for handicapped students would actually insure them access to public education.

In this chapter we will consider the legal definition of due process to understand better the context in which the hearing system was designed. We will then see how the concept of due process came to be applied to special education, a history which reflects the growing activism of advocates for children with special needs.

The Due Process Clause of the United States Constitution provides that "no state shall . . . deprive any person of life, liberty, or property, without due process of law." The clause has been taken to mean that "fair" procedures must be followed before a state can deny certain "important" interests of individuals.[1] The Supreme Court has indicated the kinds of interests it considers important enough to invoke due process protections and has specified the nature of these protections in various circumstances.

Although some specific procedures have come to be associated with due process, the concept itself does not have a fixed meaning. The right to due process is based on a normative, philosophical idea—an individual's right to fair procedures. The concept's practical application therefore demands that it be flexible enough to adapt to each new situation where fair procedures are required. The idea of what constitutes a "fair" procedure must be applicable to such diverse threats to an individual's interest as a criminal or juvenile accusation, discharge from government employment, suspension from public school, revocation of a motor vehicle license, denial of a welfare benefit, attachment of property, or some other loss of an important interest defined by the Supreme Court as within the meaning of "life, liberty, or property."

The Components of Due Process

All applications of due process share three common elements. The first is that the state is taking an action against an individual or class of individuals; the second is that the action of the state threatens to deny an individual's interest in "life, liberty, or property"; and the third is that the individual is disputing with the state over the validity of that threatened denial.

Under procedural due process, the application of safeguards is not intended to *prevent* the denial of individual interests by the state. It only limits the way in which such an action may be taken. If the state wishes to threaten an individual's rights, it may do so, but only on the basis of rational criteria applied in a rational manner to proven facts. The facts must be proven through a process which guarantees that the individual whose interests are threatened has a reasonable opportunity to challenge adverse evidence and to argue that the interest involved should not be denied.

A number of safeguards have come to be associated with procedural due process: the right to notice that one's interests are threatened with denial; the opportunity for a hearing on that action; the chance to be represented by counsel at that hearing, to present evidence, to call witnesses, and to cross-examine opposing witnesses; the right to an impartial decision maker; and the right to a specific decision based upon the application of known criteria to the facts which have been proven.

The basic principle of due process safeguards is written in the Constitution. But the specific rights protected by due process have been defined over time by court rulings and legislation. In the matter of special education, due process safeguards were applied as a result of earlier court rulings in children's and students' rights cases.

Due Process in the Supreme Court

The most extensive judicial attention to the concept of due process safeguards has been in the area of criminal law, because individuals charged with crimes are threatened with the loss of their most basic, personal rights—"life" and "liberty." In its rulings on criminal law, the Supreme Court has specified a number of procedural protections which must be accorded to criminal defendants, including notices of Constitutional rights at various stages of the proceedings, access to counsel, and a transcript of the proceedings for purposes of appeal.

Logically enough, then, the first time due process protections were specifically extended to children was in the field of criminal law. In the landmark case of *In re Gault*, the Court required that some of the procedural protections guaranteed to adult criminal defendants by the Due Process Clause must also be provided to children and youth charged with juvenile offenses.

Equally important precursors of the application of due process to special education were the Supreme Court decisions applying other Constitutional protections to public school students. *West Virginia State Board of Education v. Barnette* declared that the Freedom of Speech Clause of the First Amendment applies to public school students in the schoolhouse. In *Tinker v. Des Moines Independent School District* the Court affirmed its earlier holding in *Barnette* and gave wider scope to Barnette's First Amendment protection. In *Brown v. Board of Education* the Court applied the Equal Protection Clause of the Fourteenth Amendment to students in racially segregated public schools. The Court was beginning to hold that public school students were entitled not only to procedural protections, such as the right to certain safeguards at a trial, but also to substantive protection—laws which would actually guarantee their Constitutional rights in the public school classroom.

In *Goss v. Lopez*, the Court took the first step in specifying that public school students had the right to due process procedures in situations where their right to attend school might be denied. *Goss v. Lopez* specifically concerned only short-term disciplinary suspensions: the Court ruled that students facing suspensions of less than 10 days had the right to oral notice of the reasons for the suspension and the right to respond to the charges informally. The Court specifically reserved decision on whether more formal or extensive procedures would be required for longer suspensions. In effect, the Court was saying that the denial of a student's right to attend school was of sufficient gravity to require due process safeguards.

Goss v. Lopez set a precedent for limiting the state's authority to keep children out of school—in this case for disciplinary reasons. The Supreme Court has not yet ruled on how these safeguards might apply to a student's threatened exclusion from school on other grounds, such as "mental, physical or emotional handicap." However, this issue has been addressed by several lower federal courts.

The Lower Courts and Special Education

The landmark cases for applying due process safeguards specifically to special education are the consent decrees in *Pennsylvania Association of Retarded Children* v. *Commonwealth of Pennsylvania (PARC)* and *Mills* v. *District of Columbia Board of Education.*

The *PARC* case was a class action brought on behalf of those mentally retarded children in Pennsylvania excluded from public school because Pennsylvania school officials had deemed them "uneducable and untrainable." The *Mills* case was brought on behalf of seven handicapped children who alleged that the Washington, D.C. School Board was excluding them from public school and/or denying them a publicly supported education. In both cases, the plaintiffs claimed a denial of rights guaranteed by the Due Process and Equal Protection Clauses of the Fourteenth Amendment. In both cases, the school systems conceded the issues, and the federal courts approved agreements ("consent decrees") specifying elaborate procedural protections to govern the placement of these children into special education programs. With minor differences, the courts required the following procedural protections to be offered to parents and children before the placement or denial of placement into educational programs:

(1) notice of the proposed action;
(2) the right to a hearing before final action;
(3) the right to counsel at that hearing;
(4) the right to present evidence;
(5) the right to full access to relevant school records;
(6) the right to compel attendance of, confront, and cross-examine officials or employees who might have evidence on the basis for the proposed action;
(7) the right to an independent evaluation;
(8) the right to have the hearing open or closed to the public at the option of the parent;
(9) the right to an "impartial hearing officer."

In addition, the decrees required that the hearings be held at a place and time convenient to the parents; that the hearing be recorded, transcribed, and made available to the parents upon request; and that the decision of the hearing officer contain specific findings of fact and conclusions of law.

Congressional Action

The consent decrees in *PARC* and *Mills* gradually began to be recognized in other states through federal court decisions or through changes in state legislation. But the greatest impetus for the application of due process safeguards to special education came through the action of Congress. The final legal guarantee of due process came when the "Education of All Handicapped Children Act," P.L. 94-142, was signed into law in 1974, applying the major procedural safeguards of *Mills* and *PARC* to all states seeking federal funds under the act. This law holds that each state seeking such funds must submit to the United States Commissioner of Education a state plan containing "procedures for insuring that handicapped children and their parents or guardians are guaranteed procedural safeguards in decisions regarding identification, evaluation, and educational placement of handicapped children." These procedures must include many of the provisions specified in *PARC* and *Mills*, including provisions for:

(1) notice to parents or guardians of a change in the educational placement of the child;
(2) the right to an "impartial due process hearing";
(3) the right to access to all relevant school records;
(4) the right to an independent evaluation at the school's expense.

In addition, the act requires that parents be given the right to appeal to the state educational agency, if the initial due process hearing has been conducted by the school district rather than the state. The act also specifies the format of the due process hearing. Any party to the hearing shall be accorded:

(1) the right to be accompanied and advised by counsel and by individuals with special knowledge or training with respect to the problems of handicapped children;
(2) the right to present evidence and confront, cross-examine, and compel the attendance of witnesses;
(3) the right to a written or electronic verbatim record of such hearing;
(4) the right to written findings of fact and decisions.

Finally, the act provides for review of final administrative decisions in a state or federal district court of competent jurisdiction. For special education cases of this type, the act suspends the usual restrictions on access to the courts based on the dollar amounts involved in the controversy. Legislating rights was necessary before parents could begin to approach school systems effectively on behalf of their child. But legal rights and due process procedures do not by themselves insure "fairness." The following chapter outlines the assessment, educational planning, and appeals procedures in Massachusetts at the.time of the study. The balance of this book examines the extent to which due process safeguards actually achieved their intended goals.

Notes

1. The discussion that follows is adapted from two essays by L. Kotin published in "Due Process in Special Education: A Legal Analysis" (RIEP, 1977).

3

The Course of an
Evaluation and Appeal
in Massachusetts

This chapter presents the due process procedures in Massachusetts when this study was conducted.[1] We begin by describing the procedures for referral, evaluation, and development of an educational plan. We then detail the process of requesting an administrative hearing and the parents' subsequent options for appeal.

Getting a Child Special Help

Who is eligible?
The due process system of Chapter 766 is set in motion when a child suspected of having special needs is referred for an evaluation. The regulations specify a broad range of conditions under which this referral can be made. Since the law defines "needs" functionally rather than by traditional labels, it explicitly spells out the conditions that may place a child in educational risk. For example, a child is considered "at risk" if at mid-year s/he presents a substantial likelihood of non-promotion, has failed to be promoted, has been suspended or excluded from school for more than five school days in any quarter, or has been absent without medical excuse for more than 15 school days in any quarter.

The range of persons who can refer a child for special needs services was also purposely made broad. Such persons include school officials, teachers, parents, judicial officers, social workers, the family physician, and the person having custody of the child. A child may also refer him/herself for an evaluation. Both the person who makes the referral and the parent have the right to request an evaluation to determine what kind of assistance the child actually needs. Usually, only a partial evaluation is scheduled if the child is already in school, or if s/he has been recommended for no more than 25% time in a special program. However, parents also have the right to request a full evaluation, which is in any case mandatory for a child who will spend more than 25% of his/her time outside the regular classroom. Or, if a parent agrees, the entire evaluation can be waived if one has already been performed during the previous six months.

What does the child need?

Evaluations are performed by a multi-disciplinary team, which will then develop an educational plan for the child within 30 working school days of the time of the referral. A complete evaluation includes:

- an assessment of educational status covering the child's progress in school and current standing;
- a statement by a teacher who has recently taught the child, including a discussion of the child's behavioral style, "a statement of school readiness, functioning or achievement," and "a statement of the child's behavioral adjustment, attentional capacity, motor coordination, activity levels and patterns, communication skills, memory and social relations with groups, peers and adults";
- a health assessment by a physician who has examined the child;
- a psychological assessment;
- the parents' choice of a home visit or an interview at school conducted by a nurse, social worker, or guidance counselor.

Evaluations must also include statements of how these assessments were performed, and the diagnostic significance of the findings for the particular child.

Developing the child's educational plan.

If the evaluation confirms that the child does indeed need special services, the next step is to develop the child's educational plan. The Individual Educational Plan (IEP) is developed at a conference of the members of a Core Evaluation Team (CET):

- a Chairperson, designated by the district's administrator of special education;
- a "registered nurse, or social worker with a master's degree in social work or a certified guidance or adjustment counselor";
- a "certified psychologist or one licensed to practice in Massachusetts";
- "a physician who is licensed to practice in Massachusetts" or in another state with comparable requirements;
- a teacher who has recently had the child in his/her class;
- the child's parent;
- "the primary person, if any, who will be assisting the teacher in implementing the educational plan," for example, a resource room teacher or tutor.

In addition, parents can bring any outside professionals who are working with their child to the conference, at the parents' expense. A child over the age of 14 may him/herself be invited to the conference. The Core Evaluation Team reviews the findings and develops the child's educational plan. These procedures are reviewed in Figure 3-1.

How to Appeal an Educational Plan

Entering the process.
A parent formally enters the appeals process when s/he has been given an educational plan, rejects it, and requests a hearing. Figure 3-2 describes the law through a detailed flow chart of the procedures following a parent's rejection of the educational plan.

Within five days after parents reject a plan, the school district must report the rejection to the State Department of Education's Bureau of Special Education Appeals. Within five more days, the Bureau's central office must send parents and the school a packet of materials on the appeals process. The packet includes a form on which parents must choose a course of action: (1) take no further action; (2) go to hearing; or (3) request a decision from the Bureau without a hearing, based only on the materials submitted. This form must be returned to the Bureau within 15 days.

Both parents and school are also notified of their rights under the law, and are given the name and telephone number of the educational representative for their region of the state. This representative then contacts them for a pre-hearing meeting, possibly to resolve the dispute without a hearing, minimally to clarify the appeals procedures. This attempt to mediate the dispute was instituted toward the close of our study period.

Figure 3-1.

THE CHAPTER 766 TEAM
EVALUATION PROCESS
FLOW CHART

NOTIFICATION TO
PARENTS

The Administrator of Special Education* notifies the parents that the referral
has been made. The Administrator of
Special Education provides information
about the **766 Evaluation TEAM** which
consists of the TEAM Chairperson, the
parents, and educational professionals
from the school. The TEAM members
evaluate the student's special needs and
develop an Individualized Educational
Plan (I.E.P.)

WITHIN 5 DAYS OF THE REFERRAL

SCREENING PROGRAM

A Screening Program for 3 and 4 year
olds as well as children entering
kindergarten which identifies a child
who may have special needs.

OFFERED YEARLY

THE REFERRAL

A parent or guardian may make a direct
referral to the Administrator of Special
Education
                    or
A school official, including a teacher, a
parent, a judicial officer, a social worker,
a family physician, or a person having
custody of the child, may make a referral
for a Chapter 766 Evaluation. A child
who wishes to be referred for an
evaluation, or any other person, may
request one of the persons listed above
to make a referral. That person must
contact the Administrator of Special
Education to begin the referral process.

AT ANY TIME

PRIOR TO
REFERRAL

Prior to referring a child for an
evaluation, all efforts shall be made to
meet the child's needs within the context
of services which are part of the regular
education program.

*Whenever used, the term Administrator
of Special Education may refer to that
person or his/her designee.

THE ASSESSMENT AND PLANNING PERIOD

- The Administrator of Special Education will recommend specific assessments, depending upon the child's suspected special needs. The parents have the right to request a medical, psychological and home assessments.

- Parental approval is required in writing before assessments can be made.

- Parents can request a meeting with the TEAM Chairperson to discuss problems and ask questions about the Chapter 766 TEAM Evaluation Process.

- In an Evaluation, the following assessments may be conducted by the Chapter 766 Evaluation TEAM:

  - EDUCATIONAL HISTORY*
  - CLASSROOM ASSESSMENT*
  - HOME ASSESSMENT
  - MEDICAL ASSESSMENT
  - PSYCHOLOGICAL ASSESSMENTS
  - ASSESSMENTS BASED UPON THE CHILD'S SUSPECTED SPECIAL NEEDS* (with parental consent)

    * Required Assessments

WITHIN 30 WORKING DAYS OF THE REFERRAL

CHAPTER 766 EVALUATION TEAM MEETING

Once all the assessments have been completed, the Chapter 766 Evaluation TEAM, which includes the parents, will evaluate the results and decide if the student has special needs the regular classroom teacher cannot meet.

If the student has special needs, the Chapter 766 Evaluation TEAM will develop an Individualized Educational Plan which is designed to meet the educational needs of the student.

PARENTAL DECISION

The parent will be sent a written notice containing an explanation of the results of the Chapter 766 Evaluation and two copies of the Individualized Educational Plan.

WITHIN 10 DAYS AFTER THE EVALUATION MEETING

The parent has the right to meet with the Chapter 766 TEAM Chairperson to discuss the following options:

- **ACCEPT THE PLAN** — If the Individualized Educational Plan is accepted, the parents will be asked to sign the Plan, and it will be implemented immediately according to the dates as stated in the plan.

- **ARRANGE FOR AN INDEPENDENT EVALUATION** — If the parents disagree with the school's assessment, they can ask for an additional equivalent evaluation at the school's expense from a person certified or licensed in their profession. A parent may also obtain at private expense an independent evaluation of the child by any specialist.

- **REJECT THE PLAN** — If the parent does not accept the Educational Plan or the results of the evaluation, the **appeals process** will begin. Parents must sign the plan, and check off the box which states "I DO NOT ACCEPT."

1. REJECTION OF THE EDUCATIONAL PLAN

Parents can reject the proposed Individualized Educational Plan and start the appeals process in one of two ways:

- by checking off the box on the Plan which states, "I DO NOT ACCEPT."

- by directly notifying the Bureau of Special Education Appeals.

2. INFORMAL DISCUSSION PERIOD

Immediately upon notification that the I.E.P. has been rejected by the parents, the Administrator of Special Education may attempt to resolve the dispute informally.

3. NOTIFICATION

- Copies of the rejected Educational Plan are sent to both the Central and the Regional Offices of the Bureau of Special Education Appeals.

- The Central Office opens a master file and assigns a case number. Within 5 days of receipt of the notice, the Central Office sends the parents an informational package which explains the appeal procedures and parent's rights.

4. MEDIATION (Optional)

- The Regional Representative, or Mediator, opens a file at the Regional Office.

- The Mediator contacts the parents and the school to explain the mediation process and to schedule a parent-school conference (mediation session).

Figure 3-2.

APPEALS PROCESS
FLOW CHART

5. FORMAL HEARING

- If the parties do not wish to participate in a parent-school conference or if differences cannot be resolved through mediation, the parents or school may request a hearing. A formal hearing is held within 20 days of the request. The BSEA Hearing Officer will review the evidence and testimony from both sides and make a written decision within 25 days.

- The Hearing Officer can order the program which has been recommended by the school, order the program requested by the parent, or order an alternative program.

- The school or parents can appeal a decision to the Superior Court or to the U.S. District Court.

6. STATE ADVISORY COMMISSION

If the parents disagree with the decision of the Hearing Officer, they may appeal the decision to the State Advisory Commission which will review the evidence. No new evidence can be submitted. And, the parents are not present at this meeting.

OR

7. COURT APPEAL

If the parents disagree with the decision of the State Advisory Commission or if they wish to bypass the Commission's review, they may appeal to the Superior Court or the United States District Court.

Scheduling a hearing.

When our study began, the Bureau had 60 days to schedule a hearing from the time it received a parent's request. This time period was shortened under the regulations issued for the federal statute. Three to four weeks before the scheduled date, the Bureau's central office was to send written notification of the date, time, and location of the hearing to the parents and the school district.

But the newness of the hearing procedure caused a considerable number of delays, often beyond the required 60 days. Hearings would also be frequently postponed by either side, resulting in further delays. One parent reported that on four separate occasions the school had cancelled a hearing the night before it was to have taken place. Since it was often difficult to reach all the parties involved, hearing officers, parents or school personnel would occasionally turn up at a scheduled location only to discover the hearing was not being held. When this study was conducted, hearings could be postponed by either party at any time. After two years of the new law's operation, the high frequency of postponements had caused serious delay in resolving many disputes; hence, children had to remain in possibly unsuitable programs long after they had first been referred for other services.

In 1977, therefore, a new policy on postponements was instituted. New guidelines for the conduct of hearings were developed to cope with the slippages in time that occurred during these early stages and to regularize hearings procedures in accordance with the federal law. These new regulations guided the appeals process during the later stages of this study period. Hearing postponements would be granted by the Bureau only if the party wishing the postponement had (1) informed the other party and obtained their agreement; (2) found a mutually agreeable alternative date; (3) informed the Bureau of the new date at least seven working days before the scheduled hearing; and (4) submitted to the Bureau a written statement of such agreement. Granting exceptions to the policy is within the discretion of the Bureau's director, but only if good cause has been shown. Hence, parents in our study reflect reactions both in the early and later phases of the new law.

A hearing calendar is prepared monthly by the Appeal Bureau's scheduler, at which time hearing officers are assigned. About three times as many hearings are scheduled as actually take place, due to the frequency of postponements, successful mediations, and withdrawals of cases.

In order for the hearing officer to have some familiarity with the case, both parent and school are requested to send a file of pertinent materials to the Bureau before the hearing, so the hearing officer can review the child's evaluations. Thus the actual hearing time can be spent discussing the issues, rather than examining written reports.

The decision.

The hearing officer is supposed to render a decision within 30 days of the hearing and mail it to the parents. A form describing parents' further options is mailed to them with the decision. The form, which must be returned to the Bureau within 15 days, requests parents to choose between (1) acceptance of the decision; (2) rejection of the decision, desiring the child to be placed in a regular classroom; or (3) rejection of the hearing officer's decision, but *not* desiring the child's placement in a regular program. The last option automatically constitutes an appeal to the State Advisory Commission, which is the next level of appeal available to the parents.

Further Appeals

The State Advisory Commission.

The State Advisory Commission (SAC) serves as a state-level appeals board for parents dissatisfied with the hearing decision. The SAC's members represent the state's six regional special educational advisory commissions, appointed by the Massachusetts Board of Education. Half its members are parents of children enrolled in special education programs. The rest are regular and special public school teachers and administrators; handicapped students and adults, and the commissioners of the related state agencies, who serve *ex officio*. The SAC reviews the decisions appealed by parents, primarily to determine whether there has been an error of fact or law made by the hearing officer, and whether someone else could reasonably come to the same decision based on the same evidence. Soon after Chapter 766 went into effect, the SAC hired an attorney to help review the cases.

The SAC meetings are closed to outsiders, and no new evidence may be submitted by either party. The SAC renders a tentative initial decision which is sent to the parties for comment. Written comments concerned only with that decision, including no new evidence, are returned to the SAC for consideration and a second, final decision is rendered, which either upholds the hearing officer's original decision, reverses it, modifies it, or remands the case to the Bureau for rehearing.

If the SAC upholds the decision of the hearing officer, the parents can continue their appeal to the Massachusetts Superior Court, by filing within thirty days after they have received the final decision from the SAC.

The compliance hearing.

Another recourse for parents, instituted since the completion of this study, is a compliance hearing. Such a hearing may be called by the Bureau's director if a parent complains that the initial hearing decision is not being properly implemented. After a preliminary investigation to examine whether the complaint is justified, the compliance hearing is convened under the original hearing officer.

Parents' options.

To summarize, the possible appeal options following parents' rejection of an educational plan are:

- Parents *do not respond* to the initial Bureau notification of their right to a hearing—no action taken.
- The case is *withdrawn*; parents no longer wish to pursue the appeal and either agree to the school's educational plan or remove their child from public school.
- The case is *resolved without a hearing* and with no subsequent Bureau involvement.
- The case is *mediated*—parties reach agreement through mediation with a regional representative, or at the hearing itself before a decision is rendered.
- The case is heard and a *decision rendered* with one or more of the following consequences:
  —*No* further activity; —Parents *appeal* to the *State Advisory Committee* (SAC); —Parents *appeal* to the *Superior Court*; —*Schools appeal* to the Superior Court; or —A *compliance hearing* is held.

From the first day parents request an evaluation to the final day of possible decision by the Superior Court, a very long time can elapse, sometimes as much as two or three years. Even when time regulations were obeyed and when there was no court appeal, the process has taken up to 465 days. With any degree of slippage in any stage, this evaluation and appeals process can take even longer.

The Use of the Appeals System in Massachusetts

Since the implementation of Chapter 766, Massachusetts' hearing schedule has been a heavy one. Between September, 1974 and October, 1977, 1,470 cases were registered with the Bureau of Special Education Appeals. Of these, 30% (435 cases) went to hearing for which decisions were rendered, and 32% (465 cases) were resolved at mediation sessions before the hearing. Some 8% (118 cases) were appealed to the State Advisory Commission and 3.6% (53 cases) to the Superior Court. We do not know the fate of the 28% of the cases (409) which did not pursue their appeal. One can assume some of these cases were negotiated informally by the parents and the schools, and that others were mediated by the state mediator. An unknown number of parents simply never responded to the state agency's notification of their rights, and no further action was taken.

The State Advisory Commission.
Of the 118 cases which were appealed to the State Advisory Commission during these years, in 103 cases, the hearing officer's decision was upheld, four of those with modifications. Of the remaining 14 cases, four decisions were overturned to favor the parents, and 10 cases were returned for additional action by the Bureau.

The SAC's tendency to uphold almost all decisions has not changed. Through 1980, the proportion of parents appealing their decision to the SAC has declined from 29% in 1976 to 21% and 22% for 1979 and 1980, respectively. A 1980 state education department memorandum says: "Given an approximate breakout of 50% of . . . [initial hearing] decisions in favor of the schools, [it] is interesting to note . . . that out of those, only 50% of the parents aggrieved chose to further appeal to the SAC. In addition, the percentage of cases appealed to the SAC has decreased each year . . . I would surmise that attorneys are recommending that an appeal to the SAC, given the SAC's record of upholding the [decision] combined with well-written decisions, is not a useful option."

The Superior Court.
Between the law's implementation in September, 1974, and December, 1978, 53 cases had been appealed to Superior Court, either by parents or by the schools. Whereas parents may appeal either to Court or to the SAC, the Superior Court is the only level of appeal available to the school district. Of the 53 cases, only nine had been acted upon: in two cases, the hearing officer's decision was upheld, and seven cases were dismissed without a hearing due to the parties reaching an agreement while waiting for the Court to act. Forty-four cases were still awaiting court review (*Appeal News*, 1978).

The Appeals System in Other States

We have said that the appeals system in Massachusetts was used far more than other states. While figures for most states are not available, six states did present data to the Subcommittee on the Handicapped of the U.S. Senate Committee on Labor and Human Resources in 1979, in hearings to review the status of P.L. 94-142.

Table 3-3.
Summary of Appeals Hearings Activity in Six States

	Due Process Complaints Filed	Local Hearings Held	Local Decisions Favored		State Level Hearings	State Decisions Favored		Court Appeals
			Parents	Schools		Parents	Schools	
Georgia 1977 - 80	53	39	9	29	14	0	14	NA
Louisiana 1975 - 79	NA	41	NA	NA	13	6	3	0
W. Virginia 1975 - 79	NA	12	NA	NA	4	2	1	
Massachusetts 9/74 - 8/79	3091	NA	NA	NA	836 (Mediated/Agreed: 1311 Pending: 546)	NA	NA	
Pennsylvania 9/75 - 79	287				287 101 appealed to State Secretary of Education	NA	NA	15
New York State 1976 - 79	435	222	67	150	213	99	111	

Table 3-3 summarizes the limited amount of information supplied by these six states in response to a committee staff questionnaire. Three states (Georgia, Louisiana and West Virginia) reported low usage; only 39, 41, and 12 hearings, respectively, had been held at their local school district level since enactment of the federal act. Pennsylvania and New York reported more activity, 287 and 485 hearings respectively, while Massachusetts reported 3,091 appeals registered, 836 hearings held, 546 pending, and 1,311 complaints mediated. Clearly, Massachusetts has been the most active arena for the special education hearing, although other states' data suggest that the issues in their disputes are very similar.

Notes

1. The procedures in more specific form can be found in the "Regulations for the Implementation of Chapter 766," available from the Division of Special Education, Massachusetts Department of Education, 31 St. James Avenue, Boston, Mass. 02116.

Section II.

The Experiences of Parents Who Appealed

4

The Parents Who Appealed

This section examines the perceptions of parents who pursued an appeals hearing. In this chapter we describe how our sample of parents and children was developed and what their characteristics were. The parents in our study were mostly upper-middle-income persons, with learning-disabled children for whom they sought private school placements. As we shall see, this seems to be broadly representative of all Massachusetts parents who went to a hearing during the early years of the new law.

Development of the Sample

The major difficulty in developing a sample of hearings users is the confidentiality surrounding these proceedings. Regulations preclude any public knowledge of an appeal. By arrangement with the Massachusetts Bureau of Special Education Appeals, all parents who rejected educational plans between September, 1974 and December, 1976 routinely received notice of this project as part of the information package by which the Bureau informs parents of their rights. The notification included a brief explanation of the purposes of the project and a form that could be returned to us if parents were willing to participate to any extent. Parents could indicate whether they would allow our observers to attend their hearing; whether they would be willing to be interviewed; and whether we could have access to the records and case materials pertaining to their dispute.

Project staff received the name, address, and telephone number of each parent who returned a signed form to the state agency. When the hearing was scheduled, the parents and school district officials were informed by the Bureau that one of our observers would be present at the hearing. Verbal agreement by the parents at this time served to confirm their previous written consent. The observer was introduced at the hearing, at the end of which s/he scheduled an interview with the parents.

Eighty-one families agreed to participate in this study, representing 12% of the cases registered for hearings and 28% of all cases who actually went to a hearing during the period of this study.

Parents who rejected an educational plan were automatically registered for a hearing, but not all such parents actually went to a hearing, even during this period when no alternate mediation system existed. To get a hearing, parents had to respond to the Bureau's written request, and many never responded. It was not clear what this non-response meant. Disputes can be settled in other ways: the school system may offer a modified program that makes the rejected educational plan acceptable; the parents may change their minds and accept the original plan once they realize what a hearing will entail; they may seek a substitute program and place the child elsewhere, electing to pay the costs themselves rather than go through a costly and traumatic hearing; or they may simply fail to respond. There has been no systematic study of this failure to respond, which involved a considerable proportion of the cases registered.

Since our interest was in the hearing process itself, we had no contact with parents who rejected the educational plan but failed to attend a hearing. The parents in this study are not a sample of those dissatisfied with special education programs; they are a sample only of parents who tried to resolve their dissatisfactions through an administrative hearing.

Initial interviews with the 81 hearings parents were conducted between March, 1975 and June, 1977, as soon as possible after their hearings. Since only 12 hearings were conducted between September, 1974 and January, 1975, and since only two interviewed parents attended hearings during this period, our parent sample in effect describes the first operational years of hearings proceedings in Massachusetts, from January, 1975 to June, 1977.

In 49 out of the 81 cases interviewed, one of our observers had previously attended the parent's hearing. In the other cases, the parent was called and an appointment made for the parent interview, usually within two weeks of the hearing. In some cases, hearings had already been held by the time the arrangements with the state agency had been negotiated, but interviews were scheduled as soon as possible, usually within three months of the hearing.

In fall, 1977, parents were contacted again and 71 of the original 81 respondents were interviewed by telephone. Of the other ten, two had moved out of state; one parent refused the interview; and seven families could not be located. This second interview occurred an average of 20 months after the original hearing, within a range of 11 to 32 months. A third interview was conducted by telephone with 62 parents, approximately 42 months after the original hearing.

The data on parents' reactions to the hearing process are based on the information obtained in the first two interviews; the statistical data reported refer to this group, unless otherwise noted. The third interview was brief, and intended only to inquire into the further course of the appeal and its effects on the handicapped child.

The Types of Cases

The 71 parents who completed the two interviews can be categorized in three major subgroups:

(1) parents who had placed their child in a private special needs school before the scheduled hearing—*Private School* cases; 49 cases.
(2) Parents who requested a private school placement but kept their child in the public school pending the decision—*Leaving School* cases; 11 cases.
(3) Parents who sought different programs within the public schools than were proposed in the child's educational plan—*Staying in School* cases; 11 cases.

Private School cases.
Hearings in Massachusetts at this time most frequently involved children who were already attending private special needs schools. Forty-nine cases, or 69% of our study, consisted of these children.

Almost half of our Private School cases (24 of 49) were parents who had tried to get their children evaluated by the public schools before the implementation of Chapter 766, or during the law's first year. These parents decided to place their child in a private school when it seemed to them that the school's slow response or the belated scheduling of a hearing would prevent their child from receiving an adequate program before the start of the next school year. Since they attributed the need for private placement to the slow response of the public schools, they wanted their child's tuition and transportation costs to be paid by the school system. None of these 24 children had ever before attended private school.

The school administrators in these cases argued that since they had proposed adequate programs in their educational plans, there was no real need for the child to be in private school. Because the parents' precipitous removal of the child was the reason for the private school costs, they argued, parents should absorb those costs themselves.

The other 25 private school cases involved children who had already been attending private schools, either regular (10) or special needs (12), by the time the law was implemented. Most of the children in special needs schools had been placed even before the law had been passed, often at the suggestion of public school personnel. Other children had gone to regular private schools, but were transferred to special needs schools when they encountered problems. In these cases, the schools were asked to pay for special schooling for children who had never been in the public schools.

An additional three children in our sample had been in private schools outside the school district, with their costs paid by various state agencies. It is not clear why the schools contested these placements, since they had no financial responsibility for them. These children were guaranteed state support until they no longer required the placement or reached their 22nd birthday.

Private placement cases are unlike other appeals because the hearing decision rarely has an immediate impact on the child's school situation. Even when private school parents in our study lost their appeals, they invariably paid for the placement for at least the rest of the school year.

Leaving School cases.

The second major category, 11 out of 71 cases, or 16%, involved children who were attending public school programs at the time of their hearing, but whose parents believed the public school programs were inadequate. They wanted the school system to pay private school tuition for their child, but the schools argued that outside placements were unnecessary because their own programs were appropriate. The following examples from our sample are representative:

- A sixth-grade boy was described as "learning-disabled" by independent evaluators and as "emotionally troubled" by public school personnel. The parents wanted their son sent to a private day school specializing in the treatment of learning disabilities; school personnel wanted the boy to remain in a regular classroom, claiming that tutorial and resource room help would be adequate to treat what they saw as primarily emotional problems.
- A boy had returned to high school after a period of psychiatric hospitalization. The parents supported the hospital's recommendation

that their son be placed at a residential facility. The school system believed the boy had adjusted well to the high school program.

- A seventh-grade girl had been receiving increasing amounts of special education attention for both learning and emotional problems since the first grade, and was currently in a substantially separate classroom. Her parents requested a private school placement.

In this group, the decision of the hearing officer had an immediate impact on the child: Leaving School children stayed in a public program if they lost but entered a private program if they won. Decisions also affected the subsequent negotiations between parents and school regarding the child's future programs. Even if the child was placed outside the school system, it was still necessary to hold yearly negotiations on continuation of the placement, because the school district would seek to regain the child to minimize its own fiscal obligation. Parents who had lost their hearing were in a considerably weaker negotiating position, unless they were willing to pursue an appeal to higher levels, or to reject a future educational plan and start the whole process over again. Most parents felt this latter option to be most undesirable.

Staying in School cases.

In these cases (11 out of 71), parents were dissatisfied with the child's public school program and/or the modifications that the schools proposed, but wanted more appropriate services provided *within* the public schools. Examples of these cases include:

- A retarded 11-year-old girl was attending a substantially separate public school program. The parents had requested that her classroom be moved from the basement, where special education classes had been held before the reform; that she receive additional speech therapy and the services of a trained physical therapist; and that the school personnel communicate with them regularly so they could reinforce the child's learning at home.
- A fourth-grade boy was receiving small group tutoring in gross and fine motor skills in the public schools. The parents believed the school staff member providing this tutoring was untrained and unskilled. They wanted the hearing officer to order one-to-one tutoring with more skilled personnel, and they wanted a detailed educational plan for their son.
- A fifth-grade boy was viewed by the school system as emotionally disturbed. The parents wanted him kept in a regular classroom, while the school system wanted him in a substantially separate program.

The decisions in Staying in School disputes had an immediate impact on the child, since they would determine whether or not his/her school program would be altered. As the child's needs changed, parents and school system had to continue to negotiate an educational plan. If, as a result of a bitter hearing, the parents and the school staff continued to see themselves as opponents, the child was likely to suffer. Budoff, Orenstein and Abramson (1981) describe the total sample of these cases for which decisions were available during this early period.

In sum, this sample of 71 appeals cases includes 49 Private School cases where children were already attending private programs; 11 Leaving School cases where parents wanted a private program but kept their children in public schools; and 11 Staying in School cases, where parents sought an altered public school program.

Representativeness of the Interviewed Cases

Since the parents included in our sample had volunteered, we wanted to know to what extent they represented the total population of parents who appealed. We therefore compared them to a 50% sample randomly selected from the decisions written during the same period (September 1, 1974 through March 1, 1977). We looked at these 161 cases for six variables: year of hearing, sex of child, age of child, child's major handicap(s) (as reported by the hearing officer), and result of the decision. The data comparing the two samples on these variables are presented in Table 4-1. As can be seen, the absence of any substantial difference suggests that our parent sample does indeed represent the overall population of parents who used the hearing system.

We also compared the types of cases in this random sample with those in our interview sample.[1] Of the parents we interviewed, 69% were Private School, 16% were Leaving School, and 16% were Staying in School cases. The comparable distribution of cases in the random sample was 69%, 13% and 17%, respectively. In sum, both samples suggest that approximately two-thirds of the appeals cases in Massachusetts were Private School cases, while approximately one-sixth each were Leaving School or Staying in School cases.

This similarity on key variables between our interviewed parent sample and the 50% random sample of written decisions suggests that, despite the necessary caution in generalizing from so small a sample, our parent sample can be used to represent hearings cases in Massachusetts during this period.

Who Were the Families Involved in These Cases?

Socio-economic status.
The families that brought Private School cases were affluent and tended to be

Table 4-1.
Comparisons of Written Decision Data and Parent Sample Data

Written Decision Sample (N=161)		Parent Sample (N=71)	
Year Decision Issued	**%**	**Year of Hearing**	**%**
August 1975	27.8	August	25.4
Sept. 1975 - Aug. 1976	51.0	Sept. 1975 - Aug. 1976	56.3
Sept. 1976 - March 1977	21.2	Sept. 1976 - Dec. 1976	18.3
Total	100.0	Total	100.0
Sex of Child	**%**		**%**
Male	75.0		77.5
Age of Child			
Mean Age	11.9 years		11.2
Childs's Major Special Need			
Hearing Officer's Report:		Parent's Report:	
No Special Needs	2.9	No Special Needs	0.0
Learning Disabled	60.2	Learning Disabled	66.0
Emotional Problems	10.6	Emotional Problems	17.0
Retardation	5.0	Retardation	10.0
Other	5.6	Other	8.0
Not Ascertainable	15.5		
Parent Representation			
% of Parents represented by an attorney at the hearing	37.3		37.0
Decision Outcome	**%**		**%**
Favored Parent	34.2		46.4
Favored School	40.4		39.4
Apparent Compromise	18.0		14.1
Not Ascertainable	7.5		0.0

well educated. Among the 49 fathers in our sample, 41 had earned a bachelor's degree. Nine of these had earned master's degrees, six had earned post-bachelor's professional degrees, and six held doctorates. Among the 49 mothers in the sample, 41 had attended college, 18 were college graduates, and 11 held or were working towards advanced degrees.

Occupations revealed a similarly high status. More than half the fathers (25, or 51%) held professional positions: engineer or engineer-manager (11), lawyer (4), university professor (4), accountant (4), or architect (2). Only three of these fathers were blue-collar workers. Among the mothers, half were housewives, three were college students, and 19 women worked, with eight employed in educational institutions (in positions such as learning-disability specialist, high school teacher, and private school registrar) and two as social workers. Many of these working mothers held positions that would make them especially sensitive to educational failure and aware of their rights under the new law.

Among the Leaving School families, only two of the 11 fathers and two of the 11 mothers were college graduates. Among the Staying in School group, only four of the 11 fathers and three of the 11 mothers were college graduates.

Table 4-2 examines family income. In a period when the Massachusetts median family income hovered around $16,000, the median income of families involved in Private School cases was $30,800, with only 12.5% falling below the state median income. Among the Leaving School and Staying in School groups, seven and six families of the 11 in each group reported incomes below $15,000. Only three of these 22 families had incomes as high as the $30,000 median income of Private School families. These were parents seeking residential placements, which are a serious financial burden even for upper-middle-income families.

The handicaps of their child.

We asked parents to indicate their child's major handicap(s). The typical Private School case was reported to be learning-disabled, with secondary emotional problems that parents attributed to the history of school failure. Leaving School cases also reported their child's primary handicap to be a learning disability. By contrast, Staying in School cases included children with more traditional handicaps, such as mental retardation, cerebral palsy, etc.

Significantly, none of our 49 Private School cases included these "traditional" handicaps. Forty-two parents (86%) reported their children were learning-disabled and seven (14%) that their child's primary handicap had an emotional basis.[2] In three of the instances in which parents reported a learning disability, they indicated hyperactivity as the disability's major expression.

Parents who reported a learning disability were asked: "Does your child have serious emotional problems as well?" Seventeen of the 42 parents who responded reported emotional problems. From the detailed discussions offered by these parents, it would appear that these emotional problems were of great concern to them, though they viewed them in large part as stemming

Table 4-2:
Income Distributions for Families Interviewed
by Type of Hearing Case

Family Income	Private School Cases	Leaving School Cases	Staying In School Cases
Below $10,000	1	3	2
$10,000 - 14,999	4	4	4
$15,000 - 19,999	4	1	1
$20,000 - 24,999	6	1	1
$25,000 - 29,999	8	1	1
$30,000 - 34,999	6	1	1
$35,000 - 39,999	5	0	0
$40,000 - 44,999	3	0	1
$45,000 - 49,999	4	0	0
$50,000 or more	7	0	0
	48	11	ˋ 11

from the history of school failure. Schools often saw these emotional problems as the child's primary disability.

Among the Leaving School cases, five of 11 children were said to be learning-disabled, and three emotionally disturbed. These children had learning problems and past histories similar to children in the Private School group, and their parents sought placements at the same set of private schools. Of the three remaining cases, one child was said to be aphasic; a second, language-impaired; and the third was mentally retarded. This last case involved a child variously described as "emotionally disturbed," "learning-disabled," and "retarded" by her parents.

Among the Staying in School cases, six of the 11 cases involved mentally retarded children. The other five were a child with cerebral palsy and associated learning disorders, an epileptic child with related learning and emotional problems, two emotionally disturbed children, and only one child who was learning-disabled.

The presence of poorer families in the Staying in School and Leaving School categories refutes the stereotype that the hearing system serves only the upper-middle-class suburban family. Poorer families did pursue appeals when they felt the schools were not addressing their child's severe impairments—but they did so at great hardship. As we shall indicate throughout this book, attending a hearing exacts a high cost, in terms of both money and emotion, and it is true that the number of more affluent parents using the system is disproportionately high.

In sum, while Leaving School cases are quite similar to Private School cases in terms of handicap—mainly learning disabilities—they are more similar to Staying in School cases in terms of social class background. Those few affluent parents who brought Staying in School cases had children for whom there were few appropriate alternatives outside of the public schools. The usual Staying in School case involved a retarded child from a moderate-income family.

The Interview

Contents.

Given the exploratory nature of this research, as well as the difficulty of anticipating the types of issues that might arise, our initial interview was loosely structured. It was designed to explore the prior history of the family's relationship with the school; the expectations held by the parents when they heard about Chapter 766; the events leading up to the decision to reject their child's educational plan and to appeal; the experience of the hearing; and the hearing's aftermath. We also sought information to characterize the families on such factors as social status, parent education, and income.

We asked what the parent thought his/her child's needs were and what their expectations were for that child; what s/he saw as the future possibilities for the child; and what s/he expected would happen to the child in his/her current educational placement. We also asked a series of questions designed to determine the psychic and dollar cost to parents of their experience with the hearing system.

Methods.

Five different interviewers were employed. They were responsible for completing a questionnaire and for constructing a "case history" of each dispute, written in narrative form immediately after each interview.

The first interview was conducted before the decision was received, generally within two weeks after the hearing. The level of tension at that time was so great the parents used the interview to vent their feelings about the process. An exploratory set of questions triggered a considerable range of emotion about parent experiences and grievances. These interviews were long, averaging over two and one-quarter hours.

Approximately twenty months later, in fall, 1977, the parents were contacted again. A telephone interview was conducted, which averaged one and one-quarter hours in length. All but three parents gave permission for this interview to be recorded. Even 11 to 32 months after the conclusion of their hearing, these parents still felt keenly about their experience and again used the interview to vent their considerable frustration with the process and its outcomes. The reports in the following chapters will be based on these two interviews.

About 42 months after the original hearing had been completed, a third telephone interview was conducted to review what had happened in the interim, and what were then the prospects for the child. These subsequent events will be presented in Chapter 8.

A coder and the interviewer independently reviewed the tape recordings and coded each of the last two interviews. The coder and interviewer reviewed their findings on each case and negotiated any differences in their coding. The interviewer also compared the coding for the first and second interviews. Where there were factual inconsistencies, tapes and previous interview transcripts were examined to resolve them. On most items, multiple sources of information were available.

The next chapter presents the experiences which parents say led them to reject the educational plan proposed by the school, and to go to a hearing.

Notes

1. The child's placement at the time of the hearing could be identified in 143 of the 161 decisions. Of these, 94 (66%) were in private schools; 46 (32%) were attending public schools; and three children were not attending any educational program. Of the 46 children attending public school, we could identify where parents wished their child to attend school in 41 written decisions. They requested a private school program in 18 cases, while in 23 cases they were seeking improved programs within the public schools.

2. In one instance, the parent used the diagnosis of learning disability inconsistently, referring to her child as "mentally retarded" at several points in the interview. The school system's proposed placement for this child called for a segregated setting with mentally retarded children. The child had been denied admission to a private day school for learning-disabled children because of low intelligence. This parent eventually found a placement for her child at another day school for learning-disabled children and appears to have been engaged in a battle to prevent a more severe label from being attached to her child.

5

The Prehearing Experiences
of Parents

This chapter examines how parents came to reject the school's educational plan for their child and to utilize the hearing system. The data reported were primarily drawn from our first interview, conducted soon after the hearing, but relevant materials collected from the second interview are included as well. In both interviews we sought to have parents reconstruct their experiences with the assessment and educational planning process, in order to explain their ultimate dissatisfaction with the public schools and their consequent resort to an appeal.

Previous Experience with Their Child's Program

Parents who went to a hearing were activist parents with personal and fiscal resources, and a deep involvement with their child's difficulties. When asked, *"How much experience did you have with the school before Chapter 766?"*, 59% of the parents reported at least a "moderate" amount of experience, with many feeling they had had "a great deal" of such contact.

Parents had usually referred their child for an evaluation themselves; were aware of the nature of their child's difficulties; had sought to educate themselves about these problems; and had engaged in various activities to help their child cope with these problems before and during the school's involvement. Most parents had visited their child's school. They viewed the passage of Chapter 766 as promising more appropriate programs for their child. While many parents sought private school placements, they did not express alienation from the public schools per se, although they did have reservations about the integrity of the schools' efforts, particularly about the schools' emphasis on mainstreamed placement.

The parents in our sample originally became aware of their child's problems in various ways: by their personal observation (70%),[1] because the child fell behind in school performance (58%), or because the teacher brought it to their attention (31%). At that time, they tried to get extra help in school (61%), or place their child in private school (26%). When Chapter 766 became effective, 90% referred their child for evaluation and an educational plan.

These parents tended to see their child's future as being similar to other children, and hoped their child would lead a normal life (51%), meet his/her creative potential (42%), and be happy (38%). Most of these parents had been successful because of their own educational attainments and hoped their child would attend college (54%). These hopes indicate that these parents viewed their child's potential with optimism, regardless of the current difficulties. Given these expectations, parents became very upset when public school programs apparently failed to help their child, and they actively sought alternate solutions. They were more likely than school personnel to consider their child's handicap as severe, since the handicapping condition was frustrating their expectations for the child.

When asked to characterize their prior experience with the school, parent responses were largely negative:

- The school misrepresented the severity of the problem. (48%)
- I knew my child was falling further and further behind but the school kept telling me no additional special help was needed, that my child would grow out of his/her problem. (31%)
- The teachers acted as though we were just troublemakers. (21%)
- The school always contended that my child had emotional problems, rather than a learning disability. (19%)
- I requested that the school keep me constantly posted on the progress of my child and they failed to do so. (17%)
- The school staff said that they never had time to meet with me. (12%)
- The school told me that they did not have the facilities to meet my child's needs. (11%)
- The school never informed me of all facilities that were available for my child. (6%)

These parents had high hopes for the new law. To the question, *"With the implementation of Chapter 766, did you think that finally the schools would develop appropriate educational programs for special needs children?"*, 53% answered "Yes," while only 20% answered "No." When asked about their hopes for getting an appropriate program for their own handicapped child, however, only 47% indicated "high" or "very high" hopes, while 47% were more pessimistic.

Then, when asked what the school's response to Chapter 766 had actually been, less than a quarter of our respondents offered positive statements, for example, "good, willing to create good programs" (4%), or "attempting to comply" (20%). More often, the comments indicated negative perceptions of the school's efforts: "indifferent" (5%), "feels bothered" (22%), "poor, has tried to ignore it" (43%), and "feels threatened" (40%).

Although parents were skeptical about the immediate prospects for appropriate public special education, they insisted they were not alienated from the public schools as such. When we asked *"Do you think it is possible for your child to get a good education in the public schools?"*, 74% responded "Yes, if the public schools would devote more energy to special education." Only 21% said "No." To *"Do you have any strong feelings about your child going to a public or private school?"*, there was strong sentiment in favor of public education: 36% would prefer a public school program, but said there was no appropriate existing program; 24% believed in the principle of public education; and 24% felt their child would benefit from the social aspects of a public school.

Significantly, only 26% indicated their first response to discovering their child's handicap was to seek a private school. This group of parents expressed strong sentiment for private schools, feeling they offered superior programs (32%), or "some hope for their child to regain an interest in school" (16%). A third group took a neutral stance, stating no particular preference between public and private programs.

Most parents expressed some disagreements with the public schools' philosophy of special education, although it must be remembered that the vast majority of parents in our sample had learning-disabled children, a field which has generated far more controversy than other fields of special education. These parents generally preferred segregated placements for their (mainly) learning-disabled children rather than the schools' inclination to integrate special needs children with the non-handicapped. Parents preferred special class placements so their child would "not be ridiculed by his/her peers in the regular class" (10%) or "so s/he would get all of the individual attention and special help s/he needs" (41%). Only 18% of our parents expressed strong support for a mainstreamed program.

Of the families seeking private school placements, 53% reported they had no problems with the public schools before they became involved in the assessment process. In fact, 11 of these 49 children had already been receiving special education services in the public schools under an educational plan that their parents had accepted. These parents rejected that plan and went to a hearing because they felt the evaluation and planning process had not honored their concerns about their child's failure to progress. We shall see that parents were often offered programs at these meetings which duplicated those programs they felt had previously failed.

Many of these parents had long-standing grievances regarding their child's program: parents who had been told their child had emotional problems requiring outside help rather than an altered school program; parents who had been told their child required sterner discipline or greater maturity; parents who had not received services they had been promised; parents who had not been informed that minimal levels of special services were failing to alleviate their child's problems; parents who had been treated as "trouble-makers" when they requested altered services.

The past history of inadequate services, coupled with parents' belief that their child could progress if properly helped, undoubtedly made it difficult for these parents to negotiate with school personnel rather than confront them. School staff, in turn, tended to defend the effectiveness of their current programming and to ignore parents' unhappiness with its results. The schools' large caseloads and fears about costs created an inhospitable context for negotiations in good faith.

Developing the Child's Educational Plan

The keystone event under the special education reform is the development of the child's individual educational plan. Such a plan is a radical concept in education: parents and professionals join in an interdisciplinary assessment team to identify the child's special needs and create a plan uniquely suited to meet them. The participation of parents in every phase of the process, from the initial assessment of the child to the final formulation of the plan, was intended to ensure their ultimate satisfaction with their child's education, as well as to make use of parents' special insights into their child's needs.

A number of regulations seek to ensure the inclusion of parents in this process. Schools are required to notify the parents within five days after the child is referred for special services. School personnel must be prepared to discuss the referral with the parents, explain the parents' rights, and define the range of the concerns to be surveyed. Schools must receive the parents' informed consent before scheduling evaluations, which must be completed within 30 working days. The parents are then invited to an educational planning conference which includes a psychologist, a teacher, a social worker or guidance counselor, a physician or nurse, the parents, a team leader, other special or regular education teachers and specialists from the schools, and sometimes, professionals from outside the system who have worked with or evaluated the child.

The educational plan sketched out at the planning meeting is formally written by the team leader and approved by the school district's special education administrator. If parents are hesitant about agreeing to the plan after they receive the final form, further discussions may be held. Parents can also request an independent evaluation to check on the school's findings and the plan's appropriateness. Should parents formally reject the plan, the regulations provide for a 30-day cooling-off period to allow parents and school personnel to reach agreement or work with a state mediator.

Much of our first interview was focused on the parents' experiences during this educational planning process, and why this process led them to resort to a hearing.

What Did the Schools Offer the Child?

Table 5-1 contrasts the program proposed by the schools in the educational plan with the child's prior public school program for Leaving School and Private School cases. As this table indicates, the schools almost always proposed the same program the child had already been receiving, as illustrated by the numbers along the diagonal line in the table. The only time schools proposed increasing services was for newly identified children who previously had been receiving no services—and nine of those were still to get no services under the plan. The schools proposed to reduce services for six children. Most children were to attend a resource room for short periods of small group or individual instruction, while remaining in their regular classroom for most of the teaching day.

Only six children (10%) were proposed by the schools for a substantially segregated program, the parents' choice in Private School and Leaving School cases. Parents usually turned to private schools because they felt their child required a special class setting which would focus intensively on his/her academic and social difficulties rather than the public school's offer of varying amounts of time in a resource room. (See Chapter 9 for a discussion of parents' perceptions of segregated versus mainstreamed programs for their learning-disabled child.)

Table 5-1:
What the Schools Offer Contrasted With the Child's Prior Program

Proposed I.E.P.

Child's Public School Program Prior to IEP	No SpEd Services	10%	10%-25%	25%-60%	60%	Total
No SpEd Services	9	4	4	2		9
10% SpEd	3	4	2			3
10%-25% SpEd		3	11	6		8
25%-60% SpEd				6		2
60% SpEd					6	2
TOTAL	12	11	17	14	6	N=60

Parents Describe the Educational Planning Process

Who was there.
Table 5-2 indicates the types of people parents said attended their educational planning meetings. Almost half, (43%), said they had gone alone. The remaining parents brought advocates (17%), independent evaluators (15%), other professionals (20%), and other nonprofessionals, such as neighbors and friends.

Thus we can see that most educational planning meetings involved a large number of school personnel and an isolated parent or two, placing considerable psychological and interpersonal pressure on the parent. The school was often represented by five, six or more people: for example, special education and regular teachers, child evaluators, and a principal. In many school systems, administrators from the district office attended the meetings whenever parents had requested a private placement or when the child's serious impairment required unusual services. Parents were accompanied by outside professionals only 22% of the time at educational planning meetings. Parents whose child was already attending private school were far more likely to bring outside professionals to the meeting; 62% of such parents in our study brought either private school staff or other professionals.

How they were treated.
Parents characterized the educational planning meeting as generally unreceptive to them and their perceptions:

Table 5-2:
Parents' Reports of Attendees at Educational Planning Meetings

Parents	100% of their meetings
Special education administrator	70%
Psychologist	62%
Principal	43%
Guidance counselor	36%
Present teacher	32%
Past teacher	28%
Nurse	27%
Proposed teacher	17%
Physician	11%
Other	46%

- "The school came into the meeting with the plan written and was unwilling to change." (31%)
- "The school would not listen to anything we had to say." (28%)
- "School personnel were hostile and made us feel like the enemy." (17%)
- "The school stacked the meeting against us." (7%)

When asked, *"Did you feel the evaluation team was qualified to develop an appropriate plan for your child?"*, the parents responded:

- "No, they were not experts on the area of my child's needs." (38%)
- "Yes, but they were not doing it." (36%)
- "No, they had not seen my child." (5%)

Only eight parents, or 9%, felt the school team had adequately evaluated their child.

- We asked parents to agree or disagree that *"School personnel tried to sell me on an educational plan by misrepresenting the severity of my child's problems."* Most parents agreed (65%).

In theory, the educational planning process should be speedy and orderly— a process recognizing the parents as protectors of their child's rights and as important sources of information on their child's needs. In practice, parents in our study found child evaluations neither speedy, orderly, nor cooperative. For example, despite the rigid time requirements built into the law, one parent found:

> The reality out in the field is so different you wouldn't believe it. What happens is—and we looked at the law closely and had it pretty well memorized for a while—if you call up these people and talk to them, if you can find them, and you say "Look, it says 30 days here, 15 days here," that doesn't get you anywhere.

Many parents reported great frustration with what they saw as uncooperative school personnel.

> They hadn't developed programs. It was very difficult to get any information about the programs they already had in operation. I went to the school, wrote leters, went to talk to the head of the learning center and I would get no information. Then they had the meeting and they didn't give me a program at all. They just said there was no plan, no nothing. So I had to make a choice whether to trust them or find something else. And they were very much on the defensive because they didn't really have a program. Had they been a little bit more open, I suppose, and said "We don't have a program yet, but this is what I think we're going to do," that would have been one thing. But it was a matter of talking to one person who would say one thing, really trying to find out what would happen, and I could never find the answer.

Most parents (60%) felt they would have been able to participate productively in the development of their child's educational plan because "I know a great deal about my child's problems."

Others said they were qualified in such areas as the child's behavior outside school, but the schools never discussed those areas, or that they could have participated if the school had used less technical language.

> It's very interesting because I am a social worker myself and I attend 766 cores[2] around clients. As a social worker going to a CET I'm listened to, but if I go as a parent, I'm just an hysterical female.

* * *

When he went into the fourth grade, our communication was

strictly with the teachers, so to speak. We decided to deal just with the teachers. We didn't want another CET [assessment]. You have no idea what the CET meeting was like. It was like a kangaroo court. We had all kinds of certified people there who saw our son's problems. It was completely disregarded. It was a very prejudicial kind of meeting.

* * *

At the end of it, they handed me a blank piece of paper and said, "Sign." There wasn't anything on the paper. It was just a blank form. So I said, "I would like to go home and discuss it with my husband." And they became very angry and said I would be preventing the child from getting what he needed. They try and make the parents feel guilty for not signing a blank piece of paper.

* * *

My husband and I are not interested, not at all, in any more special education programs. I became very active in a parent group and sat in on cores with other people and I know that our situation is not unique. I think 766 on paper is very good. But I would be a person who would disagree very strongly with whether it is actually working. . . . I think it's a bureaucratic quagmire.

* * *

The people we are dealing with, you have to understand, most of them have left; some were definitely incompetent, some were just concerned with money and were not interested in anything else. And the principal, a few years ago, had some problems with some people who claimed he was anti-Semitic, and we're Jewish, and I'm not discounting that either. At the core, one woman said I don't have to worry because "She's a beautiful little girl, she'll get married." That's the kind of core it was.

* * *

They are very sexist. I felt very much discriminated against because of my sex. I think the school structure itself is a very sexist structure—the decision making, the men making the decisions in schools. They would not have spoken to my husband as they spoke to me on many occasions. I don't think anyone would call my husband "dear" and "honey."

When asked, *"Were you encouraged to participate?"*, parents said:

- "Yes, the school was receptive at the meeting, but didn't take our suggestions into account." (35%)
- "No, the school acted as though we were not qualified to contribute to the developing educational plan." (32%)
- "No, we might just as well not have been there." (26%)
- "The school came with a plan already written, and just tried to get us to accept it." (12%)

In general, parents reported two types of experiences in educational planning meetings. The larger group said they were simply not listened to:

My understanding of the law was that parents were presumed to know something about their child. In fact, the way the meetings are organized, parents are presumed to know nothing, and people who had met my child for an hour were lecturing me about her problems, and when I disagreed with them and said that their program wasn't working, the discussion stopped.

* * *

They [the evaluators] think of themselves as professional and they are there to tell you about your child. And if you disagree with their professional judgment, they are not interested.

* * *

The day before the meeting, I bumped into Mr. _____ [the school principal] and he said, "The core will definitely be held tomorrow." Remember, they had postponed it on me twice. And then he said that I didn't have to come if I couldn't make it, that it wasn't that important that I be there. I really think that summarizes the orientation of our schools.

The other group of parents found school personnel seemingly attentive to their suggestions at the educational planning meeting, but afterwards received a plan which incorporated none of their requests and was different than they had expected. For example:

After the core meeting, I thought finally they were going to give him a separate program. At the meeting, they seemed to all agree that the resource room hadn't helped him and that he needed a full-time program. Then when we got the plan, it was the same thing he had before.

*   *   *

They listened but they didn't listen, if you know what I mean. They listened, but they had their minds made up. The meeting is just really a pretense of listening, and then they write the plan they want.

These apparent discrepancies between the planning meetings and the actual plan may reflect a variety of circumstances: a deliberate tactic on the part of some educational planning teams; uncertainty within the team as to what was agreed upon; conflict between team members offering services and administrators refusing to endorse them; confusion on the part of parents as to what was discussed or what to expect in the written educational plan; or simply the school personnel's lack of experience in writing acceptably specific educational plans. Whatever the explanation, exchanges that took place at child evaluation meetings were often misunderstood. This was yet another instance of the inconsistency in the school's contacts with parents which recurs in many different forms.

These accounts parallel descriptions written by other investigators. Weatherley (1977; Weatherley and Lipsky, 1980), for example, attended over 40 educational planning conferences and interviewed personnel in seven Massachusetts schools in three school systems during the first year of Chapter 766 implementation. One of his observations was that educational planning meetings often revolved around blaming parents for their child's problems, which he interpreted as a way of pressuring parents to accept the educational plan offered by the evaluation team. Parents in our sample report similar tactics: "When you do what they want, you're a good parent. When you refuse to sign, they become angry, and you're a bad parent."

Weatherley also noticed that "technical jargon" was used at evaluation meetings "to lend an aura of science to the proceedings while making much of the discussion unintelligible to the parents." Again, he saw this as a way to exclude parents from any real decision-making role. As a member of our sample put it:

I advise parents to never attend the core alone. They talk so fast, with so many numbers—I bet half the school people don't know

what those numbers mean either—but you need someone with you
to know what they're saying. Otherwise, they get you to sign and
you don't know what you've signed.

More generally, Weatherley saw the behavior of school personnel during
the initial implementation of Chapter 766 as conditioned by the overwhelming workload accompanying the new law. With hundreds of referrals for
evaluation being made to each school department, with insufficient staff to
process these referrals, with embryonic administrative structures that resulted
in much confusion and many lost documents, and with severely limited
programming options, the evaluation process, in Weatherley's phrase,
became "routinized," so that the recommendations for a child often depended
upon what was cheaply and quickly available rather than upon the child's
needs.

Orenstein's interviews with special education staff members in a working-
class city and an upper-middle-class suburb near the end of the law's second
year of implementation provide a similar picture (Orenstein, 1976). For
example, he found that in the affluent suburb, which still had hundreds of
referrals waiting for evaluations, school personnel met together before
meeting with parents to develop a unified "front" that would induce parental
compliance.

In both communities, Orenstein found the structure of the evaluation
system to be in flux. Evaluation teams that had been attached to the central
offices of the school system were being decentralized to the school building
level. These changes increased the already considerable confusion within the
school systems, both of which were casting about for better ways to develop
educational plans that could be implemented in their schools. Many staff in
both systems told him of the financial constraints under which special needs
programs were operating. This suggested that school personnel not only were
conscious of program costs but made costs a major factor in their choice of
educational plan options, contrary to what they said at hearings.

The schools' unresponsive tactics clearly contributed to a rupture in parent-
school communication and to the alienation of many parents from the public
schools.

You see, that's the thing, the way we had to go at them to make
them pay attention, to not handle the situation like it was so many
bags of peanuts or whatever. . . . I haven't asked them, but I hate to
even talk to them now. The way they were. You can't imagine how
awful it was. And the worst was that I really knew a lot of these
people beforehand . . . I'd worked with them, and I've even studied
with some of them.

All of these responses are symptomatic of more general problems with implementing parents' rights that have been documented elsewhere (e.g., Yoshida, et al., 1977, regarding Connecticut school staff). The parents in our sample, who actually brought appeals, were highly dissatisfied with how educational planning meetings were conducted in this early period of implementation. It is likely that they and the others who appealed represent only a small proportion of those who were unhappy. Other dissatisfied parents may have felt incapable of contesting the school's proposals, feeling constrained to accept the school's program in spite of their sense of its inadequacy.

The level of alienation generated by these contacts was such that 63% of the parents in our study requested an independent evaluation of their child. Most did so because "the school's evaluation did not disclose the child's special needs" (30%), or "the school's evaluation was not complete" (21%). Only a few gave more neutral responses, such as "we wanted a second opinion" (4%), or "the school suggested it" (9%).

Variations in Child Evaluation Meetings

Educational planning meetings may occur either before or after a child has been taken out of public school. In almost half of our 49 Private School cases, the educational planning meeting was held before the placement, and it was the resulting dissatisfaction with the meeting and/or the plan which led parents to investigate other options for their child. In the other cases, when parents had already enrolled their child at a special needs school, the meeting was seen as a pro forma step in the appeals process.

The educational planning meeting triggers the appeal.

Many parents had kept their child in the public schools for years. Not until the educational planning meeting and the school's subsequent failure to keep communication open, did these parents begin searching for other options for their child.

For example, a learning-disabled child who had been receiving limited amounts of resource room attention for two years was reviewed at an educational planning meeting. His parents reported:

> We were upset by the rosy glow that the school psychologist gave to her report. "He was a wonderful boy; he has a few problems but his personality will win out." It was too rosy a glow and we decided to get another report. So we went to _____ Hospital. The test results were horrible, just horrible. So after that, we had a

conference with Dr. _____ and he said, "Get on this now,
fix him up; make him handle some of these things where he is
really way back, then get him back into the competition. Right
now he ought to go to [a private school]."

The parents enrolled their child at the private school. They never signed the
school's educational plan, and the school never contacted them to find out
why. The parents said they had been satisfied with the public school services
they had received until their educational planning meeting. Neither side
initiated further negotiation.

Another boy had been receiving learning-disability tutoring in public
school for four years, with the school maintaining that the major part of his
problem was emotional. The boy's parents had frequently visited the school
demanding increased services. They felt the principal, in particular, was
unsympathetic and punitive towards their son. They also found unsettling
the prospect of their son being promoted to the larger intermediate school
with its larger classes and frequent transitions.

Rejecting the school's first proposal, which substantially duplicated the
boy's existing program, the parents requested an independent evaluation at a
university-affiliated hospital as well as a second planning meeting at the
hospital. The parent told us:

> Our special education director didn't even take notes. We went for
> about an hour and he was going to write the educational plan and
> he didn't even take notes. . . . I think he had [already] made up his
> mind and written a plan. He obviously didn't read anything or
> listen to the input of the doctors. One doctor was there and said
> [our son] needed a class size of less than 12. They just didn't bother
> with any of the points that indicated they couldn't service [our son]
> in the public schools. They ignored those. . . . They didn't have a
> self-contained classroom at the intermediate school so they [said
> they] would tutor [him]. So we brought up that he needed small
> classes. And [the special education director] said, "Well, we'll have
> to compromise." And I said, "The law wasn't written to
> compromise to keep the kid in public school." Their plan would
> have meant nine teachers, plus a student taking him around from
> class to class.

Even though in this case the school system made an effort to stay in touch
with the parents, negotiations were still marked by bitterness and hostility on
both sides. The schools seemed to see the parents as unreasonably demanding,

while the parents felt that the school system was obsessively concerned with costs and unresponsive to their son's needs.

Prolonged delays in response trigger an out-of-district placement.

Half of our Private School children were not placed until after the evaluation. In other cases, school systems responded so slowly to the request for an evaluation that parents placed their child at a private school before the public school offered them a program. Parents who had requested an evaluation before or during the law's first year of implementation said they had to call their school repeatedly to get an evaluation. Some parents were promised assessments by a certain date, only to find that assessment personnel were unaware of the schedule or that documents had been lost by the schools, and meetings were repeatedly cancelled. Parents' frustration grew as they were unable to find anyone with sufficient authority even to reschedule the meetings, let alone conduct them. As the summer of 1975 ended, one year after the law's effective date, the school systems had not yet developed appropriate programs for the children in question. Meanwhile, scarce spaces in private schools were rapidly being filled. The parents in our sample waited from two to eight months after their initial evaluation request before they finally registered their children at private schools.

The problems of delay and disorganization which triggered half of our Private School placements were common throughout our sample.

> All those meetings we had, all that time, every one of those, I made them do. They wouldn't have done any of them if I hadn't called them every day for five months. I had to force them to allow me to get a second opinion. I had to bring a man from the [State] Department of Education to the school to tell them, yes, I have a right to a second opinion. They kept saying, if I wanted to do that, it wasn't their responsibility. They thought it would be bad for my child, at least that's what they said. I had to teach them the law. They weren't smart enough to read it on their own.

* * *

> If I waited for them, he would still be rotting away in the third grade. Every time they would cancel something, I would get on the phone and call every 15 minutes until they would answer and I would say, "You can't do this to my son."

* * *

We said there should be some psychological testing. And they said, "Oh, no, that's not necessary." And at the hearing they said they had talked about it to us. Well, they never did. We never got anything back from them. We never got any appointments. Everything was always just left hanging. And anytime I would try to force it forward, it would have to be me. And they, of course, implied at the hearing that they were doing all this. *They* were having all of these meetings and *they* were trying so hard. If I hadn't been pressing them, none of these discussions would ever have taken place and yet they implied they were really anxious for this to work out.

*   *   *

This appointment was set up and it was with the understanding that even though it was a summer vacation, [the school system] would come with their teachers, with their therapist, because we wanted our son in a program for the fall. Two days before the meeting was supposed to take place, [the special education director] stated, "You know, Mrs. _____, so-and-so can't be there next Monday," and I said, "Why?" And he said, "Well, this is summer term," and I said, "Well, this was all discussed in June and I have a memo to that effect." And he said, "Why don't we cancel?" and I said, "No, I want my boy in a program and I have made arrangements for that meeting with five or six people from [the psychiatric facility the boy was at] to come. You can't cancel again." When it finally went to the Commissioner of Education ... and [the Associate Commissioner of Special Education], [the school's lack of timely response] was all documented. They were out of compliance in [many] respects.

The newness of the evaluation process and the unexpectedly large number of referrals may have been partly responsible for the schools' disarray. However, parents anxious about their child's progress interpreted this disorganization as evidence of the schools' lack of good faith and unwillingness to take their child's problems seriously. They came to question the schools' ability to provide effective programming, no matter what the educational plan called for:

Dr. _____, who was the psychologist on the core team, said he would provide one-to-one counseling. We were appalled by that, because he was stretched so thin that he wasn't able to fulfill his obligations as a member of the evaluation team. This was a very important objection at that hearing.

Eleven Private School families in our sample had accepted an educational plan during the previous year, demonstrating their willingness to cooperate with the schools. Yet some of these children had not even received an evaluation by the end of this first year. In three instances, parents had received a letter informing them their child was to be placed in a special program for the law's first year. They accepted the school's judgment though there had not been an educational planning meeting. Most parents told us that the program they initially accepted was not provided fully and their child experienced difficulties. By the end of the first year, these parents expected increased services; when the schools offered the same plan a second time, the parents sought other options.

Evaluation meetings after the child was placed.

Even when parents had transferred their child to a private school before an educational plan was developed, a child evaluation meeting was eventually held. To enter into the appeals system, parents needed to formally reject an educational plan, a document which could only be produced after a meeting.

Both parents and school personnel usually saw these meetings as a formality. As a consequence, these meetings sometimes developed an ostensibly cordial tone with little attempt by school personnel to negotiate the proposed plan with the parents.

> [The school officials] read their reports and we said what we felt [our son] needed. . . . We had brought the director and his teacher at the [private] school and they said what he needed. And they listened politely and a few days later they sent us an educational plan that was completely different than the things we had stressed.

In other instances, these evaluation meetings were hostile and adversarial:

> At the evaluation meeting, the director of special services, Mr. —————— , yelled at me, literally yelled at me, that I was trying to bilk the city.

> *How were evaluators from the [private] school treated at the core meeting?*

> As if they were trying to drum up business. Throughout the whole meeting, the underlying message was "You're here to rip off the

city." I suppose they wrote as good a plan as they could, given what
was available in the system. But there was a lack of sensitivity. We
pointed out to them that while our son did relatively well in
structured situations, anything unstructured was disastrous. What
would happen in the lunchroom or at recess? So their proposal was
to have a tutor follow him around at those times. And we said,
"Does that sound like a good idea to you, having a grownup
walking behind him all the time?"

* * *

I think they saw [the meeting] as a last chance to prevent an appeal.
They knew they were in the wrong, that they had violated all the
procedures by not giving us a core for almost a year. And now they
were going to prove to us that they could beat us at a hearing by
giving us a good plan, on paper at least. So they had a new teacher
in the resource room, who had never seen our daughter, and she
said she could do anything. Anything we wanted, her program
would do it. Well, we tried to explain as good as her program was,
it was just not the same kind of experience as she was getting at the
[private school] and we had been through resource rooms for three
years. I was really not trying to attack her, I'm sure she's an
excellent teacher. But she became very defensive and the principal
became very angry and the meeting just sort of broke down.

Whatever the tone of these meetings, their focus was not on maintaining
communication and considering future plans for the child but on developing
a written document which would serve as evidence at the hearing. Neither
parents nor school staff spent time on repairing their relationships, on
developing guidelines for the child's future education, or on determining how
to ensure a smooth and timely transition back to the public schools. Once
parents decided to pursue an appeal, parents and school personnel ceased to
communicate about the child's needs.

The high frequency of cases in which an evaluation meeting was conducted
after a child had already entered a private school—about half the Private
School cases—has undoubtedly reinforced the stereotypes school personnel
hold about parents who appeal. Given the pressure of the heavy workload, it
must surely have seemed futile and discouraging to develop assessment
reports and educational plans for children who had already been withdrawn
from the public schools. To newly hired staff unfamiliar with the past
histories of these cases, it must have seemed that these were parents who had
given the schools little opportunity to prove themselves. And, to parents, these

attitudes must have further reinforced their sense of the schools' lack of understanding and commitment to the child's special needs.

Differences in definition of the child's problems.

Disputes between the parents and schools in our study were based on three major issues: how to define the child's special needs (the diagnosis); what types of services were required to meet those needs; and what degree of program intensity was necessary. Most disputes involved the latter two factors. Sometimes there were substantial differences on the diagnosis, which surfaced at the educational planning meeting to become a key issue in the appeal. Some examples:

> The brick wall for us came when he had already repeated first grade once and his second grade teacher said, "He's a fine student, he has no acting-out problems, everyone likes him, but he simply can't read and write and I cannot in good conscience send him on to the third grade." But he can't repeat second grade because he had already repeated first grade before and at that point [the city] didn't have any set-up whatsoever. Again, this is in legal contention but that is my perception. They had absolutely nothing to offer him and the guidance counselor of the school was telling us, in a long complex series of conferences with all the bigwigs of the school, that the basic reason for dyslexia was that the child was emotionally disturbed. . . . She had this theory, so she wanted to send him off to an emotionally disturbed classroom at the other end of town. . . . Since the [private school] was closer to our home than the local school, and since [their staff] seemed interested and sympathetic, we thought it was an easier and more responsible parental decision to ship him three miles rather than eight and a half miles.

* * *

> He would run in at six in the morning screaming, "I don't want to go to school." And the school system kept telling us that it was us— that we were putting too much pressure on the child. And we kept thinking, maybe it is us. But we couldn't see that we were doing anything to pressure the child.

* * *

* * *

What the school tries to do is say the kid is emotionally disturbed and blame it on the parents and say that the parents are bad parents. But he isn't, he's all together.

* * *

This shouldn't have happened to anyone. I was always very nice. I didn't want to rock any boats and neither did my husband. We felt she was in school and really, they could deal with any problems. It was just a matter of getting them to understand. We tried very hard to play ball with them and to preface everything with "I know you're trying very hard." However, our daughter was coming home every day crying that the other children were calling her retarded. And their response was that they didn't see it; that she was a very happy, well-adjusted child, and their program was working 100%.

* * *

In January [of 1975], I went to see what was going on. I was getting all this stuff written all over her papers and our daughter was so unhappy down there. And I got the same thing—she was emotionally disturbed and they wanted me to take her to [the local mental health center]. Nothing about a learning disability. I never fought them. I did anything they recommended. The year before I went to [the mental health center] on their recommendation and they saw my daughter and me privately, and my husband privately, and me and my husband, and me and my daughter; it went on and on. So the second year they told me that, I said, "No." I had already gone that route. That's when I decided to take her to a neurologist at _____ Hospital and they told me that she was super, super sane and had no emotional problems at all. [But she was living] under this harrassment, just about, I call it child abuse really. I told them [at] the school evaluation that they had emotionally abused my child, and they didn't like that. But I asked for her confidential report. And I found out that from second grade on they knew about the learning disability but they never told me. They had records of it, and they never told me. Fortunately, we are not in that position, but if I had to wash floors, I would never put her back in that school system.

* * *

He was just a disaster in the first grade. His emotional well-being. He was frustrated. After one month at the [private school], he was just a changed kid. We were desperate is why we put him there. I think I would have kept him home rather than put him back in public school. They offered him nothing. They insisted they were right and wouldn't talk about it. It was June, at the re-evaluation meeting, when they decided, after three months in a program, which was very minimal to begin with, that this child was ready to go to second grade. My God! He was a disaster! They [took] him out of the classroom twice for 20 minutes for three months and said he was cured. They didn't recognize that the kid had become an emotional wreck.

* * *

I kept going to the school to find out what was wrong and they would say that he wasn't applying himself, that he needed greater discipline, and it was my job to discipline him to make sure he did his work. And I did it. I would punish him, and he became worse and worse. And I would go to the school, and they would say, "Keep at it. We'll turn this boy around yet." It was cruelty. These are educators. They should know about things like learning disability. I'm just a parent and if I could find out about it, they should have known about it and not put him through all that torture. Finally, we went to a doctor at _____ Hospital who said he was learning-disabled. And the next term, it started all over again. They would punish him for not doing his work. And I went to the teacher and I said, "You can't punish him anymore. Now we know what's wrong with the boy." But it went on. And I went to [the special education director], and he said, "Well, the doctors have their opinion and I have mine." These people have no interest in children.

In some of these cases, by the time the dispute reached a hearing, the school system had developed an educational plan for the child based on a learning-disability definition in order to counter the parents' request for a private school placement. Although the original planning meeting had been premised on a different diagnosis, sometimes on an outright denial of any learning disability, school systems deemphasized this difference to make a better case at hearings.

School Actions After the Educational Planning Meeting

If parents failed to return the completed educational plan promptly, the law allows school personnel to contact them to negotiate any differences. According to our respondents, however, the schools made few attempts to maintain communication with them after the planning meeting. In our opinion, this lack of communication was particularly detrimental in view of parents' anger, and the need for a continuing long-term relationship between parents and schools on behalf of the child. Moreover, the schools' failure to follow up on unsuccessful planning meetings may have been the deciding factor in some parents' ultimate choice to remove their child from the public schools.

Parents reported varying amounts of contact with school personnel. At one extreme were three families who never even received a written educational plan. Other parents who received a plan but did not approve it said they never heard from the school system again. To the parents who had already decided to use private schools, these responses may have been irrelevant, but some parents said they still felt considerable uncertainty after their planning meeting:

> The school wanted to keep him in the resource room but he didn't seem to be getting anywhere and he seemed so unhappy in there that I decided we should get another opinion. I took him back to Dr. _____ at _____ Hospital who had seen him the year before. And he said that there had been no improvement and that it was time to get to work on this, and so that's what we did.

* * *

> I think my biggest fear was what it would do for him in terms of his friends, going to a special school out of town. So I talked with Mrs. _____ , who had a child going to [the private school], and

she said that you just have to work on it—make sure he goes out for Little League, be a den mother in the Scouts—that it was a problem but that it could be overcome, and she was very happy with [that school].

It wasn't an easy decision. We are public school people. My husband, myself, my children. We've gone to public school all the way. We are just not the type of people who go to private schools. And, of course, there were the costs to consider. And, truthfully, I felt he should be able to make it in the public school. Those are the people he has to be able to make it with in his life. I was very torn up about it.

We cannot know whether this parent might have been persuaded to accept the school system's proposal even if the school had offered more services. However, without efforts by school personnel to discuss the parent's unhappiness with the educational plan, there was little chance the child could be retained. Certainly the following parents might have been persuaded to retain their child in the public schools:

During that whole summer, from the time we rejected the core to the time of the hearing, [the school system] never contacted us. We kept on sending them letters—lawyer's letters—asking them to please reconsider, to please rewrite the plan; that if they couldn't, we would have to make other arrangements. They never responded to any of them. So when the fall came, we made arrangements to have her go to [private school] for the year.

Interestingly enough, of all our cases, those parents who had not yet removed their child from public school—Staying in School and Leaving School cases—reported the most frequent attempts at negotiation. We cannot say whether schools were more receptive to these parents because their child was still in public school, or whether the parents were more receptive to negotiation because their choices were limited by costs and the availability of outside services for more traditionally handicapped children. Clearly, however, schools' efforts at continuing negotiations with parents were a crucial, and often neglected factor in resolving parent-school disputes.

Even when parents did have further contact with the school system, these encounters were usually unsatisfying. About half of the families who put their children in private schools after the planning meeting said they had been in touch with school officials again, most often with the system's special education director, but occasionally with a higher-level administrator.

But by the time these contacts occurred, both parents and school personnel were frustrated and angry. For parents, the months of seeking a program through the school system had produced unacceptable results, and they had become increasingly convinced that only a private special needs school could help their child. Since their highest level of contact was usually with the special education director, parents tended to blame this administrator personally for refusing to provide a more appropriate program, or to pay for a private one. The administrator was seen not as an impartial professional considering the child's best interests but rather as a bureaucrat pursuing the school district's interests. Under these conditions, it would have taken considerable skill on both sides to focus the discussion on resolving current issues rather than on assigning blame for past failures, a skill which the administrators in our sample seemed to have lacked.

Parents reported that school administrators were generally unwilling to modify their proposals. Sometimes, these discussions were amiable:

> He said that the program they offered was what the school system had to offer and was appropriate to our son's needs. Mostly, he talked about keeping the appeal informal; that he would not use a lawyer if we wouldn't. We recognized we were at an impasse, but I didn't become emotionally involved in it and neither did he. I can see how other parents would.

More frequently, though, negotiations were used to vent frustration rather than to reach an accommodation which both sides increasingly viewed as unattainable:

> He said that the school program was a good program and that was that. If we wanted a private school, he wasn't going to be a part of it. He as much as accused us of never seriously wanting our son in the public schools, and going through the whole process so that we could win some money off of them. My husband got very upset and said some very intemperate things to him.

* * *

> I do think that . . . the school administrators felt they should develop an adversary relationship with parents who take this up to a hearing. Maybe some parents are bullied by hearing the school people say, "We have all of these special needs kids and no one

finds fault except for those of you who have removed your kid and you're bad to do that." That's too bad. It's one of the reasons you need a lawyer, to protect you from those kinds of attacks.

The Massachusetts Bureau of Special Edcuation Appeals ultimately recognized how antagonistic relations between parents and school personnel had become and by 1977, the law's third year, they began to provide a state mediator to try to resolve disputes informally. However, these mediators soon came to believe that many disputes were not possible to mediate because of the alienation resulting from the educational planning process. Also, mediators often became involved only after the child had already been placed at a private school, when the only remaining issue was who should pay the tuition.

Parent Visits to Programs

Many school districts invited parents to visit the programs proposed for their child, either before the educational planning meeting or after the program had been prescribed in the plan. These visits were poorly organized, and often provided far less favorable impressions of the public school's program than the descriptions offered at the educational planning meeting. For example:

> First, they wanted to put him in a resource room all day. You must understand that these meetings really devastate me. I think they are appalling. Anyway, the school principal finally spoke up and said shouldn't he at least be associated with some type of classroom, and I think it was on my mind too, so we rejected [the resource room concept] . . . so then the school said that they did have another classroom at another school. Now this was a big shock to us because I had no idea that they had a separate learning-disability classroom anywhere in the system. So we set up a time that we could go to meet this teacher who was in the other class. And my husband and I, really, to think of paying $4,000 a year [for a private school], it's out of the question for a family like us.

> We couldn't get home fast enough to burst into tears. It was a classroom with borderline retarded children, very morose children. If I had a child in that category I might have accepted it. The teacher was a nice person, but she is not geared to teach children with problems like my son.

* * *

We made a date . . . and I visited this lovely third-grade classroom.
She was a very nice teacher, an extremely pleasant room, but, and
this isn't just one thing but it's one thing that stands out, I made a
comment about my son's handwriting. I noticed on the board the
math papers. Math is a terrible problem for him and the math
papers [had] tiny writing compared to the way he writes all over the
page. I just made a comment about that and the [third-grade]
teacher said, "Oh, we'll have him doing that in a month." [The
mother reacted negatively to what she perceived as the teacher's
lack of understanding of her son's difficulties.]

* * *

At the core, [they said] they would give us anything we wanted all
day—the kitchen sink, carpeting. Then I went to the junior high
school to meet with his actual teachers and they gave me a schedule
of his classes. When I got home and added all the time up, he had
two hours of gym with kids his age and one hour of shop. Except
for three hours a week, he was going to be stuck with low-
achieving, delinquent boys all day. He was going to go through
school like that. Well, he was tested out in science as being in the
eleventh grade. There just seemed to be no flexibility for what he
could do well and sort of a fixed idea of what he could do. And yet
we were promised everything by the core team. It was very hard.
When we went to the [private school], we got a schedule: here are
his teachers, here is what he is going to get, and these teachers are
all trained. . . . That was it as far as we could see; that was what we
were looking for. . . . It is hard because his friends all go to the
junior high and it's hard [for him]. He wants to go back all the
time.

* * *

What they said they were going to give him didn't exist. We went
down to the school and it wasn't there. And the principal said, "I
had better have my lawyer here before I speak to you."

* * *

The learning centers in [our public school system] were the most
depressing, oppressive places—barren, so little stimulus to
genuine education. It was all full of the Mickey Mouse business of

how you teach kids to read; it became a sort of coercive affair. You have to do this and that and the other. But there was no motivation to learn.

In arranging program visits, the lack of coordination among school personnel meant that parents usually observed school programs alone, unaided by personnel from the Child Evaluation Team who could explain why this particular program was appropriate for their child. Staff might have described the aims, techniques, and even the daily length of the program in different terms than these had been presented at the educational planning conference. Unaided parents could easily develop serious misgivings about what the public schools were offering them.

Some parents were sent to observe programs that would begin operating the following year but were not yet operating. Clearly, this was a confusing experience. A number of parents were sent to programs in which the severity of the handicaps of the other children was greater or more visible than the parent had been led to believe. Finally, in two instances, it was not made clear to parents that they had to schedule an appointment for a visit and their appearance at the school was met with distress by program personnel.

How Parents Explain the Schools' Behavior

We asked parents how they explained the behavior of school personnel and why they felt the school system was unable to develop an acceptable program. Parents viewed the school system's response to Chapter 766 in general, and to their child in particular, as reflecting an unwillingness to comply with the law.

When we asked, *"Why do you think the school designed the program it did?"*, the most frequently selected alternatives were "because they had the facilities to realize that program" (38%) and "to provide a program 'adequate' enough to comply with the law" (22%). The implication was that the schools' response was minimal, the least they could "get away with" under the new law. The least frequent response was "because they thought it was best for the child" (4%). Clearly, parents were profoundly cynical about the motives of school personnel.

In the view of many parents, school personnel used illegitimate tactics— such as pressuring them into signing nonspecific or inadequate educational plans or refusing to negotiate more acceptable programs—because personnel were too much concerned with program costs and too little concerned with children's welfare. Some parents did distinguish between special education administrators and evaluation personnel, who worked more directly with their child. For example,

> When the educational planning meeting started, [the child evaluator] seemed to feel that [our son] needed an outside placement. But when the director of special education walked into the room, they changed what they were saying, almost in mid-sentence. Now I know it's their jobs that are on the line. [The special education director] doesn't want any more private schools and that's it, no matter what the condition of the kid. But really, some of these people who sit on these teams and have buckled under, how can they live with themselves?

* * *

> There is a difference between what you are told publicly and what you are told privately. Some of the evaluation people knew what was going on and privately they told me they had nothing for [our child]. But publicly they had to write an inadequate plan because they are not free to recommend what the child needs.

Other parents distinguished between evaluation team members and teachers:

> Her teacher told me all the things in the plan they had been trying and hadn't gotten anywhere. And she said I should go out and look at what was available. Now here is a woman who knows our daughter and has her best interests at heart. The core team are people from outside of the school, and they're members of the administration, really.

* * *

> I talked to the resource room teacher [privately] and she sounded much more pessimistic than she had been at the meeting. I think she couldn't say it in a group, but she was trying to give me a signal.

Still other parents distinguished between school staff and the school board:

> Mine was the very first case [in the town]. It was terrible. I had no problems with the core team but the school board wouldn't pay.

This is a very stingy town and they felt if I got a [private placement], everyone else would be asking for it.

* * *

[The special education director] told me that if it was his child, he would be doing the same thing. But his hands were tied by the school board. He said he would have to fight me but that when we got to the court, he didn't think he would win.

As these comments reflect, a significant reason for the lack of consistency in the schools' positions was that parents were being given different advice by different levels of the bureaucracy. Generally, those staff who had more interaction with the child were seen as more concerned with the child's needs and less concerned with costs. Some parents even reported being offered certain services by personnel at one level and then having the offer specifically retracted by higher-level staff.

Whatever the level at which financial pressure occurred, parents felt that the evaluation system was unduly influenced by it.

They're in tremendous financial difficulties. [Chapter] 766 is costing the town a half million more than they expected it to. The town doesn't want to fund these programs. They don't want to fund children outside of the school, in the worst possible way. They don't even want to fund programs within the school. I think it's purely financial. I think the people don't like me either. But that's not why they're continuing this. If money wasn't the issue, there wouldn't be a fight.

* * *

At every meeting I went to, I had the question of money thrown at me.

* * *

When I heard that the school wouldn't pay for private placements, no matter what the circumstances, I just broke down and cried. We'd been hoping for something for so long.

* * *

Money, money, money. That's all I heard.

Clearly, most parents did not see the school systems as acting in good faith. Educational planning teams were seen as recommending programs more because they were cheaper and available than because they would be appropriate.

A small number of parents did not share this economic interpretation, but had a more extreme view of the school's behavior: that the actions of school personnel reflected personal malice.

I stood up to them and I said "No." They can't stand that. They want parents to do whatever they say and they're out to teach me a lesson.

* * *

Oh, I have no doubt it's a vendetta against me.

Other parents interpreted the school's behavior as simply incompetent. When we asked, *"Did you feel the child evaluation team was qualified to draw up a program for your child?"* 36% of our parents responded, "Yes, but they were not doing it." However, 38% chose "No, they were not experts in the area of my child's needs." When we asked parents to agree or disagree with the statement *"The school system did a good job of evaluating my child,"* only 20% agreed.

Quite apart from parents' assessment of financial pressures, they felt considerable skepticism about the school system's assessment capability:

When I went to [an independent evaluator], she looked at the school's records and told me they had given him the wrong test.

Many parents reported that some school personnel who attended their child evaluation meeting had never seen their child, yet, as one parent put it:

They took a formal vote as to what kind of plan [he] should [have]. Some of the people who were voting knew nothing about the case. They had never seen him. And yet they were voting on what his education should be. It was insulting.

One parent reported that a school psychologist had seen her child for one hour:

At the core meeting, he gave this big report, with lots of numbers, as if he knew something about this child. I was with him for no more than an hour, maybe forty minutes. He tried to come off sounding like he really knew the child, but you can't know a child after forty minutes.

Other parents reported:

They tested him and their psychologist said that he did not have a learning disability. Very nice lady but very incompetent in her field. [Our boy] was very upset by the testing, because she was giving him the answers to the test, telling him what to put down. Now he's no dummy, he came home extremely upset.

* * *

Look, these people didn't know anything about learning disabilities. The law was new, and these were the old people. One of their testers used to be a physical education teacher. You know how school systems protect and bring along athletic-looking incompetent males. So the law came in and they reshuffled titles. But they didn't know what they were doing. Today, they have a whole new staff. But back then, they didn't have the people who were specialists and they were just making do.

Many parents felt that not only were the evaluators incompetent, but the teachers were unqualified as well:

That's one of the big points we made at the hearing. At the [private] school they are all qualified people who know something about these problems. The public schools don't have those kinds of people. They didn't then, maybe they do now. What they had [then] was people who had taken two courses at a teachers college, not people who could handle real trouble.

In sum, consider the parents' responses to the question: *"Why do you think the school allowed this to go to a hearing rather than negotiate with you?"* We allowed parents to choose as many responses as they felt were appropriate. Among all the respondents, 70% chose the category "Money," and 29% said "Because the school wishes to prove it is competent." Other responses were: "The school believes the demands of parents are unfair" (21%); "Because the school feels indignant" (19%); "To make an example of us" (19%); "Out of spite" (10%); and "Because they knew they could win a hearing" (2%).

In contrast, parents often saw their own actions as not simply protecting their own child but as fulfilling a social obligation for other handicapped children as well:

> We discussed with our lawyer whether we should drop the whole thing and just pay the tuition. And then we decided that if the law says children deserve this attention, parents have to call the school system on what they are doing if the law is ever going to work.

* * *

> My appeal hasn't gotten me anything. After all this time, I have nothing to show for it. But maybe it's taught them a lesson, and the parents who can't afford to appeal will get a better deal.

One parent—out of 71 cases—held a very different opinion when she viewed the educational planning meeting two years later. She now felt that:

> Some of the things that the evaluation team was saying about my child I just couldn't accept at that time. . . . Perhaps an educational planning meeting, which is a big, formal affair, is not the best situation for trying to bring parents to an understanding of their child, but I think that's what they were trying to do, and I wasn't prepared for it.

Parents' Need for Support During Decision Making

This discussion has focused on the sense of betrayal that was generated by the educational planning process. But these reactions cannot be considered in isolation. The parents in Private School and Leaving School disputes came to believe that, regardless of the process, public schools were offering them inferior programs and private schools had better ones. Parents did not come to this position unaided; they required significant social support. The most important sources of this support were professionals outside the school system attached to hospitals, university clinics, child guidance centers, and in private practice.

Consider a parent who was told by her school system that her child was emotionally disturbed. Upon the advice of a friend, she had the child tested for a learning disability at a major Boston hospital. She reported:

Finally, there was someone who was listening and who didn't treat me as crazy. After all that time, I finally got to someone who seemed to know what he was talking about and seemed to know how to talk to me about it.

There were often considerable differences of opinion between school- and nonschool-based professionals over the needs of learning-disabled children. We have no data on parents who sought outside evaluations and were advised to keep their children in the public schools. But many parents in our sample found outside evaluators who recommended private placements.

They told me that no school system had the facilities to handle children in as much difficulty as my son.

* * *

They said I would be wasting my time fooling around with more resource room programs, that they are for children with minor problems and that our son needed something much more intensive.

Frequently, parents not only were told that public programs were insufficient but were specifically directed to particular private schools.

Almost all the parents in our sample, regardless of their plans for their child, took their child to an outside evaluator. In 44 of the 49 Private School cases, the child had at some point been evaluated by nonschool professionals: 27 children received learning-disability evaluations, usually at Boston hospitals or university-affiliated clinics; 17 children received both learning-disability and psychiatric evaluations. In the 22 Staying in School and Leaving School cases, all but three children were evaluated independently. In most instances, these outside evaluators testified for the parents or provided supporting documentation at the hearing. In general, parents did not transfer their children to special needs schools without first seeking independent evaluations. This information played an important role in legitimating the parents' claims, either to private placements or more intensive school-based programs.

Many parents reported that the school staff tended to ignore outside evaluations when planning their child's program, action which further exacerbated parents' frustration and alienation from the public schools.

The Decision to Appeal

While we have been concerned with parents' decisions to accept or reject an educational plan, the parents in our sample also made a second decision—to resort to an appeal.

Some parents not in our sample but with similar complaints about their child's lack of progress simply placed their child in a private school and did not appeal. In one instance, parents feared an appeal would damage their relationship with school personnel who were serving their other children. Another family considered a legal action distasteful.

Even among the parents in our sample, some had transferred their child to a private school before they knew about the appeals system.

> I think the first we heard about [the law] was at the [private] school. We had heard about the law, but I probably thought it was for blind children, retarded children. I hadn't thought of it as applying to [our learning-disabled son]. When I was talking to [the director of the private school] about the problems we had been having with the public schools, he told us that it was the kind of situation that the law was intended to correct.

We asked parents whether they had intended to use the appeals system at the point at which they decided to reject their educational plan. Some 25% said they had "definitely" been planning on an appeal; 28% said they had not heard about the appeals system or that it was not yet operating; and 17% were aware of the appeals system but were not sure whether they would use it. Many parents told us they first learned about the appeals system from other parents at private schools or from private school staff members.

Sometimes parents were directly aided by private school staff members in preparing for their hearing. The director of one special needs school acted as an advocate free of charge for 11 of our 49 private school parents, presenting their case for continuation of the placement. Seven other families had private school staff members appear without charge as witnesses at their hearings. Most of this direct involvement came from a single special needs school at which 21 of our 49 Private School children were enrolled. In five other cases, a former staff member of another special needs school helped parents prepare their cases and represented them at hearings for a fee. Parents were directed to use this advocate by that school's current staff. Three families used lawyers who were recommended by their private school's staff. In addition, staff at private schools frequently accompanied parents to child evaluation meetings.

Parents of Leaving School and Staying in School cases rarely had access to this support, making an appeal more difficult for them. If the parents had enrolled their child in a summer program, they could develop a relationship with private school staff. Otherwise, these parents had to develop their supports themselves, or with an advocate or attorney's help. This requires considerably more personal initiative and money.

The Role of the Private Learning-Disability Schools

Massachusetts has a long tradition of private sector schooling for regular and special education students, and supports a well-developed professional community of physicians, psychologists, and educators supportive of private schooling. It is not surprising that when parents become disenchanted with public school programs, the professionals to whom they turned for advice were likely to direct them towards private education and to offer them significant support for this choice.

A select set of private learning-disability schools moved quickly to make use of the promise of special education reform. They encouraged parents to use the hearing system to pressure school systems into providing more appropriate programs for learning-disabled students. One headmaster in particular moved quickly to support parent appeals, evidently reasoning that once a school system had been forced to pay private school tuition, it would develop its own learning-disabled program. Several persons directing these private schools had been trying for two decades to stimulate the development of learning-disability services in the public schools. They seized upon the new law as an effective tool.

Private schools not only offered a visible and respected alternative to the programs available in the public sector, they actively urged parents to use the appeals system to get reimbursed for private tuition. When parents went to a hearing, these private schools were often ready with sophisticated support, resulting in many early victories for parents in the early days of Chapter 766, when public schools had not yet implemented the new law and did not know how to organize themselves for a hearing. Private school personnel, on the other hand, offered an array of services and free expert testimony.

Usually, parents would visit the private school before deciding whether to place their child outside the school system. They found private schools cordial to them and their inquiries. They discovered they were able to communicate with the director and staff members more effectively than they had with the public school staff. These positive contacts with private school staffs contrasted dramatically with their often acrimonious disputes with the public school. In five Private School cases, the child had attended a summer program at the private school and had a successful learning experience, often his or her first. The quality of these contacts strengthened parents' resolve to pursue an appeal.

As a consequence, private schools have had a dramatic influence on programs for learning-disabled children in Massachusetts. Special education administrators who lost early appeals, or saw other communities losing, recognized the need to develop programs for these children rapidly if they were to avoid paying high private tuitions. To blunt the arguments raised at hearings by parents and private school staff, they had these private school programs available to serve as models for their own services.

The central role played by private school staffs also suggests the extent to which even privileged parents require a support system in order to be successful in the hearing process.

Summary

This chapter has described parent experiences with public special education personnel, and how these led them to file appeals during the early years of Chapter 766. The typical appeal in Massachusetts involved high-status parents with high expectations for their child who had become frustrated by the child's failure to progress in mainstreamed public school programs even with added special education help. Parents were also frustrated by the inability of school personnel to evaluate their child properly, or to communicate with parents in an open and collegial manner. Although some of these difficulties were undoubtedly due to the rapid expansion of school services, parents interpreted them as incompetence and a lack of concern on the school's part. They then looked for other ways to address their child's problems, coming into contact with a wide range of independent evaluators who legitimated both their perceptions of their child's needs and their demands for more intensive programming. Such programs were mainly available in the private schools.

The schools' failure to negotiate with parents in good faith stands out as a major reason why parents requested hearings. We have the impression that many school administrators have striven for better communication with parents since the early years of the law and have expanded their programs to better serve the learning-disabled child.

Parent criticisms of the public schools are particularly striking in light of their generally favorable assessment of private schools (see Chapter 9). Data from the follow-up interviews we conducted four years after the hearings strongly suggest that many of the children in this study made considerable gains at private school, after one or more years of failure to progress in public school.

Even if we assume public schools were offering learning-disabled children adequate programs, the schools' defensiveness and rigidity clearly prevented them from developing responsive relations with these parents. The private schools saw the parents as their clients, and sought to be responsive to the parents' concerns, an approach which parents appreciated. While these schools were working with the child's problems, they also worked to help the parents understand the child's situation. Public schools' staff tended not to see the parents as clients, and resented the parents' attempts to hold them accountable. The resulting conflict led frequently to the adversarial confrontation of a hearing.

Notes

1. Percentage of the 71 parents making a given response is indicated in the parentheses. Parents often provided more than one response to the questions, so percentages often add up to more than 100%.

2. When the original Chapter 766 regulations were written, they called the child assessment group the "Core Evaluation Team" (CET) to denote the minimal number of specialists and parents who had to be involved in the assessment of the child. The world of Chapter 766 soon adopted the expression "core" to refer to the assessment process and the educational planning meeting. Hence, children were "cored." Subsequent state regulations changed this expression to the TEAM. It is too soon to know whether children will now be "TEAM'd."

6

Parents Go To a Hearing

We have seen that the first users of the Massachusetts appeals system sought services for their handicapped children at a time when schools were overwhelmed by the problems of implementing comprehensive special education legislation. Their experiences with the disorganized evaluation and planning process caused many parents to feel considerable anger. Parents came to view school personnel as incompetent, insensitive towards their children's needs, and as sabotaging parents' rights to help plan their children's programs.

School personnel also entered the appeals process with a good deal of anger towards parents. Parents were often viewed as illegitimately using limited special education funds to obtain private schooling for their children, or as venting on the schools the anger that really grew out of their own inability to deal with their children's handicaps.

These disputes intensified because of the continuing lack of communication between parents and schools. The conflict escalated as parents became more assertively involved. School personnel felt uncomfortable talking with parents in a collegial, participatory fashion. Parents and school staff tended to have no contact after parents rejected the child's educational plan, ignoring the 30-day "cooling off" period which was designed to further negotiation. When parents and schools did meet, their contacts were often so hostile that even mediators had difficulty keeping the discussion focused on the substantive issues.

With few prior attempts at meaningful communication and negotiation, with high levels of nervousness about the process, and with a good deal of anger toward each other, the parties entered the hearing. The contending parties were arrayed against each other in a formal confrontation: presenting their evidence, calling their witnesses, cross-examining the witnesses of the other party, being subjected themselves to hostile or legalistic questioning from the lawyer or advocate of the opposing side. A hearing officer rendered a written decision, which for all practical purposes named a "winner" and a "loser."

A more complete picture of a hearing's rules and procedures is presented below in Chapter 12. School administrators' views of hearings are covered in Section III. In this chapter, we present the hearing from the point of view of the parents, describing both the nature of their experience and some salient difficulties they encountered with the process.

The Use of Representation at Hearings

A central feature of the hearing as it has developed in Massachusetts is that both parents and schools make relatively high use of representation at hearings, in the form of lawyers and advocates.

Among the 71 cases in our parent sample, lawyers represented 26 parents (37%) and 34 schools (47%).

Parents secured two other types of representation. In 13% of the causes, they used paid advocates, usually a former learning-disability evaluator at a private day school. In another 15.5% of the cases, they secured free representation at hearings, usually a staff member of the private day school their child was attending. A few parents were represented by social workers, other parents, or similar interested parties. Thus, a total of 65% of all parents in our study were represented. In these early hearings, parents were more likely to be represented than schools, who used attorneys only 47% of the time. Some parents were doubly represented, by both lawyers and private school advocates.

Representation varied by type of case. Parents who had placed their child in a private school were most likely to be represented. Among the 49 Private School cases in our sample, 69% had some sort of representation (39% lawyers, 16% paid advocates, 12.7% unpaid advocates). These findings were similar to our analysis of a 50% sample of the decisions from the first two and one-half years of hearings. That study found that among 91 Private School cases, 78% of the parents were represented by an attorney or advocate, while 61% of the schools had attorneys. Private School parents are more often represented for two reasons: (1) they are wealthier than other parents, and (2) their children are already enrolled in private schools so that they have an immediate financial interest in the hearing's outcome. Public schools are likewise more often represented in these cases because they have a considerable stake in avoiding a decision that might require them to pay costly private tuitions.

Parents and schools are least likely to be represented in Staying-in-School cases. In our parent sample, only three of the 11 parents involved in these disputes were represented (27%); while schools used attorneys in four cases (36%). The 50% sample study also showed that in the 23 Staying-in-School cases, parents were represented only six times (26%) and schools only eight times (35%). These cases usually involved poorer parents who were less able to afford representation. Since parents were usually requesting relatively inexpensive modifications of school programming, the schools were also under less financial pressure to win.

Among the 11 Leaving School cases in our study, parents were represented in five cases (45%) and schools in seven cases (64%). Again, the 50% study corroborated our findings: in the 18 Leaving School cases, parents were represented in seven cases (39%) and schools in nine cases (50%). In Leaving School cases, parents tend to be poorer and have often had no prior contact with private schools. Even though a loss in these cases is costly to the schools, school personnel told us they were reluctant to use attorneys when parents could not afford to do so.

The situation for poorer parents has improved somewhat in recent years, as several advocacy agencies have trained staff to aid those unable to pay a private attorney. However, such resources are still severely limited, with serious consequences for parents who cannot afford representation. Without some help in facing the intimidating experience of a hearing, parents feel unable to exercise their right to an appeal.

The Perceived Need for Representation

Although less than two-thirds of our parent sample used lawyers or advocates, almost all parents we interviewed said they would definitely advise other families to use them. Less than one-fifth recommended against such help or said it was unnecessary. For example, only three of 11 parents who brought Staying-in-School cases used attorneys or advocates, but nine of these 11 parents said they would recommend representation to other parents. And of the 58 parents who recommended representation, 47 felt that parents need a lawyer rather than just an advocate.

In explaining their need for support at hearings, parents emphasized a number of interrelated themes which provide a portrait of parents' reactions to the hearings. Attending a hearing is upsetting to parents. We asked, *"How did you feel when you actually arrived at the hearing?"* Seventy-three percent of our subjects used adjectives like "nervous," "scared," "apprehensive," and "angry" to characterize their feelings. Only a few recalled themselves to be "determined to win," "relieved," "confident," "calm," or "uncompromising." This high level of tension suggests one reason why parents need an outsider's support.

> It is very important that you have someone with you and the reason is that it is a very emotional thing. It's your child and someone else can present things you couldn't.

* * *

> An outside person can present things without becoming upset.

Parents saw attorneys and advocates as a means of protecting themselves against losing control of their emotions during the hearing:

> Yes, I would certainly take a lawyer, without any question. Mr. _____ [the Special Education Director] is the kind of person who would make me furious if I didn't have an attorney to get furious for me. That happened to a friend of mine. At the hearing, he sort of flew off the handle when he heard the school's arguments, which really amounted to nothing more than an attack on the parents. That sort of behavior on the part of parents does not appeal to a hearing officer. I needed—I'm sure most of us need— some help in preventing the hearing from becoming simply another confrontation.

* * *

> Parents, I think, get too emotional. I mean, I wanted to burn the school with everyone locked in it. A lawyer can be more objective.

Hearings are experienced by parents as very formal procedures. When asked to agree or disagree that *"My appeals hearing was very formal, like a court case,"* 61% of the parents perceived this to have been true. Among parents bringing Private School cases, 30 of 49 agreed; among parents bringing Leaving School cases, 10 of 11 agreed. Only three among the 11 Staying-in-School cases agreed, but theirs was the kind of case where representation was used least by either side.

The formality of a hearing intimidates parents and makes them feel unable to act on their own behalf. For example, we asked, *"Why did you choose to have a counsel or advocate at your hearing?"* The most frequently selected response—chosen by 55% of the represented parents—was that "I didn't feel confident enough to present the case myself." One-third of these respondents said friends and acquaintances had told them they needed counsel to win at a hearing, while one-tenth felt that "an attorney could cut through the emotional, adversarial build-up that had developed between the school and the family."

Part of the formality of a hearing involves an emphasis on procedural details and rules of law, which parents feel they need help to address:

> There are a lot of legal snags, loopholes that the schools try to use. An attorney doesn't help you very much in presenting the problems and the history, but you need them for the legal part.

* * *

> If I hadn't had a lawyer, I would have thought the appeals system was biased in favor of the schools. And the reason for that is that at the hearing, a number of technicalities were brought out which I had never heard, but my lawyer was absolutely competent. He was much more conversant with it than the school system itself, because this is a thing he's made his speciality. It is a legal proceeding in which the schools try to avoid the issue of how appropriate their services are for the child and instead simply maintain that they are within the law. There is also a great deal of personal attack on the motives of parents. In our case, the school kept saying that we wanted our child in a private school for social prestige types of reasons, even though the special education director knows that we have two other children enrolled in the public school system. There were continual objections as to whether evaluation reports and other types of documents were admissible and whether things we had learned at the evaluation meeting and in conversations with the various school personnel were hearsay. There was a good deal of discussion about what the time limits in the law and other parts of it actually meant. For these types of issues, one needs an attorney. I would have been very uncomfortable going it alone.

Many parents attributed their own need for representation to the actions of the school's attorney:

Yes, definitely, I would take an attorney. It's just too complicated
and if the school has an attorney like [ours did] it becomes a total
fiasco. . . . He twists everything around and doesn't obey any of the
rules set down. You take a lawyer like [our school system's] and he
goes through the hearing as if you're in a courtroom, which was
not the intent of the law as near as I can tell. So he destroys the
whole concept with his approach.

* * *

We were not emotionally or intellectually prepared for the
adversary relationship that evolved and we remain astounded, I
think is the proper word, at what we perceived to be the viciousness
of the town counsel [who represented the school]. We are not at all
convinced that the town counsel represented the [opinions of all
parts of the] school system, but, on the other hand, he was
operating on the direct instructions of the School Committee. The
hearing took two whole days and the town counsel objected to
everything, literally and absolutely everything. Like the testimony
and evidence we wanted to present. We would offer an opinion and
he would object because it was an opinion. We were shocked. It got
to be so ludicrous that by noon of the first day, we hadn't presented
anything yet because he was objecting to every little point and
detail, challenging the right of the state to hold such a hearing.
The suggestion was made to break 45 minutes for lunch and he
objected to that. . . . When a town makes that type of presentation,
of course parents need an attorney.

There was considerable variation in the tasks actually performed by
advocates and lawyers. Some advocates went so far as to prepare dossiers of
testing materials and other documents to present at the hearing, even
recommending to parents that additional evaluations be obtained or
conducting such evaluations themselves. Other advocates and lawyers
expected parents to compile their own materials. Most lawyers made an initial
presentation to the hearing officer, though some had parents make the
presentation. Most lawyers and advocates cross-examined witnesses; a few had
parents do this. Some lawyers restricted their participation to points in the
hearing when matters of law and procedure were in dispute. Despite the high
rate of representation in our sample, parents invested considerable effort of
their own in preparing and presenting their cases.

Many parents indicated that lawyers acted "as a mediator between us and the school" (42% of parents who used them) or "as a counter force to the school counsel" (48%). (Parents were allowed to give more than one answer.) Almost half the represented parents (45%) reported that an attorney or advocate "added a feeling of authority to the evidence."

Some Dissenting Views of Representation

Close to 18% of our parents did feel that representation is unnecessary or counterproductive. This belief may reflect the difficulty these early hearings users experienced in finding knowledgeable attorneys. They also found attorneys to be unfamiliar with the educational jargon and testing material presented by the schools. This situation has improved as more attorneys and advocates have specialized in special education appeals cases.

Some parents thought attorneys might deflect attention from the real problems they had with the schools, stressing legal matters at the expense of educational issues. Parents often reported that lawyers and advocates increased the formality of hearings by emphasizing rules and procedures in their presentation. Some felt this made it harder for them to convey the history and details of their dissatisfaction with the schools. As several parents told us:

> My advice would be not to use an attorney. In fact, I consulted my attorney and his advice was that no good attorney knew these regulations well enough to provide adequate representation. And the cost of retaining a good lawyer would be $10,000. I found during the hearing itself that when the school department tried to harp on technicalities, my simple statement that this was bull and that we were here to discuss a child's education and not technicalities was enough to convince the hearing officer. Perhaps that was just the hearing officer we happened to draw. I have friends who used [a paid advocate] and they were very satisfied. But from our experience, I think a parent can feel confident that they will get a fair hearing by themselves.

* * *

> We were told by several sources that we would be better off if we had an attorney because the hearings were so technical. We were very sorry that we hired an attorney. She hurt us more than she helped us. We have since advised parents not to bring an attorney unless the [attorneys] are familiar with their child's needs. [Our attorney]

did not adequately represent us. She didn't know our case as well as she should have and didn't even read over the notes, the records, until the morning of the hearing. Then she asked the kinds of questions—legal, quibbling questions—that could only make the hearing officer vote against us. These are very specialized hearings and attorneys simply don't know the child and his history. So I feel that parents are better off if they simply present what they know themselves.

* * *

Lawyers don't know the story. They have little set things that they say. So for our second hearing, we presented the case ourselves. I must tell you that my husband worked on this till three or four o'clock in the morning for the last three weeks and I was right next to him. It took a tremendous amount of work but once you did it, you told the story. It's better without a lawyer. My husband did the cross-examination. We had planned it out as if it were a script. Lawyers, I think, get in the way of presenting the story.

* * *

Our attorney sat through the whole thing and didn't say a word. I had to present our case. He kept saying I knew it better and could express it better. I wasn't prepared for that. The town had an attorney and he was very clever and our attorney was worse than useless. It was money thrown down the drain.

Some parents who had used attorneys thought that advocates would be better:

We found the same problem with a lawyer as with [the school system] in trying to evaluate [our son]. The lawyer didn't know the boy either and it was really up to us to try and bring out the differences. Also, a lawyer is not familiar with these tests and what they mean so they can only help you with lawyer-type arguments. I have heard that some of the advocates are educators and know the terminology and this score and that score. I have had three or four parents call me about the hearings and I've recommended that they find an advocate. I don't think that any parent in her right mind should go in alone, but I don't think it is the kind of thing lawyers are trained for.

Other parents reported negative experiences with advocates:

> The advocate was very helpful in drawing together all of the papers that you need, compiling the test scores and telling us what we would need to get. [But] at the hearing, I thought her presentation was very weak. I would not recommend her for that reason. I thought we were poorly represented. On the other hand, it may be that only parents can really represent themselves at these things. No one else knows the real history behind it.

* * *

> [Using an advocate] was the worst mistake of my life. We showed that the school hadn't offered us any plan, and gave the doctor's reports and said what his program was now. And then [our advocate] said we should leave, that that was all that we had to present. So we left. We didn't stay for the school's side of the argument, and they had a very smart lawyer, and he apparently convinced the hearing officer.

Despite this testimony, we found few parents who expressed acute dissatisfcation with their representation. Among represented parents, 69% judged their representation to be excellent or good, and 20% "fair"; only 9% applied a rating of "poor." As we shall see, however, when parents lost an appeal, they tended to explain their loss in terms of the effectiveness of the school's counsel and the ineffectiveness of their own representation.

How Parents Saw the School's Case

Besides the formality of a hearing and the need to keep emotions under control, three other aspects of a hearing led parents to want help: the schools' ability to present more witnesses than parents can; the surprising and often questionable nature of the school's testimony; and the perception that parents were being personally attacked by the schools.

The use of witnesses.
Just as parents felt outnumbered at the educational planning meeting, so did they feel disadvantaged at hearings by the school's greater number of witnesses.

School systems regularly bring a broad range of personnel to hearings: special education teachers; child evaluation personnel (diagnostic teachers, psychologists, social workers); and administrators such as the child's principal and the director of special education.

Parents' witnesses were most frequently teachers, private school administrators, and advocates connected to private schools. Less frequent witnesses were specialists who acted as independent evaluators of the child.

Written decisions usually provide a listing of who attended a hearing and what their affiliations were. While the people in attendance may or may not provide evidence, their presence indicates who was available to testify for each side. Table 6-1, compiled from the 50% sample of decisions written during the same time period as this study, presents data for 135 decisions which include attendance listings.

The average hearing was attended by 3.2 school staff and 1.1 persons for the parents in addition to the parents themselves. Attendance varied by the type of case. When children were still in public school and had not been independently evaluated, parents brought few witnesses. Of the 23 identifiable Staying-in-School cases from the decisions sample, the average attendance at hearings for parents was .2 people, in addition to the parents themselves, while schools averaged 2.5 people. In 18 Leaving School disputes, parents averaged only .4 additional people in attendance while the schools brought 2.8 people. Both parents and schools had more witnesses in Private School disputes: 1.4 for parents; 3.4 for schools.

Representatives of human services agencies, who attended 14 hearings, and "others," who attended 72 hearings, could not be identified as belonging to either side; they are excluded from the tabulations. We have included advocates for parents as potential witnesses, since advocates were often educational evaluators or private school personnel who also provided testimony.

In our study sample, 63% of the 71 children had independent evaluations which parents presented at their hearings as reports. Few of the psychologists, psychiatrists, and independent educators who conducted these evaluations actually appeared at the parents' hearings (19%, .6%, and 13%, respectively).

By contrast, the school personnel who prepared evaluations and the educational plan often attended the hearings, as did the people who were going to implement the proposed program. Parents felt that written reports had less impact than the physical presence of a witness:

> The purpose of the independent evaluation is to get the best opinion on what should be done. We got the best opinion. Then we went to the hearing and those opinions were disregarded. The [school's] lawyer kept saying that we didn't want our child in the public schools, that we were against the public schools. It was never that we were against the public schools. It was that he hadn't

Table 6-1.
Attendance at Hearings Based on Written Decisions for 135 Hearings

Hearings Attended by Parent Representatives

Attended	# Who Attended	% of Hearings
Mother	134	99%
Father	111	82%
Parent Advocate	47	35%
Administrator of Private School	40	30%
Private School Teacher	35	26%
Psychologist	18	13%
Medical Doctor	5	4%
Psychiatrist	5	4%

Hearings Attended by School Representatives

Attended	# Who Attended	% of Hearings
Director of Special Education	86	64%
Special Needs Teacher	59	44%
School Psychologist	55	41%
Director of Pupil Services	51	38%
Child Evaluation Team Chairperson	51	38%
School Social Worker or Counselor	39	29%
School Principal	31	23%
School Superintendent	28	21%
Regular Class Teacher	22	16%

gotten anywhere and the best advice we could get was that he needed the kind of program we were asking for. But when you get a hearing, they twist everything around. If there are people who are supposed to be experts, a hearing officer, who is a lawyer and doesn't really know anything about these matters, should not be discounting the advice of the best people. Now one problem, of course, is that Dr. _____ [the child's evaluator] from the _____ Hospital couldn't attend. You can't ask him to spend a day there. But he did send a very strong letter saying that [our son] needed such and such a program. But this tends to be discounted at hearings, at least it was in our case. The school had everyone there. They would have had the janitor testify if it would have helped them. And whatever he needed, they promised they could do. They made a good impression and we didn't have the people there who could contradict it.

* * *

I felt that recommendations from the _____ Hospital and the _____ Medical Center should stand by themselves. I never expected that written reports would be ridiculed at the hearing and taken so lightly.

* * *

You felt alone. My husband and I went through it totally alone. They brought [the special education director] and [a psychologist] and [a special education teacher], and we brought ourselves. Now, luckily, I'm a collector. I have every scrap of paper since kindergarten. When they said that in third grade she had a particular teacher, I brought out the papers and showed them that she never had that teacher. And I prepared my speech. I started out, just like I did with you, way back in first grade. And [the special education director] kept cutting me off, saying this has nothing to do with the matter. And I kept saying, yes it does. These are the reasons the child has acted in the way that she does. This is the treatment she has received in the public schools. This is the lack of capability of dealing with it. I spent three whole days laying this thing out in my mind. We reworded and reworded so that everything would come out with complete clarity. So that it couldn't be disputed, because they twist words on you. I just wouldn't allow them to get the upper hand. It was like an obsession with me. They were not going to be able to contort any longer because they had been doing it all along. This is how they have treated my child and this is why I want her out of that school. I had to do it all by myself. I went to a lawyer, but [the cost] was just prohibitive. Besides, a lawyer wouldn't know the story. But it would have been better to have someone besides my husband and myself. I worried about whether they would think, "This is just another crazy parent."

In our parent sample, 35% of parents but only 7% of schools were without witnesses at their hearings. Even though they presented written documentation of their child's needs, parents felt that their relative inability to command the physical presence of specialists put them at a disadvantage. Ironically, school personnel often felt that the evidence supporting parents, given by child evaluators from prominent hospitals and clinics and by personnel from prestigious private schools, was given greater credence by hearing officers than the evidence of school personnel, even though the outside evaluators often knew little or nothing about the child's school experience and had often seen the child for only a very short time.

Truthfulness at hearings.

Parents were less concerned with the number of witnesses schools brought than with the quality of their testimony. We had frequent reports that this testimony was unexpected and even dishonest. We asked parents *"Was the school's testimony what you expected?"* Fully 73% said "No." We asked, *"If not, why not?"*, and allowed parents to choose as many responses as appropriate from among ten types of reasons.

The item most frequently selected—by the parents who had said "No"—was that "the school was more belligerent than we had expected." For example:

> As much as the school led me to believe that they wanted the best for [our son], when they got to the hearing, they had all kinds of reasons why the boy couldn't have private school. They came very prepared. What happened was that I wasn't prepared at all. Because [the special education director] promised me on the phone, "Don't worry, Mrs. _____ , we want him to have everything he needs." Still, when we got there, he had a folder, and he had all these things, and he had an attorney. And they were very nasty to me. Their lawyer tried to trip me up on questions. He tried to put words into my mouth. Then he said I could only answer yes or no to things. I broke down. Whenever they had a criticism, it was levelled at me.

* * *

> We were dumbfounded at how vitriolic the special education director was at the hearing. He in effect accused us of lying about our son's problems.

* * *

Their argument at the hearing was that he is all right, that it's just maturation, and that I'm crazy. These are people I had worked with in the schools. I was really amazed.

* * *

They want to win in the worst way. I don't think I fully realized how little they care about the children they are supposed to be protecting until we got to the hearing stage. The kinds of arguments they used, the kinds of lies. These are supposed to be professionals who care about these children, but obviously the only thing they cared about was winning.

Some parents felt they were simply unprepared for the formality of the school's presentation. Perhaps because these parents were early users of the appeals process, they had had insufficient access to information about hearings; a number felt they had been deliberately misinformed. For example, five parents claim to have been advised by school personnel that it was not necessary to use an attorney or advocate and then discovered at their hearing that the school system had brought its own lawyer. More generally, 14% of our sample (10 parents) reported they had not anticipated the school would bring a lawyer, and 10% had not anticipated the number and types of witnesses the schools would present.

We approached this whole thing in a somewhat naive fashion. We read the law and we thought it meant that parents had a status and almost an obligation to take this thing through themselves. We felt that we could argue it as well as anyone. And while it worked out well in our case, we were surprised at the extensive preparation that the school seemed to have undertaken. The town counsel [acting as the school's lawyer] was there, which we hadn't anticipated. In fact, the special education director presented the school's position, so that the presence of the town counsel had no great effect. They also brought one of [our son's] teachers, which we hadn't expected. I suppose our image was that we were going to tell our story and [the special education director] would tell his story. Perhaps we thought of it as more of a negotiation than a hearing.

* * *

I didn't know what I was getting into. I didn't know I had to make an opening statement. I thought it would be much more informal than it was. It was a regular court case. They had a lawyer and a prepared statement.

* * *

At the time of the appeal, I had the choice of hiring a lawyer. Three weeks before the appeal, that's when the school system decided to hire a lawyer. Before that, they said they wouldn't, and I made a choice not to. I had no idea it would be quite the way it was, that it was like going to court.

Not only did many parents feel the school's testimony was unexpected, they saw it as decidedly dishonest. One-fifth of these 71 parents claimed the educational plan presented by the schools at their hearing was different from the plan initially presented to them. One-fifth claimed that "the school falsified the progress of the child." Fifteen percent reported that "the school claimed a loss of evidence," indicating the school suppressed those evaluation documents not in their favor. Twelve percent felt that the "school brought in new, unknown information," often interpreted by parents as information that had been tampered with.

[The school] said that they were doing a wonderful job and everything, and they claimed that they were doing things that they weren't. We just sat there. It was all we could do to bite our tongues the way lies were flowing some of the time. The lawyer just kept telling us, "Calm down, we have the evidence."

* * *

When we went to the hearing, they claimed that I refused to have her tested. That was an absolute lie. They said by June they were going to have all the testing done, and they never did it. They said at the hearing that I refused to sign but the thing of it was, I was never asked to sign.

* * *

The school psychologist told us many things that she denied at the hearing. They said they would take the child in the morning at one school and then bus her across town after lunch to another school. Now a hyperactive child can't stand confusion. But at the hearing she said, "Oh, no, I never said that."

* * *

There was very definite, purposeful lying on their part, and there was mudslinging. The psychologist that we had said he had never seen such disgraceful behavior, such unprofessionalism, as he saw that day.

* * *

My husband and I try really hard to set an example. The boy in question was at the hearing and he heard his guidance counselor say things that weren't true. And he sat there and listened to it and for him to hear these people who play such an important part in his life lie like that, I thought it was just terrible.

* * *

They had a new educational plan that I had never seen and if I didn't have a lawyer, I might have lost or panicked. But the lawyer had been there before and knew this man and knew this is what he might do, because [these were] his tactics.

* * *

When we put her in the school, we went down to this psychologist and she said, "Yes, that is the kind of thing that [Chapter] 766 should pay for." Nothing in writing, mind you. But that's what she told us. We contacted her while my daughter was in nursery school and we said, "We'll pay for this year. But you'll pay for next year—her kindergarten year." And she said, "Fine, there will be no problem whatsoever." She totally denied it at the hearing.

* * *

We stood there and said, "We have a right to a full core evaluation by law," and they wrote a plan without doing the evaluations, with two people who never met, had never seen [our daughter]. Then they said we didn't have a right to a new core, because we had asked them for a plan. And we kept reading them from Chapter 766. They were using evaluations from a full year before and we said that they were not allowed to do that. This all happened to us. Do you know, at the hearing, they changed the dates on the evaluations. None of their testimony about the sequence of things was true.

* * *

At the core they kept saying that he didn't have a learning disability. At the hearing, they said they had offered us a program for learning-disabled children. It was that blatant.

* * *

At one point, I didn't dare to go to any of these meetings [with the school] by myself. I asked [an advocate] to go with me. At the hearing, they refused to have [the advocate] testify as to what went on at that meeting and the man across the table from me told a story as to what went on that was absolutely untrue. But they wouldn't let her testify.

* * *

Of course they lie. They had paid for a consultation with a psychologist, and he told us that he would recommend an E.D. [emotionally disturbed] school, because that's what [our son] needed. At the hearing, he completely changed his testimony. Three weeks later he was hired by the school system. I do not think that is an accidental happening.

* * *

The teacher totally supported any statement [the special education director] made. I couldn't believe the woman would talk that way. Whatever the special education director said or inferred, she just stood up and lengthened the lie.

* * *

The school lied about things, even under oath. They would say things that they really didn't do.

Because reports of dishonest testimony have been so frequent, we have discussed these charges in detail with selected parents. Four factors were suggested which may have contributed to such reports.

First, in the process of securing a school system evaluation, parents worked with people at many levels of the school system. Regular classroom teachers, special education teachers, evaluation personnel, and administrators each had different connections to the child and family and different organizational commitments. In all probability, various staff expressed different opinions to parents about their child's performance and needs. Then, several months after these contacts, the staff had to prepare for the hearing by formulating a coherent argument in support of their proposed educational plan. Testimony at hearings would naturally seek to justify current claims and prior actions, with earlier informal communications forgotten, or "reformulated" to support the system's current position as determined by the special education director or the school's lawyer. Thus, the school district's official case did not necessarily reflect the teachers' views of the child's needs nor the adequacy of existing programs. Parents said that teachers often privately encouraged them to find an alternative program for their child, then testified otherwise at the hearing. Not surprisingly, these parents felt betrayed.

Second, school personnel saw themselves as having honestly attempted to meet the child's needs in the midst of the organizational crises generated by the new law. But parents saw the schools' response differently. Many parents had waited months for an evaluation, felt they had to harass school administrators to get any response to their requests, and then felt intimidated at evaluation meetings. To them, school personnel's claims of "good faith" seemed hypocritical and false.

Third, parents said that at the hearings, school personnel often described what was theoretically available to a child in that system, rather than what had actually been offered in their child's educational plan. Some parents noticed that as the hearing progressed, the schools began to include new elements in their proposed program, evidently designed to counter the complaints made in parents' testimony:

> If you could reverse the process of the hearing so that the school system had to present their evidence first and they were not allowed to change whatever they came in with and were not allowed to bring in other things and say, "Oh, yes, we have this or that in the school system too," then I think parents would have a better chance.

* * *

> Really, they never offered us a plan. From one meeting to the next, it kept changing. When it finally got to a hearing, it kept changing, too. What they were trying to say was, whatever we want, it is available here in town. What we were trying to say was, we want a clear definite program. Decide what the child needs and supply it. Instead, their presentation at the hearing came down to, "If the [private school] can do that, we can do it too."

While many parents interpreted such changes in educational plans as deliberate falsifications, the changes may in fact reflect the uncertainty of school personnel about what parents desired and the child required. Parents reported their own considerable uncertainty about what they had been offered, because of poor parent-school communication. Due to the pressure of their workload and the very general phrasing of many educational plans, especially the early ones, school personnel might themselves have wondered what programs they had actually offered.

Finally, parents felt they found dishonesty among school staff about the quality of programming. Many parents had been promised programs which had not been delivered or were incompletely delivered, but at the hearings, school personnel described the promises, not the reality:

> What was on paper and what they were giving the boy were two different things. And at the hearing, they claimed he was getting what was on the paper.

* * *

> What I feel, here in town, they know how to write up their records, and they write up their records to make the state happy, and they say, "We're great; we're doing a great job because we've written up these records." But I found very few people that I have talked to that were satisfied with what's going on in the programs. At a hearing, they give their records, and the woman from the state, she doesn't know that they are just records. The school people tell her that's what they are really doing for the children. The school people have to say it's real, because it's their jobs that are at stake. So the hearings take place in a world of imagination, not a world of reality.

Based on past experiences, many parents were also cynical about promises of future programming and viewed such promises as unrealistic falsifications:

> They had no one in the system trained in the Gillingham method [a method for working with learning-disabled children]. We eventually saw a copy of a memo which I believe we were not intended to see, but which we obtained honestly, where the assistant superintendent argued that the school needed to hurry up and hire somebody so that they would be covered on that issue at the appeal. But this wasn't done. What was done was that a teacher whose background and experience was in handling emotionally

disturbed children was shifted over to the L.D. [learning disability] classroom. That didn't give us a lot of confidence that they were going to seriously address our problems even within the framework of their own educational plan.

* * *

They had a young girl who just came into the school say what a fine program she would have given [our daughter]. She had never seen her but she felt that anything [our daughter] needed, she could do it. Now they know that's not true. In a crisis classroom, when you've got one kid who is emotionally disturbed because the family is divorcing, when you got a kid with one problem or another, and your kid has still another problem and they're setting her in a class with four others, you're complicating her problem; you're not helping it. But they made out as if it was just the program [our daughter] needed, designed with her in mind. Now these people are not stupid. They know the crisis classroom is a kind of grab-bag. But it's what they had, so they hid the problems when they talk about it. At a hearing it's not what's best for the child, or even what's good. It's what they have, so they embellish it. However good they made it sound, they know it's not that way.

Parent perceptions of low-quality school programming often led parents to interpret as dishonest school personnel's efforts to describe or defend the quality of their programming. The need for school personnel to put the best possible face on their program in an adversarial setting like a hearing clearly contributed to parent complaints about lying.

All of this accords with our perception that hearings widen the gulf between parents and schools. To the extent that hearings have this effect, they make it more difficult for the contending parties to cooperate in future educational planning for the child.

Personal attacks.
Parents describing the school's testimony often said they felt they were "on trial" at their hearing. Rather than focusing on the child's needs, schools often directed attention to the parents' behavior and supposed motives:

It was very uncomfortable. It was hard, emotionally very hard to do. I've said to other parents, if you can possibly not [go to a hearing], don't do it. Maybe if the roles are reversed. You think you are bringing the school system to court, but, in fact, they are bringing you to court.

* * *

They blamed me for everything. Whenever they had a criticism, it was against me.

Many schools attempted to denigrate the motives of parents who sought private placements:

Their lawyer made it seem that I was a person who always sent her children to private schools and that this was just another way to get the money.

* * *

The special education director told the hearing officer that I was using Chapter 766 as my own form of social welfare. That's a direct quote.

* * *

Instead of admitting that I had legitimate concerns about my child's progress, they tried to make it appear that I was in it for the money.

Besides impugning parents' motives for seeking private schools, the schools challenged their integrity in much more damaging ways that were clearly not relevant to designing the program most beneficial for the child. For example, one Leaving School case involved a teenaged boy who had returned to a public high school after a period of hospitalization for emotional difficulties. Staff at the hospital submitted written evaluations urging the child be placed at a residential facility. According to the reports of both the parents and the special education director, the school system successfully argued at the hearing that since the mother had remarried, the child was an embarrassment, and therefore the mother wanted him out of the house. In addition, the school argued that the child could easily function in the local high school. The mother reports:

I felt very naive, very stupid. We felt that we were made fools of. The whole thing was turned around like we stuck [our son] in the hospital for four months because we wanted to get rid of him. They twisted everything around. That's just not the way it was.

In the case of an epileptic girl, the parents said, the school system argued that the family was psychologically unable to accept their child's disability. A similar argument was used by a school system to explain why a retarded child was behaving appropriately in school, according to school personnel, but acting out at home, according to the parents. In another case, a parent described the testimony at her hearing as insulting and painful:

> Their social worker testified that we had never accepted [our son] [who was diagnosed as retarded at age three and one-half]. So our lawyer asked her, what happened after [the parents] found out? How soon did they go for help? And she said, that's not the point. She kept saying, that's not the point. Finally the hearing officer said would she please answer the question. And she said it was January 1 of the same year [almost immediately after the diagnosis was made]. And the hearing officer turned to me and said, "It doesn't sound like you were in shock."

                                        * * *

> I don't feel that we should have been forced to go through something like that. I feel that we weren't on trial. We were there because we love [our son] and want to do something for him. It got my husband so upset. His face started to get red.

Parents had told us that staff at educational planning meetings had called their child's problem a "home problem," caused by faulty parenting, using that analysis to curtail service demands on the schools. Parents felt that schools also used this line of attack to "win" the hearing. Whether or not a school has any substantial evidence for such a charge, the danger of presenting such interpretations in the adversarial context of a hearing is that the school may so alienate parents as to make all future communication close to impossible.

> The guidance counselor, who I didn't get along with when [our daughter] was in school, said that I didn't want her in the public school because there was a crippled child in the room. Which is not the truth at all. And I wanted our lawyer to jump on her, and he felt it was irrelevant, so he let it go. But to make that kind of comment. I have seen her since then and we have been polite to one another. But I won't have anything to do with her and she won't have anything to do with my child.

In sum, part of what parents meant by the "unexpected" belligerence of the school was the school's evident attempt to interpret parent complaints in terms of the parents' motives and lifestyle.

My advice would be to bring witnesses. The people the hearing officer listens to are the so-called experts. If they are not there testifying for you, then what the school does is attack the parents. "It's a home problem." "It's bad parents." They do the same thing they do at the cores. "It's a family problem." That's what the schools say all the time. I hear it from other families in town and if you have skeletons in your closet, you end up fighting with your husband. If there's anything you feel ashamed of, you start feeling guilty, and then they got you. Hearings are the same. It's your word against theirs, and there are more of them. We had someone to speak for us, and I don't know what I would have done without her. She would keep interrupting and say, "Do you mean that this type of test score in the doctor's report comes from home problems and there is nothing a school should be able to do about it?" If she hadn't been there, the way they made me out, I wouldn't be able to bring them back to the point. I was a crazy parent, interfering with all these good things they were doing for the child, half of which they'd never done. You need witnesses and you need people to speak for you to show that it's them, it's not you.

As a final indication of the testimony at hearings, we asked parents what they saw as the most important and damaging aspect of the school's testimony. Thirty-four percent felt it was the "quantity of testimony by school personnel." Seventeen percent felt it was the "school's contention that programs must be tried before they are rejected," an issue frequently raised when parents had transferred their child to a private school before an evaluation meeting or before the child had entered the proposed program. Fifteen percent felt the most damaging argument was the school's "contending that we never wanted a public school program," while 15% felt it was the school's "promising to get teachers and facilities if their plan was accepted."

Parents also indicated another theme that the school frequently stressed at hearings: since private day schools were segregated settings, they did not meet the requirements of Chapter 766 to place the child in the "least restrictive" setting possible:

They said that the [private day school] was a restrictive placement for [our son] and their obligation was to place [him] in the least restrictive placement. Their argument was that the rules specified categories of placements starting with regular schooling without any help; then resource rooms; then self-contained classes; then day schools; then residential schools; and that if he would function at all in the public school program then the law demanded that is what he receive. It was a very technical argument based on a kind of legalistic reading of the law. Our argument was that the quality of the help at the private school was so much greater than was available in the town that the desire of the lawmakers to promote integration was not an appropriate criterion in this instance.

* * *

Their basic argument was that he should be mainstreamed.

Was that because it would be good for the child or because the law requires mainstreaming where possible?

I think they argued both positions. Their view of the law was that if he had been in a public program all along none of his problems would have occurred and that putting him back in the schools would in some way help him.

Many parents of learning-disabled children argued that the mainstreaming requirements were inappropriate for their child, though appropriate for the mentally retarded and physically handicapped chilren for whom Chapter 766 was originally intended. School personnel argued that mainstreaming was an important criterion for evaluating the programs of all handicapped children.

Parents View Their Own Cases

We asked parents to identify the most important aspect of their own presentation. Twenty-nine percent felt it was "having convincing independent evaluations from reputable organizations." Fifteen percent selected each of the following choices: "demonstrating the child's lack of progress in previous school placements"; "the poor quality of the school's educational plan"; and "demonstrating the lack of good faith and compliance of the school." Fewer parents indicated "the age of the child and the severity of his/her condition" and "having convincing professionals as witnesses."

These responses omitted an argument raised by many parents in their remarks: that their child's previous failures in a public school program lowered the possibility of success in any new public program. Thus, the services being offered by the public schools may have been appropriate given the child's clinical problems but were not sufficient given his prior failures. For example:

> Our major arguments were that the personnel were unqualified, that what they had promised in the past had never come true, and that even if it came true this time, his self-image was so defeated that he needed a new environment in which the stigma of his former failure would not interfere with his learning.

In contrast, the schools tended to argue that past failures would not affect the child's ability to benefit from new programs.

The Costs of a Hearing

Two types of costs represent major barriers to parents desiring a hearing: economic and emotional.

Economic costs.

Easiest to measure are the economic costs to parents. Three major types of expenses can be identified: the costs of representation, expert witnesses, and independent assessments.

Representation can be especially costly. The nine parents in our study who used paid advocates spent an average of $266 each; the overall mean fee for representation was $674. This figure, however, is misleadingly low, as many cases in our sample were handled free of charge by one excellent advocate from a private school, and four cases were handled without charge by private and public child advocacy agencies or public interest law firms. The range of fees provides a more accurate indication of the costs of representation: parents spent from $200 to over $2,000 for advocates or attorneys. Legal costs are currently closer to the higher figure, although more free advocacy services have become available since this study was completed. One attorney reports he accepts only one of three clients for hearings because of the high total cost required to assure winning.

Second, while more than half the witnesses who testified for parents did so without charge, 16 parents paid for expert witnesses. The average cost per witness was $68; the average cost of witnesses per case was $107.

Third, parents often pay for independent assessments. There is considerable controversy over these fees. In 14 cases, parents claimed they had been promised reimbursement by the schools which they never got. In 17 cases, parents paid for their own independent assessments to prepare for their hearing. Excluding assessments covered by insurance, the average cost per case for assessments was $261.

Parents face other out-of-pocket expenses, such as photocopying documents, transportation costs, telephone calls, job absenteeism, and their own psychological counseling. In two instances parents said they lost jobs because of repeated absenteeism necessitated by the educational planning process in schools and the preparation for hearings.

As reported in the next chapter, many families continue to be involved in litigation after the initial hearing. Parents may appeal the hearing officer's decision to the State Advisory Commission, or to the Massachusetts Superior Court or Federal District Court.

Fifteen parents reported expenditures beyond their initial hearing, while other parents continued their conflict without additional expenses. The average additional expense was $730, but four families had expenses that exceeded $2,500, while the costs for 15.5% of the sample were more than $1,300.

Expenditures for representation vary by type of case. The average expenditure for the first hearing of a Private School case was $395; for a Leaving School case, $391; for a Staying-in-School case, $280. Total average expenditures were $573, $512, and $389 for these three types of appeals cases, respectively. Two Leaving School cases were seeking residential placements, and these higher-income families incurred high legal fees. Without these cases, the mean cost for Leaving School cases would be less than $100.

In general, the more costly the parents' requests, the higher the legal fees expended by both parties. The mainly higher-income families in the Private School cases, who had placed their children prior to the hearing, incurred higher legal fees than the middle- and lower-income families seeking private placements or an altered public school program.

In the years after this study was conducted, there was considerable activity by publicly and privately funded child advocacy and public-interest groups to insure that parents have access to free or low-cost representation at hearings. At the same time, the dramatic increase in private lawyers' activities in this area tended to make knowledgeable representation more easily available, but also more expensive.

Clearly, participation in an appeals hearing involves a considerable financial cost. When parents were also paying private school tuition, the total costs sometimes required adjustments in the family's living standard. For some families, the increased economic costs of going to a hearing undoubtedly increased their emotional involvement in the outcome of the dispute. Consequently, they may have been even less willing to work with the schools or to compromise.

Emotional costs of a hearing.

Less easily measured is the emotional trauma experienced by parents over the course of meetings, preparation for a hearing, and the hearing itself. When asked, *"How upsetting is it to parents and families to participate in an appeals dispute?"* 56% of the sample found it "extremely upsetting" and 19% reported "somewhat upsetting." Only 24% chose "not very upsetting" or "not at all upsetting." Asked to agree or disagree that *"the emotional costs of using the hearing system are high,"* 70% agreed. These structured responses do not begin to convey the sentiments of some parents.

> I've been through seizures and everything else with her, and this has been the worst affair of my life.

* * *

> It's really very rough and frustrating, and you feel like an idiot at times.

* * *

> It's been hell. Absolute hell. I very seldom speak about it, even to my husband, because I find that it gets me very upset. And once I start thinking about it, I get the feeling that I become very obcessed by it, and that's all I can think about. My husband spent hours and hours with the papers, stacks and stacks of papers, for nearly two years. The lawyers' bills are atrocious. The tuition is very hard to come up with. My opinion is that the whole thing is stacked against the parent. It's such common knowledge that you can't beat the system. I have a friend who went to a doctor, and she said [her daughter] needs [a private school], she needs it desperately. But you don't stand a snowball's chance in hell of winning. It's the worst I have ever been through.

* * *

> My hands right now are shaking as I'm talking to you about it. I'm cold and I get that same horrible feeling all over. Maybe if I had

been a different kind of person, but I feel that it is very difficult to go in and sit across from someone two or three feet away and have them lie blatantly and not be able to say anything about it. You present your case. They present their case. And there is no way to go back and say, "Look here, that never happened." You can't say that. There's no way to combat the lies.

* * *

I'm sorry I'm so vague on the factors. It was just a time of my life that I purposely have tried to wipe out.

* * *

It's horrible. It's just so horrible. It aggravates me so that I can scream.

Even among parents who felt they had experienced little trauma, we elicited such comments as the following:

Of course, if you become emotionally involved, it can tear you up. But I chose not to become involved in that route. I chose the route that I had a right to a hearing; that's what I pursued. You know, it took well over two years before I got a hearing. The [school's] lawyer pulled every trick in the book to postpone the hearing and prevent it from ever happening. I just put it out of my mind. It was in the hands of a lawyer, there was nothing I could do about it, that was not my fault but the fault of the process, which is not a functional process. So we just waited, and I knew I would get my day in court.

* * *

The whole thing is the most dreadful experience. But we are among the fortunate ones. Our child was in a good school. We can afford it. Throughout, we have been convinced that our actions have been perfectly proper, that we were asking for no more than the law says our child is entitled to. It is an aggravating procedure but not a disturbing or traumatizing one.

The absence of reliable information about the hearing process for these early users increased the emotional pressures. In an extreme case, one parent reported being told by a special education director there was no such thing as an appeals system. More generally, our sample had great difficulty knowing what to expect from the procedure and often reported that schools withheld information or provided incorrect information.

Preparing for a Hearing

The high level of parent effort required to be suitably prepared for a hearing increased emotional pressures and also imposed an enormous burden of effort. Our interviewers have entered living rooms stacked with documents relating to a hearing: multiple evaluation reports, multiple education plans, memoranda of meetings, letters to officials, etc. As one parent put it, "This has become my second job." Another explained:

> We've spent hundreds of hours on this. It's an incredible amount of work. If my husband got his usual fee, we'd be rich. Whenever you call anybody, they are not there, and no one in the entire state ever returns a phone call. You spend half your life on the phone. Just to get my son's records from the school took two weeks of constant calling. . . . I've been to dozens of meetings, with the public school, at the private school, with advocates, with lawyers, with doctors, with other parents. . . . We've had to read through every document. It's like getting a Ph.D. in educational testing. . . . For a while there, I had the regulations pretty well memorized. . . . None of the meetings are easy to arrange. If you want someone from the public school and someone from the outside to sit in the same room, it's the parent who has to arrange it. The school cancelled our hearing date twice, and each time it meant I had to arrange new times with the witnesses, which was almost impossible. . . . You can get advice from advocates and lawyers but it is the parent who knows the problems and knows the child and in the end has to be the one that organizes the materials and the presentation. . . . You need a tremendous amount of determination. It's tremendously discouraging. It's bureaucracy, and a new system is being implemented. But I think part of it is deliberate.

Detailed record-keeping of the treatment of handicapped children by the schools is required under special education laws as a way of opening the school's decision making process to the hearing system and to the courts, thereby protecting the due process rights of children. School personnel often complain that these requirements are so burdensome they diminish the time available for serving children. It is easy to forget that parents are also subject to these requirements. When they wish to protest the school's decision, they, too, must compile numerous and detailed records, as well as coordinate the activities of a variety of specialists. While they may receive advice from lawyers and advocates, in most cases parents have the major responsibility for developing a record of their dispute. There can be little doubt that the parents who have used the hearing process have needed unusual abilities to cope with complex bureaucratic processes through extensive work and preparation. This experience has reinforced their antagonism toward the schools and increased the trauma associated with the use of the hearing system.

The Hearing's Effect on the Child

We asked parents a variety of questions about the effects of the appeals process on their child, and they consistently reported little or no effect. While most children were told about the dispute, many were too young to appreciate its implications, and parents claimed to have shielded their children from their own anxieties. During our interviews, however, parents described in graphic detail their own frustrations and their extraordinarily high level of effort. It is highly unlikely that their children have not found meaning in these events, though how such interpretations might be elicited has eluded us.

Parents' Final Assessment of Their Experience of Going to Hearings

Our initial interview with parents came shortly after their first hearing. We asked, *"Would you use the hearing system again?"* Twenty-eight percent reported they would not. Among parents giving this reply, 70% reported the major reason for their answer was that "hearings are too traumatic," while 30% of parents chose one or more of the following replies: "Even though we won, the school did not change anything"; "the whole process is so disorganized, unprofitable, and inconsistent that the merits of the case have little to do with whether you win or lose"; and "because one agency is being monitored by another agency and is biased in its favor." During our second interview, nearly two years after the initial hearing, we asked parents if they would use the system again. This time only 17% said they would not, with a more even split between those who commented on the emotional trauma of a hearing and those who complained that decisions had not been enforced.

These parents now felt that through the hearing they had obtained for their child an opportunity s/he might not otherwise have had. In spite of the heartache, they felt the improvement in their child's performance after many years of school failure ultimately made the effort worthwhile. Some parents, with this hindsight, felt they had fought a social as well as a personal battle in confronting the schools' inadequate response to their child, since their precedent might have benefited other children.

A small number of parents actually found positive features in the hearing experience:

> In some ways, it has been good for us. Particularly for the children. It showed them that it wasn't just mother worrying about her youngest, that there were real problems, and that we were willing to do everything necessary.

* * *

> Well, I've certainly had to learn much more about learning disabilities and that has reduced some of the feelings of helplessness.

Summary

While a high proportion of these parents chose to be represented at hearings, an even higher proportion recommend representation to others. This is an important indication of parent experiences. Hearings were reported to be emotionally straining, overly formal, and primarily concerned with procedures and rules of law rather than issues of substance. The schools, particularly school attorneys, were reported to be belligerent and to engage in personal attacks on parents. The truthfulness of the school's testimony was frequently questioned by parents, who felt "outgunned" by the number of witnesses the school could present. All of this was experienced as so intimidating and threatening that parents felt unable to act on their own, feeling strongly the need for an attorney or advocate.

These descriptions of parent experiences emphasize the need for mechanisms to reduce the conflict between parents and schools. The high costs, the long wait for a hearing, the ceaseless preparation, the anxiety about the hearings, the win/lose atmosphere, and the long wait for a decision all operate to increase alienation and sustain antagonism. Parent reports of schools lying and attacking them personally are potent indicators of the extent to which the hearing process engenders and supports anger. If a hearing officer's decision were final, in the sense that the contending parties would no longer have to work together again, the absence of any means of conciliation might be less damaging. However, as the next chapter shows, parents and schools must continue to maintain contact after a hearing, and negotiate the details of the child's program. After the hearing's end, parents and schools tend to resume their conflict.

7

Outcomes of Going
to a Hearing

For the first parents to use the appeals system in Massachusetts, the outcomes were rarely satisfactory. Almost the only happy parents we found were those whose fiscal resources enabled them to bypass the system by placing their child privately and so eliminate all contact with the public schools.

Fueled by the antagonistic evaluation and hearing process, parent-school conflict often reemerged soon after the hearing decision was rendered. Parents and schools frequently disagreed over the interpretation of the decision, particularly over its exact requirements for the school. Sometimes school staff felt that parents had also failed to comply.

Occasionally, schools would contest an order in court. More often they simply failed to act, tacitly or explicitly ignoring the order when they lost a decision. Some systems failed to pay private tuitions promptly or failed to pay them at all, forcing parents to pay tuitions while resuming costly legal action. Parents who could not afford this double expense had to withdraw the child from the private placement they had won.

Recognizing that schools might not always comply with decisions, the state created a "compliance hearing" near the end of this study period. The Bureau of Special Education Appeals would schedule a hearing on a school's compliance with a decision if the Bureau's investigation substantiated a parent's complaint. The compliance hearing represented some attempt to respond to school district failures, but the burden was still on parents to insure enforcement of the decision.

In almost every case when children remained in public schools after a hearing, parents reported continued conflict regardless of who had won the hearing. Children who had been placed in private schools before the hearing tended to stay there, regardless of the decision. Even when parents won a decision, they frequently faced an annual hearing, because the required annual re-evaluation of the child's progress provided a convenient occasion for schools to argue once again for their original educational plan. When parents were ready to have their child leave a particular private special needs school, the prior conflict had usually so embittered them that they tended to transfer him to public school only when the child insisted on being with neighborhood friends, or when there was a new administrator with whom to negotiate re-entry. Many parents had suffered a major loss of faith in the ability of the public schools to serve their handicapped child, even while they continued to enroll their other children in public school.

This dismal record is relieved by scattered parent reports of marked improvement in their treatment after their hearings. But almost all parents in this study felt they had lost their hearing, either immediately by a negative decision, or more slowly, through the nonimplementation of a positive decision. We consider that children also lose when their parents become so alienated.

After a Hearing: The Parents' Options

After a negative decision, parents may appeal to the State Advisory Commission for Special Education, or to the courts. Or they may refer their child for a new educational plan and start the appeals process all over again. Parents in our sample tried all of these options; none proved satisfactory.

The State Advisory Commission.

The State Advisory Commission (SAC), composed of educators, school administrators, and citizen representatives, serves as a state-level appeals board for parents only. Schools wishing to appeal must use the courts. The SAC is composed of representatives of the six regional special education advisory commissions appointed by the Massachusetts Board of Education. Half of its members are parents of special needs children; the rest are regular and special needs teachers and administrators, handicapped adults and children, and commissioners of related state agencies, who serve *ex officio*. (For more information on the SAC, see Chapter 3.)

Upon receipt of a negative decision, parents can request a SAC review simply by signing a form. Some parents also filed a formal brief. When schools heard of a parent appeal, they sometimes filed a brief of their own. Both parties are informed of the SAC's preliminary judgment and given time to submit written commentary before a final decision is rendered.

Of parents who lost Private School disputes and then requested a SAC review of their decision, most submitted briefs with their requests. While a request for review required minimal effort, preparation of a brief was a substantial and expensive undertaking, often requiring the services of a lawyer. Most parents felt the procedure had done little good.

No Leaving School cases and only one Staying in School case in our sample were reviewed by the SAC. In this one case, the SAC sustained the parent's request for individual rather than group tutoring for a learning-disabled boy.

Court appeals.
The final level of appeal under Chapter 766 is the Superior Court of Massachusetts. As of October, 1977, under the federal legislation, P.L. 94-142, parents can also appeal to the Federal District Courts.

Four Private School parents in our sample appealed to the Superior Court. By the time of our second interview two years after the hearing, two cases had been heard and two were still awaiting court review. Six sets of parents who had won private school tuitions had been taken to court by the school system, and in four of these cases the schools withheld payment of the tuition pending the court review, causing the parents considerable hardship. None of these cases had been settled by the time of our second interview.

Seeking a new educational plan.
The SAC is most likely to uphold the hearing officer's decision, and court reviews are slow and costly. Some parents therefore chose to request another educational plan, which they then rejected. Thus they went to a second hearing to argue again for private placement. While parents seeking payment for private tuition could not be reimbursed for previous costs in this way, a decision in their favor at a second hearing would make the school system responsible for all current and future costs. Two sets of parents in our sample took this route; both lost their second hearing.

What Happened After the Decision

Let us now consider the actions of parents who lost hearings, and document the sources of disillusion for parents who won. The experiences of both groups reveal major shortcomings in the hearings system.

Part 1 of this chapter examines the outcomes of Staying in School and

Leaving School disputes. The major ongoing issues were parents' reports of schools' noncompliance, and parent-school confrontations over new issues that arose. The mutual ill feeling engendered previously made further negotiations regarding the child's program difficult.

Part 2 concerns parents who lost Private School disputes. The major issue here was parents' disillusionment with the decision and their frustration.

Part 3 Examines the subsequent histories of parents who "won" Private School disputes but who later faced continuing legal disputes they did not anticipate when they entered the appeals process.

The data reported in this chapter were drawn from parents' reports during the first two interviews, one of which occurred within weeks of their hearing, with the second about two years later. Events and perceptions during the subsequent two years are reported in the next chapter.

Part 1. Outcomes of Staying-in-School and Leaving School Cases

Of the 22 children, only three stayed in public school programs without further conflict; one was resolved after parents won an appeal to the SAC. Six children were awarded private school placements; in four of these six cases there was no further conflict.

Thus, 13 children remained in public school while parent-school disputes continued over months or even years. Half of these 13 cases led to further appeals actions; the other half involved no further appeals, but conflict continued. Often conflict ended only when the child graduated, or when key administrators in the dispute left the school system. Sometimes parents ended the dispute by removing their child from special education, or from the school system itself, decisions which may have hurt the child.

When further appeals actions did occur, it was almost always unsatisfying to the parents. In three cases parents scheduled or attended a second appeals hearing; in two cases they scheduled or attended a third hearing. In one case, a child was home for a year and a half without any program at all while her parents waited for their appeal to the Superior Court to be heard. Parents described a number of reasons why their conflicts continued, some of which are addressed below.

The Ambiguous Decision

In four of the five cases that were heard more than once, conflict over what services had been ordered by the first decision erupted soon after that decision was received. Parents and schools continued to disagree over future plans for their child. The situation of one language-impaired and emotionally disturbed boy illustrates the problem.

The boy's parents applied for a second hearing four months after the first decision was received, a decision which the parents felt was being ignored by the school. Throughout those four months, the parents continued to have frequent hostile contact with school personnel. The second hearing was held three months later, at which time the parents argued that the original decision had never been implemented: their child was in a resource room rather than a self-contained classroom; specialist services were erratic; the staff was unqualified; and no meaningful psychological counseling had been provided.

The school conceded most of these points, though they felt their program was improving. They volunteered payment for the outside program originally requested by the parents. The hearing officer ordered this placement, as well as the psychotherapy requested for the child. But by not specifying the type of therapy for which the school was responsible, the hearing officer unwittingly laid the groundwork for a third hearing. The parents preferred family therapy, which requires the participation of the parents as well as the child, but the school refused to pay the added cost of the parents' involvement. "You're asking for too much," the special education director told the parents, who then scheduled a third hearing to determine what type of psychotherapy had in fact been mandated.

Similar ambiguities have occurred in other cases, usually resolved only by a second or third hearing. When other decisions specified such services as "regular class placement," "psychotherapy to be paid by the local school district," or "a half-time placement in a self-contained classroom," disputes surfaced immediately afterward over the specific meaning of the decision.

Noncompliance.

Parents frequently complained that schools did not comply with the hearing officer's order, a complaint common to four cases that went to new hearings.

> The decision was great but [the schools] have no way of implementing the decision. [The state has] no way of forcing the schools involved to go ahead and present [that] program. [The

schools] can present it to the hearing officer on paper, but that doesn't mean they will install the program.

* * *

When you go to a hearing, everything seems okay when you're there, but there is no follow-up to it. I got nothing from the hearing.

One reason for the frequent complaints of noncompliance was that hearing officers were ordering programs that schools seemed unable to deliver. Compliance problems occurred most often when schools were forced to serve children not previously served, or were required to deliver services not traditionally offered by the schools. Some examples in our sample concerned a school that had no personnel skilled in toilet training a retarded child; a high school that had not viewed a delinquent child as a special needs child; a school that had no self-contained program for language-impaired children; and schools unequipped to provide specialist services such as occupational, physical, or speech therapy.

Two Staying-in-School cases involving mentally retarded children from the same community illustrate these problems. At her hearing, one of these parents demanded that the class for retarded children be moved from the school's basement, that regular speech therapy and adaptive physical education be added to her child's program, and that a program in fine motor coordination be developed. This parent was explicit in seeing her dispute as a demand for system-wide change:

I don't have any problems with the school department. I think [the city] is fabulous for its schools. The only place they are lacking is because it has been an undercover department for so many years in so many schools, and they have just not brought in the best people to get the best progress out of the handicapped children. Those who are trying to develop the program for this school system are no more well-versed in it than I am. I don't think my child is better than any other child, but I just make a few waves because I want change. Some of the mothers who have these children have just numbed up; they have just drawn the shell right inside. They don't want to be bothered. They don't know what to do for the child and they just tolerate the child.

Neither set of parents reported any immediate compliance with the hearing officer's decision and both engaged in continuing and rancorous disputes with school staff. However, within months after the decision was received, a new special education director made some changes in the program. While both sets of parents still indicated grievances, they did see some progress.

Commonly, when hearing officers ordered new services, schools tended to use existing programming arrangements and personnel to provide them. But even when this was done in good faith, their distrust and previous conflict with school personnel often led parents to perceive that the school was not trying to comply. And in fact, some administrators did resist provision of these mandated services, even when their costs were moderate, for fear of setting a precedent for other children's needs.

"Making Progress"

In two other cases that went to new hearings, the initial decisions favoring the parents were implemented for a considerable period of time but the children still did not make progress. The parents of one learning-disabled boy rejected a second educational plan and again requested a private school placement. While the school's testing showed modest gains for the boy, an independent evaluator reported little or no progress. In addition, the parents felt the child's self-image would suffer in a mainstreamed public school program in contrast to the private school.

The parents of an aphasic girl who had received the speech therapy ordered by a hearing officer for more than a year and a half appealed to place their daughter in a school for the deaf. School personnel had told the parents they had difficulty "reaching" her and had offered a new plan calling for more intensive speech and language training, but the parents felt that only new programming options would promise improvement.

Both sets of parents expected improvement as a result of the "appropriate" public school program ordered by the decision. In the absence of discernable improvement, they sought proven private sector programs.

The "Bitter Cases"

Some particularly complex cases in our sample illustrate how vitriolic and adversarial these disputes can become. All the parties to these disputes acknowledged that these situations had "gotten out of hand" and were at an impasse by the time of the second interview. We give three examples.

The first case involved a retarded child whose parents were particularly concerned with his speech and self-help skills, especially toilet training. The child had been withdrawn from the public schools before the first hearing because he had become a behavior problem. The parents also felt the school's program was hurting him. After a decision requiring some changes in the program, he was withdrawn a second time when the parents claimed noncompliance with the decision. For example, the half hour of speech instruction each morning and afternoon was not delivered for the first two months, and when it finally was delivered, the therapist was changed frequently:

> Every other week it was a different teacher. So I said to them, you can't be switching teachers on him because they have to get to know him.

At the second hearing, a different hearing officer reiterated the first decision, though toileting and self-help skills were not mentioned, which disturbed the parents. Three months after the second hearing, the child, whose behavior had become progressively worse, was expelled from school at a meeting to which the parents were not invited. They were told, "We will get in touch with you in a few weeks." The parents decided to force the school to pay attention to their child by dropping him at the school each morning and leaving him for the day. This continued for nearly two weeks, until the school offered an assessment by an outside evaluator. At the time of our second interview, the child was without a program; the school had promised to pay for a residential program but had not been able to locate one that the parents considered acceptable.

As viewed from the parents' reports, this scenario might be considered prototypic of Staying-in-School cases. The parents felt the school had tried to slander them at their first hearing by suggesting they had not "accepted" their child's retardation. Since that hearing, they felt school personnel had been "vindictive" towards them because they "stood up" to the school. Over time, new issues have arisen, for example, whether the child should learn sign language and whether he should be given a summer program. Each new issue added a new layer of acrimony, since the previous hostility has made constructive communication between the parents and the school virtually impossible.

These arguments, in turn, led to a virtually irreversible alienation from the public schools. The parents came to feel the direct service personnel were incompetent, hence their poor response to their child's needs. They felt that though some teachers wanted to be helpful, others were repulsed by the child's toileting problems. The parents saw the administrators as concerned with costs and little else. The mother told us that at one meeting after the first hearing, she had to prevent her husband from coming to blows with the special education director. At another meeting, the parents became furious at a guidance counselor who suggested the child be "put away." Through all this, the parents watched their child's behavior deteriorate. They felt school personnel had lied at the hearings by not admitting they were also having difficulties controlling him. While no lawyer was at the first hearing, the parents did employ a lawyer at the second hearing, making the hearing more expensive for this middle-income family. The parents were convinced their child's program had hurt him and were completely disillusioned with the ability of the appeals system to rectify the situation. They accepted the proposed residential placement at great emotional cost, since they wanted their son at home, but felt there was no way for them to secure an acceptable public school program to make this possible.

A second case involved a teenager with multiple problems who was confined to a wheelchair. By the time of their third hearing, her parents argued that their child was still not receiving due process protection, because even a hearing every half-year did not prevent the arbitrary and capricious actions of school personnel during the intervention period. In the parents' view, school personnel had acted unreasonably towards them over such a long period, had violated so many of the regulations of Chapter 766, and had shown such wanton disregard for their daughter's needs, that it was no longer reasonable to assume that parents and school personnel could reach agreement on any important aspect of the child's educational plan. The parents therefore asked the hearing officer to appoint a monitor to attend all meetings involving the child, either to mediate disputes as they arose or immediately to render a decision. This request was refused.

The parents' concern at their first appeal was that the car transporting their daughter to and from school needed to be modified to allow her greater self-sufficiency. At two subsequent hearings, the parents attacked almost all aspects of the school's special needs program. At each appeal, new issues have arisen, for example, whether a history course could have been modified to meet the child's needs. Old issues were never fully resolved. The parents saw no other way to protect their child, except to maintain a combative posture until she graduated.

The most serious disruption of a child's educational career in our sample involved a girl with a variety of problems, most prominently epileptic seizures that could not be controlled with medication. She had been home for nearly 18 months at the time of our second interview while her parents awaited their appearance in Superior Court. At her first hearing, the parents had asked for a regular class placement and occupational therapy administered by a teacher's aide, though supervised by a specialist, plus a variety of other supportive services not in contention. The parents objected vehemently to a segregated special class because they felt that a previous placement with retarded and emotionally disturbed children had damaged their child's self-image and increased her seizure rate.

The dispute had an involved history. The child had received multiple and conflicting evaluations. The parents had previously removed her from school when they felt her program was unsatisfactory; the school thereupon referred the case to the Department of Public Welfare, seeking to remove the child from the guardianship of her parents. Given this history and the attitudes of parents and school personnel toward one another, no hearing decision could possibly have averted further conflict. When the hearing decision favored the school's position in all respects, the parents refused to comply and petitioned the Superior Court for a reversal.

What is striking in this situation is that the alternatives seemed to consist only of legal confrontations, a type of action which had been singularly unsuccessful at providing programming in the first place. Some attempt by an outside agent to work with the parents' beliefs about appropriate programming, helping them to explore their sense of the child's needs and their own feelings about these needs, might have resulted in effective compromise. In another system, trial placements might have been ordered, subject to change.

What was required was a procedure which would minimize the conflict, a means to re-establish constructive contact—anything but the continuing legal confrontations. The legislative grant of parents' rights had legitimized parental involvement in educational decision making for their handicapped child. It sometimes seems also to have erased schools' understanding that parents still need help in understanding and accepting their handicapped child, and that these needs are best addressed in an atmosphere of negotiation or even counseling. School professionals' major focus should be to maintain the child in an appropriate program. Unless schools can show real or potential harm in a parent's proposal, the conciliatory stance of "let us try out your placement approach for a few months" can prolong cooperative dialogue with the parents, while keeping the child in school. Parents' assertion of their rights appears to have turned schools toward confrontation, as staffs defensively proclaim their "professional" prerogatives against parents. This orientation toward confrontation distorts the special education reform's intent of granting parents the right to share in their child's educational career.

Withdrawing the Child from Special Services

Given the rampant antagonisms that persist, it is not surprising that a few parents have taken actions that might be interpreted as hurting their children. For example:

- Because of poor communication with his teachers, the parents of an aphasic high school boy broke off contact with the special educators who had been providing some speech therapy, counseling, and resource room instruction. Instead, the boy attended regular high school classes, which the father supplemented by paying the boy's classmates for tutoring. The father hoped his son "would pick up a smattering of high school knowledge."

- The parents of a retarded high school boy removed him from public school three months after an unfavorable decision was received and continued to argue with school personnel over the original issue: whether their child's small group instruction included so many children with behavior problems that the teacher could not adequately serve their child. A new issue had also arisen: the child had formerly eaten lunch in his classroom but, after the hearing, school personnel insisted he go to the lunchroom, where he felt rejected and refused to eat. In addition, the parents wanted school personnel to begin instruction with Cuisenaire rods, with which he had been successfully learning from a privately paid tutor. Feeling that "time was running out" for their son, they removed him from public school and placed him in a two-day-a-week program at a significant traveling distance from his home. Both the parents and the child seem content with this program. However, from the parents' description, the program evidently de-emphasizes academic instruction in favor of expressive instruction through dance and other physical activities, although the child is clearly capable of doing academic work. In our opinion, the dispute created a situation that was clearly damaging to the child, limiting his options for more academic development. While the schools were not to blame in this situation, good professional practice dictates that they should have found ways to maintain contact with the parents on behalf of the child. Again, had avenues of compromise been available, the child might have benefited.

- A child was awarded five months at a private, learning disability day school, after which he was to return to a public program. Upon his return, the school system reiterated its contention that his problems stemmed from the parents' divorce rather than from a learning disability. After a series of angry meetings, the school offered limited special education services for that year. They offered no services for the following year. At our second interview, the parent had enrolled her son at a small private school with no experience or skills in the remediation of learning disorders. It is the only school she can afford and she recognizes that her child is having a "terrible" year. Asked why she did not appeal to get a more satisfactory public program, the mother said that the schools are now adept at writing seemingly acceptable educational plans and that she would need a lawyer to challenge this at a hearing, which she cannot afford.

Among the 16 cases in which children were required to remain in public programs after their initial hearing, we found three children who were attending no school program at all at the time of our second interview. One parent simply dropped her handicapped child at the school door to protest his lack of a program; another set of parents used "political pull" in their community rather than the appeals process. Other parents felt that school personnel had treated them "vindictively" because of their participation in a hearing. Consider that six of the 16 cases continued to subsequent hearings or court appearances and seven saw continuing disagreements of other kinds. When only three cases out of 16 continue without further conflict, adversarial hearings are clearly not resolving these disputes amicably.

Part 2. Parents Who Lost
Private School Cases

In 49 cases in our sample, the major issue was reimbursement for past private school tuition and/or the continuation of such placements at public expense. In one case, after parents testified at their hearing, the school system agreed to pay the tuition and transportation costs requested and the hearing was terminated without a decision. All other cases were ruled upon by a hearing officer.

In 57% of these cases, the hearing officer ruled in favor of the parents. The decision held that the school system had not offered an adequate educational plan in a timely fashion, and so should pay both for past expenses, usually from the time when parents first requested an educational plan, and or current tuition and transportation costs.

In the other 43% of these cases, hearing officers found for the schools, and the parents had to pay all private school costs. Not surprisingly, these negative decisions exacerbated parent-school conflict and mistrust.

Parents Interpret Negative Decisions

How did parents view their loss of a hearing? As might be expected, they disagreed with the outcome. Some claimed that hearing officers had seriously misinterpreted the evidence. For example:

The hearing officer ruled that [the city] had offered us an adequate educational plan for '74-'75. Now, in fact, they never even held an educational planning meeting until January of 1976. So how could he rule such a thing?

Do you have any idea why he ruled against you?

Because he's a fool. I honestly don't know why. We presented a case and evidence from two doctors at two notable hospitals. Both doctors said [our daughter] needed a small, self-contained classroom. The school was offering a resource room for half a day and a large first grade classroom. And the hearing officer ruled that the school's program was precisely what the doctors were talking about. I don't understand it. Maybe he couldn't read. I don't know. He didn't understand.

* * *

A lot of our case depended on the fact that [the school] just never offered us anything. Whether it was good or bad was really secondary. They just never held the meetings or did the testing. But the hearing officer seemed to have gotten confused about the timing of things so that in the decision, she includes as part of what was offered to us as a program things that were offered only after [our son] was already going to [the private school].

But parents saw misunderstanding of the facts as less important than the hearing officer's assumption that the school was acting in good faith. Most parents who lost were unable to share that assumption:

In our case . . . the school did not follow at all the rules and regulations that the state set up. . . . I don't know why they make rules and regulations if they aren't followed. By the time [the school] presented us with a plan, we [only] had a week to decide whether we would accept it or not. And they had no books, no teachers, no room, no program, and we were supposed to say, fine, we'll send our child up for this program. And this is what the hearing officer said, that they were acting in good faith. But our experience with them in the past had not indicated it to us. So I mean, how do you argue that situation? They broke all the rules and regulations that the state had written and the state hearing officer was well aware of it and he decided in their favor. The state was in terrible financial difficulties, maybe that explains it.

* * *

The hearing officer said that the town had a program, and the fact that they sent us a letter in August was sufficient to inform us that they planned to provide a program. The law was just coming into effect and at that early point a letter was enough of a response to show they meant to do something. So after two years of my haranguing them not to torture the boy, the fact that they had the smarts to hire a typist lost me the case.

In a number of cases, their presumption of the school's good faith did lead hearing officers to accept educational plans they recognized as faulty, as indicated by decisions which accepted the school's plan but also included suggestions for strengthening the proposed programs. Some decisions acknowledged the school's plan to be inadequate but asserted that the school would be capable of providing adequate services. Parents were very upset by this type of reasoning.

The hearing officer ruled that the major part of the educational plan was not in compliance with the law, mainly because [the school had] neglected to write down tests, or goals, specific or general; they neglected to write down when the goals would be achieved. . . . This is how stupid the whole thing is—he ruled in favor of them even though they had a crummy plan, and told them to rewrite the plan. So in January, they rewrote the plan as if it were June of the year before and they put down goals and whatever. They still weren't any good. They even put down what testing they were going to do in September, the September that had already passed. The whole thing was the weirdest thing I've ever seen. They sent this in to the state and the state, of course, never looked at it. No one ever looked at it. Why should anyone look at it? She wasn't even in the school system anymore. They submitted it to us, so we rejected it again, thinking that maybe they would give us another hearing on that also.

It was a very poor educational plan by any standard. That was admitted by the hearing officer in the decision. He pointed out that there were many things in the plan that were not adequate. I think that right there we should have won our case. The way the law is set up, the plan is a kind of contract, and what is in the plan is what the parent is supposed to use in making a decision about the program. But the real standard they are using is not what is in the plan, but what they feel the parents were told at all of the meetings and how good a program the hearing officer thinks could have been produced for the child. So the hearing officer makes all kinds of inferences. The people from the school get up and say, "We told the parents this and that," some of which they said, some of which they didn't say. Of course, the problem is that they say so much and at different meetings [that] what they say is often so contradictory that you don't know what they are saying. And they have teachers stand up and say what good classrooms they have. And so what really was offered the parents, which is in the educational plan, and is the only thing that the school is responsible for giving you when you sign the plan, becomes only one of the factors that the hearing officer considers when he is deciding these things.

* * *

[The hearing officer] managed to get [the school] out of adhering to any of the regulations that they are supposed to adhere to in the law itself. He managed to slap them on the wrist and say, "Oh, you naughty boys, you didn't write out what you were supposed to," and then he prescribed his own plan that the school system never agreed to. I then got a letter from the school system because I sent them [a copy of] my reply to the hearing officer. And they were shocked and dismayed that I could possibly feel this way and they were looking forward to taking care of my child in the fall.

A few parents interpreted the hearing officer's presumption of good faith in more sinister terms:

I think it was predetermind before we ever got there. . . . No parents were going to win any more cases. It's just a feeling I have that the state is handcuffed. They can't enforce their own rules.

* * *

[The hearing officer's decision] really went against all of the evidence. It seems to have been a political decision on his part because six weeks later, the hearing officer moves to an administrative position.

* * *

> I just feel that he had been reached. He seemed to know the superintendent. It's just suspicion on my part but I feel he was reached.

As an indication of their feelings about the hearing process, we asked parents to agree or disagree that *"In general, I think the appeals system is biased in favor of the schools."* Among 22 parents involved in Staying-in-School and Leaving School disputes, 41% disagreed. When asked how the system was biased, more than half of these parents cited the hearing system's lack of follow-through which allows decisions to remain unimplemented, rather than actual bias at the hearing. But among the 21 parents who lost Private School cases, fully 76% felt the system was unfair. Their most frequent complaints were that the schools have abundant legal and other resources to defend themselves at an appeal and that hearing officers were more sympathetic to the school's position. Significantly, of the 28 parents who won Private School disputes, only 25% saw bias in the system.

As might be expected from their descriptions of hearings, many parents felt they were "beaten" by an adept attorney for the school. Other parents could not understand why the evaluations provided by authorities from hospitals and university clinics were not given greater weight by hearing officers. Some parents felt the benefit of any doubt was always given to the schools except in the most extreme circumstances.

> Our feeling is that you need a lawyer and my husband feels it's not worthwhile [because it's too costly]. The only time they do rule for the children is when it's a very obvious case of negligence—like putting these [learning disabled] children in with the mentally retarded. It seems that those are the only ones who win, unless you have a lawyer.

* * *

> Perhaps we would have had better luck if we had let the schools destroy our son completely before we went to a hearing. In some cases, the state can't help but vote for the child but where they can, I think they vote for the city.

To summarize, many parents felt betrayed by the hearing and angered at what they perceived as the school's successful use of illegitimate tactics. However, Chapter 766 does give these parents appeal options by which to pursue their dispute. Their use by parents who lost Private School disputes is discussed below.

Appeal Options

The State Advisory Commission.

In 14 of the 21 losing Private School disputes, parents requested a review of their decision by the State Advisory Commission (SAC). Eleven families submitted briefs with their requests, which was a substantial and expensive undertaking.

In one Private School case, all documents relating to a hearing were lost by the SAC and the parents were awarded a second hearing, which they lost. They subsequently appealed their case directly to Superior Court, the ultimate review authority.

In a second Private School case, the SAC overturned a hearing decision and ordered that the child be given a private school program. The school system subsequently appealed to Superior Court, where the case had not been heard as of our second interview, two years after the initial hearing.

When parents did not request a review, the reason typically given was disillusionment with the state's ability to enforce Chapter 766:

> After seeing the decision, we just felt that was enough. We have so many papers and we've been fighting it for so long and you get nothing for it. They have a law and they say, "Aren't we wonderful? We have this progressive law!" but they really don't want to back it up. We just thought it was hopeless.

Parents who requested a review but did not file a brief often felt the considerable effort required to prepare the brief could be wasted:

> We signed the paper asking for review, but all we ever got back was another copy of the decision. Terrific! Just what I needed! Maybe I could paper the walls with them. At that point, we got off the merry-go-round. They say they are going to protect these children and they really have no intention of doing so. The whole thing is an nightmare. It's good for the professionals. Look how many people they are employing—ex-teachers, hearing officers, lawyers, administrators. The only ones they don't think about are the children.

In all other instances in which parents did not pursue their conflict further, they expressed dissatisfaction with the decision but felt that a continuation of the dispute would be expensive and/or ultimately futile.

Superior Court.

Four of 21 parents appealed to Superior Court. Two cases had been heard, and were awaiting court review at the time of the second interview. No decisions had been rendered.

Asked why she took her dispute to Superior Court, one parent explained:

> I never push things. But when I'm pushed and I'm right, then I'll go to the very ends of the earth. The cost of the lawyer is so great that I've thought, let's just pay the money [for private school] rather than take the chance [on having to pay more legal fees]. But like I say, there are principles behind it and to me it was worth taking a chance to push the system.

Another parent said:

> This all began when I went to the school because I thought he should be doing better. I'm not even sure now what I had in mind; maybe an hour or two of tutoring. But the reaction of the school was just so insensitive, so callous—you're just a parent and you should know your place—that I took him to Dr. _____ to see what was really going on, and I had never realized how much trouble he was in. Fortunately, we are well able to afford [the private school] but I am going through with the court case because some day I want to be able to go to a School Committee meeting and say, "Now look what you have done. You have to pay all this money and you have had to pay all of these bills and you have been made to look foolish before all of the community and you could have prevented it all. None of it would have happened if you had listened to me as a concerned parent and not had a system of pushing parents around." Two years ago if they had said, "Yes, we'll try and work with him more and we're glad you brought these problems with his homework to our attention," I probably would have just gone home and thought I had done my best for the child. But they have been nasty; they have lied. And when I go to the School Committee when I have won this, I am going to tell them how I think their employees have behaved and that they have some responsibility for it.

In a third case, the parents explained their use of the courts in terms of cost:

We have big debts. You should see the bills. We've run over $14,000 in debt on this thing so we can't stop now. We have so much invested. If there was a chance that I was wrong, I would stop. But I know I'm right. We've been to every specialist from here to Rhode Island and they all say the same thing.

However, for a number of parents it is the additional cost of continuing the conflict that prevents a further escalation:

I wanted to take it to court. I would have wanted to go on. I may be wrong, but I think a judge would have seen it in a legal sense, that they had done so many things illegally to us. But my husband didn't want to. He said it would just take more money to pursue it than not to pursue it.

* * *

After a point it becomes impossible. I can't afford more lawyers' bills when I have to pay these tuitions.

* * *

Go to court? Are you serious? First, I'm still paying the lawyer for the hearing. Second, it's like a crap shoot, because no one has any idea of what the courts will do with these things. Third, I've had enough of it. You want me to suffer through more?

Rejecting a second educational plan.

Parents can also reapply to their school system for a new educational plan, reject this plan, and take the dispute to a second hearing if they lose a decision. A positive decision at this second hearing would not relieve parents of the responsibility of paying for previous private schooling but would make the school system responsible for current and future costs.

Two sets of parents in our study who lost Private School cases went to a second hearing in this way. Both reported they were offered the same programs they had previously rejected, a resource room rather than a self-contained learning disability program. Since school personnel knew these parents were seeking to reverse an earlier decision, their relationships were strained throughout the evaluation process. Both families lost their second hearing.

In sum, parents who lost Private School cases had various options. Some of these parents requested a court review or rejected additional educational plans in order to secure a new hearing, but most had their decision reviewed by the State Advisory Commission, and over half submitted briefs. That so many submitted briefs, even though this required continued involvement in the dispute and additional legal expenses, is a reflection on the strength of parent belief in the legitimacy of their demands, the depth of their commitment to the dispute, and their perception that the adverse decisions were not justified.

For most parents, however, the added costs of continuing the dispute, their sense of futility, and the trauma associated with past hearings have led them to end their conflict by paying for the private programs themselves.

Among the 21 families who lost Private School disputes, only two returned their children to public school because they could no longer afford private tuitions. Other children returned because private schools advised parents that no further remediation was warranted, the child wanted to go to school with his/her neighborhood friends, or negotiations could now be conducted with a new special education administrator. In general, once parents committed themselves to private education, they expressed extremely high levels of satisfaction and were willing to pay for this schooling no matter what the hearing officer ruled. This commitment held even though 10 of the 19 parents in this category reported these costs entailed considerable financial sacrifice for their families.

Part 3. Parents Who Won Private School Cases

The paradoxical outcome of the appeals process in Massachusetts is that even parents who won Private School disputes remained embroiled in continuing legal controversy. The school may continue the dispute in two ways: (1) by appealing the case to the Superior Court, or (2) by preparing a new educational plan, as part of the required annual review, which proposes placement in a public school program and thus forces a new hearing.

Schools Go to Superior Court

The parents in our sample won 28 of 49 Private School cases. School systems took six of these disputes to Superior Court. In four of these six cases, schools withheld payment of past and current tuitions pending outcome of the court review. The parents who won had to contest the court action by the schools by engaging and paying counsel (see Note 1), meanwhile paying the tuition which the hearing decision had said was the responsibility of the schools. Winning an appeal led to a continuing conflict lasting longer than the parents had envisioned when they chose to appeal the educational plan.

Some schools simply failed to meet the obligations ordered by the decision. For example, one family brought the school system to a compliance hearing at which the original order was reaffirmed. The school system was again ordered to pay the mandated costs, but eight months after the compliance hearing, the school system had still failed to meet this obligation. At the time of our second interview, this family anticipated their next step would be to sue the school system.

A second family, which paid over $1,200 in legal fees for their first hearing, concluded after eight months of nonpayment that the school system would not reimburse them for private tuitions as ordered, and they ceased their attempts to secure reimbursement. The family needed to conserve its limited resources to pay the tuitions it had "won," and eventually was forced by the fiscal pressure to return their child to a public program. They are bitter about their experience:

> When we left the hearing, we knew we had won. The school system was just so unprepared that the hearing officer had to rule for us. But then I saw that the people from the school were smiling and I wondered why they were smiling. Now I know. They knew we had won but they knew we hadn't won anything. They have just refused to pay. They drag things out so long that parents just give up. I couldn't keep paying a lawyer when I had to pay $5,000 bills from [the private school]. So what did I win? I won nothing.

In one instance, a family could not be reimbursed because the private school they selected included nonhandicapped children, a provision of Chapter 766 of which they had not been made aware by school personnel, nor by their own lawyer.

Two years after their hearings, six of the 28 families in our sample that "won" Private School cases still had not yet received tuition reimbursements. This situation caused a high rate of return to the public schools among this group.

Multiple Hearings

The most frequent strategy by which schools prolonged a dispute for parents who won a Private School case occurred at the annual re-evaluation. If the school system continues to pay for private schooling, the conflict between parents and schools subsides. However, if the schools recommend a public program at the annual review meeting, the parents face three options: (1) they can transfer their child back to the public schools; (2) they can reject the proposed educational plan and take the dispute to a second hearing; or (3) they can decide not to use the appeals system and pay the private tuition themselves. Many parents whose child had experienced a modicum of success in the private school wanted to retain the placement. They faced an annual negotiation and, potentially, a new hearing each year.

Only four of the 28 children whose parents won Private School cases were not subsequently re-evaluated: two children graduated the year after the placement, one child was moved to a regular private school, and one family enrolled their child in the public schools without further special educational services.

In 10 of 24 cases when a child was re-evaluated, school systems did agree to continue funding private placements. In the other 14 cases, school systems offered parents a public program, forcing parents to choose whether to use the appeals system again (6 cases), to pay the tuition themselves (3 cases), or to accept the school's proposal (5 cases).

Of the six new appeals, four were won by the parents, while two were still awaiting a hearing at the time of our second interview. In two cases when parents won the second hearing, the school system took the disputes to Superior Court, arguing the decisions neglected relevant evidence. Both of these cases came from the same community, in which the special education director was particularly antagonistic to paying private school tuitions. In one of these cases, the schools were preparing a third educational plan, and the parents feared they would have to prepare for a third hearing.

All of these parents felt forced to mount new appeals each year just to maintain the program for their child which they had supposedly won in the hearing. One parent, whose university affiliations provided access to free legal services, complained:

> I become upset when I think of the necessity of going through it again. What do I do after the next thing [a Superior Court case] is over with, even assuming that I win? Do I have to keep fighting this alone, year in and year out? I feel that I need and deserve some assistance from the state. I don't mean monetarily, but some advice.

The parent is really helpless because the school system is able to pay for its representation, but individual parents are frequently very badly off. I have met some people, particularly some Black parents, who don't have the connections to get quality legal representation. I have had access to a lawyer which no one else would have. What happens to the poorer people? This is the tragedy. I was brought up in the public schools all my life. I would like more than anything to strengthen the public schools. But I don't think [the special education director] is helping them. I mean, let the private schools do what they can do best.

Another parent complained:

If they give you the same plan—a 502.2 [less than 25% special services]—over again, why should you have to go through the whole thing again? Why should you have to spend the money on a lawyer again and they spend tax dollars on hiring an even bigger lawyer for the second hearing than they had at the first one. I think the state should really get after these towns and see what they're doing.

Clearly, there is also a residue of bitterness in these disputes which makes it less likely that future negotiations regarding new programs will succeed:

It was very hard for them to write another plan. I had phone calls with Mr. _____ , the head of the L.D. [learning disability] program, and he said to me, "You beat me once, but you won't again." To me, I don't feel I beat him. I just got the best services for my youngster that my youngster deserved, and he felt I was attacking his program, which I wasn't, but he would hang up on me. We have had very poor relations with him. As for the plan he finally gave me, it was a very generalized thing. Absolutely no specifics. It could apply to any youngster in their entire system. They did not specify his needs, they just made a general outline that he would do better in the mainstream with his peers than at a special school but they did not indicate what kinds of services he would be provided, by whom, or what level the youngster was functioning at. It was just a bad job.

One family which won two hearings has refused to allow the schools to prepare a third educational plan:

My husband decided that we've just had enough. We've gone
through two of these things. Each one is wrenching. We have been
insulted and browbeaten by [the special education director]. I
would never put my child back into any school that he had
anything to do with. I have given up on this so-called due process.
In fact, I've advised parents to stay away from it if they can, to just
pay the costs.

The option of ending the conflict by paying the private school tuition
themselves was adopted by three parents. Although they rejected the new
educational plan, they decided not to appeal because of the emotional cost of
attending a hearing. In one case, relations with school personnel remained
hostile and bitter. A new evaluation meeting was not held for the child; the
parents were simply mailed a new educational plan calling for a public school
program. The mother explained their decision not to appeal:

This year it came up again and I could have gotten my ducks in a
row and taken them to a hearing again. I decided not to do it. . . . My
hands right now are shaking as I'm talking to you about it. I'm old
and I get that same horrible feeling all over. Maybe if I had been a
different kind of person but I feel it is a very difficult thing to sit
across from someone and have them lie blatantly and not be able to
say anything about it.

In five cases, the parents accepted the offer of a public school program. One
of these cases involved a kindergarten placement in which the parents had
already planned for their child to attend a public first grade. The other four
families returned their child to the public school when their re-evaluation did
not recommend a private placement. Two families admitted financial
problems were a significant element in this decision:

[The private school] said he was able to go back [to the public
school] but he might have some problems. I suppose in the best of
all worlds, he would have spent another year [in private school].
On the other hand, the superintendent was saying he would do
everything in his power to provide for her in the public schools,
but if not, we would have to fight it over again. And I felt, at that
point, the strain. I'm sure you've talked to many parents. I really
didn't feel that I was strong enough to go through it again. Also,
it's been hard paying the tuition and I'm still fighting them to get
what they owe me. So it would have been another fight. So I
relented.

In ten cases, children were re-evaluated, and the schools did volunteer to continue paying private tuitions. Parents offered a variety of interpretations of this rare victory:

> We have been delighted with their change since the hearing. They visited the [private school] program and sat down with us and said, "Yes, that is what he needs now and we can't offer you similar services." They have been very cooperative.

* * *

> I think they're scared of us. They know we'll take them to another hearing so they're giving us what we want.

* * *

> You have to understand that the people have all changed. It's not a result of the hearing. It's that the town got rid of the old special education director, so that the situation has changed for everyone, not just us. We sat down with [the new special education director] and he was very frank in saying that they just didn't have the facilities for her yet so that he felt obliged to continue paying, but that when he did have a program and he could assure us it was a good program, he would expect us to bring her back.

In three of these ten cases, hostilities have ended. In each case, the school system paid for one additional year of private schooling after the decision, and then offered parents a public school program which they accepted. In two cases, parents are currently satisfied with these programs. In the other case, a child attended the public school's tenth grade for three weeks, found the experience emotionally traumatic, and was moved to a regular private school at the parents' expense. These parents interpreted their child's negative reaction as due to his past history of failure and social rejection rather than to any inadequacy in the public school's program or in the cooperation of school personnel.

In four cases, hostilities subsided. In two cases, the public schools volunteered one further year of tuition; in one case, for two further years. In the fourth case, the school system certified the child's special needs but the parents' difficulties were with a previous state statute.

In three remaining cases, the school volunteered payment for an additional year of private schooling but at a second evaluation wanted the child returned to the public schools. In one case, the parents rejected the plan and went to a second hearing, which they lost. In two cases, the parents were discouraged from using the appeals system by the risk involved. For example:

> We looked at the other families and saw that schools are now winning. They write much better plans, though we felt they still didn't have the people in the schools who could carry through. But to win, we would need a sharp lawyer. So we decided not to risk it. It's like everything else: if you're rich, you can fight them. But if we lost, we'd be out the tuition plus the lawyer. So we couldn't do it. So now we're paying the [private school] tuition. I don't know what to do about it. We're really hurting financially.

In sum, parents who won Private School cases had to engage in annual negotiations over their child's program. Such negotiations can be difficult if the school seeks to recapture the child. In 14 cases, the school's new educational plan recommended public school programs, forcing the parents to consider a new appeal. With a few exceptions, parents who accepted this new plan ascribed their choice to financial difficulties. Parents who did not accept it either went to another hearing or paid the tuition themselves. Of the 28 "winning" cases, 52% of the parents attended subsequent hearings or went to court. Another quarter of these parents ended the conflict by paying the tuition themselves, often because of the school's default or intransigence. In 74% of these "winning" cases, then, there was continuing parent-school conflict. "Winning" an appeal involved a complex and extended conflict. These parents were not happy winners.

Summary

This section has described the events which followed attendance at a hearing. These histories provide little basis for optimism about the exercise of parents' rights. When children were returned to or retained in public programs, there was usually subsequent conflict over implementation of the programs ordered by the decision and the consequent changes which the child needed. When parents lost Private School disputes, their limited resources and their need to end the trauma prevented continued conflict. Even when parents "won" Private School disputes, most remained involved in continuing controversy which they had not anticipated.

Almost 40% of the families in our study had scheduled or attended second hearings or had court appearances; many appeared at hearings or in court more than two times.

However, this is only the most visible indication of the continuing discontent among these families. In some cases the continuing conflict caused parents to remove children from the schools or from special education, with probable damage to their children. Some children were returned to public programs, or parents were forced to pay the ordered private school tuitions themselves because of the schools' failure to obey a decision. Other parents confronted school personnel directly because they perceived a second hearing to be pointless, but they too met with little success.

If we consider the various problems described, 61% of the families in our study experienced serious, continuing difficulties. The fewest problems arose when parents lost Private School disputes—only 38% of these cases resulted in a second hearing or court appearance, but this is because many of these parents chose to pay the private school tuitions themselves. Parents who could not afford such costs were in an especially difficult position. In Staying-in-School and Leaving School disputes, 27% of the cases had additional hearings or court appearances, and continuing difficulties of other types dogged 41% of the cases. When parents "won" Private School disputes, 52% of the cases resulted in additional hearings or court appearances and 22% more had continuing difficulties, such as a failure to pay tuitions.

This incredible record of ongoing conflict may be an unintended consequence of the adversarial approach to resolving these differences. But an adversarial model scarcely seems suitable for determining educational priorities. It is not structured to permit consideration of the best interests of the child in a system in which parents and school personnel must cultivate long-term relationships on the child's behalf.

Some suggestions for more effective practice may be indicated even within the constraints of this adversarial model, however. First, the appeals system must take responsibility for the children who come before it. While the compliance hearing procedure helps somewhat, it still requires parent initiation. In our opinion, the appeals system must institute routine procedures to monitor compliance, in order to assure that the child's interests are protected over time. Thus, disputes which arise after the original hearing may better be addressed simply by re-opening the hearing upon request without starting each round from the beginning. Having become involved, the original hearing officer, when necessary, should be able to maintain jurisdiction.

Some of the worst situations we uncovered are common to human service systems—the children who fall into the jurisdictional cracks in the service delivery system. As the people established to consider the programming needs of children, hearing officers are well positioned to direct the schools and other agencies in meeting their responsibilities to the child who requires a comprehensive range of services from many sources. Legally, hearing officers do not have jurisdiction over non-educational agencies, though perhaps their applicable range of authority might be broadened, given the mandate of comprehensive services provided in the special education laws. Even so, they could more actively pursue avenues to assure the services delivered are integrated and appropriate for the handicapped child. Instead, the Bureau of Special Education Appeals has interpreted the hearing officer's mandate narrowly, and due process safeguards for children have not received their active advocacy.

Without routine follow-up of decisions, parents are left to continue a difficult initiative, with little support even when they have "won." Mechanisms must be developed to insure implementation of the decisions by active follow-up and negotiation—a continuing presence—until implementation is achieved. Failing this active role by the hearings staff, a monitor might be appointed with an active surveillance role to assure that the ordered program is implemented, with power to request the hearing officer to reconvene the hearing or to take some other appropriate action to attain compliance.

Notes

1. In some later instances, the Massachusetts Attorney General's office has entered a dispute on behalf of the parents, after a decision was rendered in their favor.

8

What Happened
Four Years Later

Even four years after the original dispute, the hearing system had failed to resolve most cases. When we conducted follow-up interviews in 1980, we found that cases appealed to Superior Court still had not been heard, "winning" parents were unable to count on the tuition and programs they had supposedly won, and many parents had opted out of the system entirely, preferring to pay their own tuition than to engage in seemingly endless confrontations with the schools. Only in districts where new administrators had been hired, allowing parents and schools to "start over" in their negotiations, did we find any substantial incidence of resolution of disputes.

Of the 71 families in our interview sample, we spoke with 64 for this third interview, which took place an average of 42 months after the initial hearing. (We could not locate three families. The other four refused to talk further about their hearings, saying it was a time in their lives they would rather forget.) We asked these 64 families about the current status of their cases, and about the impact of the appeals process on their special needs child. We found a level of bitterness about the hearing process which had diminished little over the years. Ultimately, it seemed, the appeals process had only weakened support for public education among parents who had once considered themselves advocates of the public schools.

Staying-in-School and Leaving School Cases

Children who stayed in school.

Of our study's original 22 Staying-in-School and Leaving School children, 16 had remained in public school (10 and 6, respectively). We interviewed 13 of these families (two could not be located, while one dispute had ended with the child's graduation from high school).

Only three of these 13 cases had gone on to litigation since the second interview. This was a small number, especially since seven cases had indicated satisfaction and no conflict at the time of this second interview. One of these 13 cases had gone to a new hearing. The issue concerned whether psychotherapy for the child should be included in the educational plan. This dispute continued four years later.

Parents in the remaining two cases had taken their appeals to Superior Court. Neither case had been heard at the time of our second interview, even though one child had been out of school for two years, and the other had been kept in a program which her parents felt was damaging. Although both cases were resolved by the time of this third interview, neither resolution was achieved by the court. The long histories of conflict had stymied negotiations in both cases, which were resolved only by the hiring of new administrators with whom parents felt they could work.

One case involved an epileptic girl who had been removed from school for three years pending action by the court. She returned after the new special education director and the principal persuaded the parents to accept an interim program. While not enthusiastic about the interim program, the parents were very excited about the program proposed for the following year. The mother thought it was "the best plan [the city] had to offer" and "exactly what we requested four years ago."

The other case had gone through three hearings and an appeal to Superior Court. The parent of a girl confined to a wheelchair had become convinced that hearings only increased antagonism, but they did feel able to work with the new special education director, who was hired late in their case. The new administrator helped change the emotional climate of the dispute. The parents adopted a strategy of developing informal agreements with school staff, avoiding formal educational planning meetings. Although the parents did feel their wheelchair-bound daughter continued to be excluded from extracurricular activities, the dispute terminated with the girl's graduation from high school.

Both disputes had been marked by a steadily escalating sequence of hostile confrontations between parents and school. The special education director ultimately referred the first case to the Welfare Department on a petition that would have awarded the child's custody to the state. In the second case, both the prior special education director and the parents accused each other of malice and malfeasance, with the parents attacking almost every aspect of the special education program at each of the three hearings, even seeking a monitor to oversee the school's efforts for their child. It is unlikely that Superior Court action could have resolved these cases since their problems were caused by lack of communication and trust, rather than matters of law. In such an emotional climate, probably no program would have satisfied the parents, and in fact, the second dispute was resolved more by the change in emotional climate than by any specific program offering. When administrators new to the dispute actively worked to defuse the conflict, they were able to create the basis for a new parent-school relationship.

Private school placements.
We also interviewed five of the six familes in these two subgroups who had won private school placements. Two of these five families felt that Chapter 766 and the appeals process had served them well: in both cases emotionally disturbed daughters had been awarded the requested residential placements. The other three families were less pleased. Although initially satisfied with their private placements, they still had to renegotiate their child's program each year as the schools reviewed their educational plans. Parents saw the schools using these reviews as an excuse to try to return their children to inadequate public programs. Whether or not this was true, the atmosphere of conflict generated by the hearings had surely increased the mistrust on both sides.

For example, one decision originally split a fourth grade boy's program between a private day school and a public school. After two years, when an independent evaluation showed he was making little progress, the parents informally negotiated a new program calling for a full-time private placement which the school covered for two years. Then the system proposed an "alternative class" at the junior high school, which the parents rejected, leading to a new hearing the following spring over who would pay for the previous year at private school. The parents told us they would appeal to Superior Court if they lost this hearing, because they felt the private day school had finally produced real progress. They were angry over the school's attempt to return their son to an "inadequate" program, an attempt which further eroded their faith in the public schools.

A second private placement was awarded an emotionally disturbed boy whose only education at the time of the hearing had been home tutoring supplied by the school. Although the parents had not even requested it, the hearing officer ruled for a residential placement. After two years at this placement, the school system wanted the boy moved to a private day school, against the advice of the residential staff. This resulted in a new hearing that the parents won. The following year, however, the parents gave in and accepted a plan for a full-time segregated placement at their local high school, but they were not satisfied with their son's progress and felt "the school is waiting for him to quit."

These cases reflect the difficult personal problems of the children involved. But their difficulties were compounded by the uncertainty inherent in a hearing system whose decisions are only valid a year at a time. Schools are also reluctant to assume responsibility for remediating solely emotional problems that have family-based causes. And when children whose parents have undertaken these extended disputes do return to the public schools, parent-school communication still reflects the earlier antagonisms, thus renewing and sustaining the conflict. A last case illustrates the problem:

A sixth grade boy was given six months at a private day school by a hearing officer "to make up for lost time" when he had not been getting appropriate public school services. When he returned to public school, staff again diagnosed him as having no learning problems. After a dispute over this diagnosis which continued for two more years, the mother placed her child at a private school she felt was inadequate, but the only one she could afford. At our second interview, the mother had claimed to have "given up" on the public schools, though her son was having a "terrible year" at his new private school. Two years later, this private school refused to re-enroll the child because he was failing in almost all areas. The mother requested a new evaluation from the public school, which she again felt to be inadequate, but she saw no choice but to re-enter her son in the public eleventh grade, where the services he had received are reportedly "nil" and where he continues to do poorly. The mother is bitter about the hearing system, which she feels did not insure the provision of an adequate program for her son and assured him no support when he returned to public school.

Private School Cases

When parents win private school cases.
Parents clearly had ample reason to mistrust the hearing system even when they ostensibly "won" their dispute. Nowhere is this more clear than in "winning" Private School cases. When we spoke again with 23 of these 28 winning families, we found more than half of them still engaged in litigation.

Winning Private School parents had a much higher rate of subsequent litigation than any other subgroup in our sample. Eleven of 23 had attended additional hearings: four second hearings continuing the original dispute, and seven new hearings to prevent schools from returning the child to the same public school program that parents had rejected the year before. The child's evident progress in private school made the stakes even higher for these parents.

These cases had various scenarios, but all were characterized by mounting parent-school conflict. In one case, the public schools volunteered to pay for one additional year. The parents lost their appeal for the subsequent years. In a second case the parents did win another year, but decided to place their child at their own expense to escape the seemingly endless round of hearings.

In four cases, the school developed a new educational plan immediately after a losing decision and a new hearing was held within a year. Two parents won and two parents lost this appeal. None of these children were returned to the public schools; all were kept in private schools. None of the parents subsequently requested educational plans: the yearly cycle of confrontations ceased because parents opted out of the game.

Five cases were appealed to Superior Court, but almost four years later only one case had been heard, and no decision had been rendered on that one. In two cases, parents reached a financial settlement outside of court. Two cases are still awaiting court action. The outstanding issue in each case was the schools' nonpayment of tuitions the parents had won.

When parents lost private school cases.

We interviewed 16 of the 21 families who had lost Private School disputes four years later. Two families had attended a second hearing. Five had been involved in litigation after their first hearing: four of these had appealed adverse decisions to Superior Court, while one family had been taken to court by the school system. Four years later, two of the five court cases had been heard, and only one decision had been rendered. The pending disputes have been of three and four years' duration.

One example particularly illustrates these cases. The family based their appeal for reimbursement of tuition on the school's denial of a child evaluation. During the second year, the parents requested an evaluation but were told the child's problems must be reviewed by a pre-evaluation screening committee. This screening committee, constituted to inquire into whether or not the child could be served by the regular education program, concluded the child was emotionally troubled, not learning-disabled, contradicting other diagnostic findings. This delay caused the parents to seek private school space while the school was still conducting its evaluation. The judge ruled the parents had been denied their right to an evaluation, but subsequent appeals for private school reimbursement were denied at a later hearing.

The Subsequent Educational Career
of the Private School Children

We asked the Private School parents about the subsequent school careers of their children. We wanted to know to what extent their parents' disputes have affected these children's education. In our third interview, four years later, the parents reported that their children had generally made considerable progress, especially in private learning disabilities schools. But we were troubled by their continuing estrangement from public special education, although their other children usually attended local public schools.

Who Returned to Public School?

By 1980, an average of four years after their initial hearing, about 40% of the children who were attending private special needs schools had eventually transferred back to public school programs (18 of 44), while 30% transferred to other private day (10) or residential schools (3), either regular or special needs. Although most children spent only two or three years at their original private school, 30% did stay longer. The children who moved to different special education schools went to facilities with more intensive services, for example, residential placements. The parents of all such children had won their hearings and the move was possible only because costs were being paid by the school system. No child whose family lost a hearing moved to a second special education school.

Parents who lost Private School disputes were somewhat more likely to return children to public programs than parents who had won—50% of losing parents returned their child, as against 35% of winning parents. But the difference is misleading because some of these parents never intended to keep their child in the private placement. Of the 18 "losing" parents, five always planned to enroll their child in the public school program at some point. For example, two losing parents were seeking reimbursement for a special kindergarten, but had always intended to send their child to a public first grade. Three parents had been advised before their hearing that their child had already progressed to the maximum in the private special needs school. Only two children were returned to the public schools because their parents could not afford to pay the private school tuitions.

The remaining eleven losing parents either kept their child at a private special needs school or transferred their child to a regular private school. These parents expressed continuing antagonism toward the public schools. The unresolved bitterness engendered by the educational planning process and the hearing procedure led many to maintain their child in a private school even when educational problems no longer required it. For example, one parent reported that "at times" her son "wishes he could go back to the public school because many of his friends are there and because the workload at the [private] school is heavy." However, she will "never" let him go back because of the "horrible experience" the family has had. The phrase "I will never let him go back" occurs in almost all the interviews with losing appeals parents. One family that did want their child back in public school sold their house and moved to a new community, so they would not have to interact with the same school personnel.

Families who had won their cases were actually more willing to use public schools than those who lost. While only 9 of 26 winning parents returned their children to public school, only two of these nine did so for economic reasons. The other seven were returned "to give the public schools another chance." However, most winning parents were still reluctant to use public school programs. When their child left the original private school, he went to another private school, either special needs (5) or regular (8).

Asked why they had decided for or against the public schools, parents suggested a number of factors. First, children differed in their willingness to return to public schools. At one extreme:

> A psychologist recommended [an alternative high school program], and we registered him there but he wouldn't go. He said he would rather be miserable in the [town's] high school and be the same as everybody else than be different. He really wanted desperately to get back. It was his choice. I think kids his age want to be the same as everybody else. They don't want to be different.

* * *

> He wanted to go back. I think he matured to the point where he thought what he would find here was adequate. He was not totally enthralled with private school life. He could see that was limited too and that he has to compete and make friends among his peers.

At the other extreme:

> We originally thought that it would be very important for him to go back to public school, psychologically important to be successful where he had previously failed. My attitude on that has changed. He has experienced such success at [the private school]

that I wouldn't want to risk him going back. When it came time to pick, we discussed it, and he had no desire at all to go back. He said he wanted another school like the [private school] so we never seriously considered him returning.

* * *

The public school has so many negative connotations to him. He was miserable for so long and was met by such lack of understanding that I don't blame him for not wanting to go back.

A second factor affecting placement choice among winning families was the perception that it would be hard to deal with school personnel:

It would be very difficult to work with them. They pulled every dirty trick in the book on me and, frankly, I have lost respect for them as people who are sincerely doing their job. I think they might not be too happy with me either. I don't think they like parents they cannot dominate.

However, families who use the public schools reported they could often avoid contact with those staff who were the major actors in their dispute. One family moved to a new community for this reason. A number of parents said the presence of a new special education director eased the problems they had feared. Others said their conflict had been with administrators, whereas their decision to return had involved lower-level personnel, who bore them no animosity.

A third factor was the difficulty some parents experienced in finding appropriate private secondary schools that would accept learning disabled children. For example, one family could only find a residential school for their son, but was unwilling to have him leave home.

Parents were more willing to send younger children back to public schools. Among children who were transferred to private programs, all but one was past the seventh grade. Since there was no major difference in the time spent at a special needs school between older and younger children, it may be that younger children were viewed as more capable of re-entering public programs, not having experienced as many years of failure there. Parents expressed concern about the inferior quality of both regular and special education services at the secondary level and were fearful of placing a child who had had problems into a junior high school with few resources.

Generally, the children who returned to the public schools needed only small amounts of special services, so that parents could avoid the special educators involved in their disputes. For example, four of these returning children received no special services upon their return to public school (with parental agreement) and three received less than three hours a week, sometimes just increased guidance help. However, not all such children returned to public schools: the eight children who transferred to regular private day and residential schools also required minimal services; half received no special help and half only limited tutoring.

Finally, prior experience with private schools affected parent choices. Some children had never attended public school. The children who had attended regular private schools before their disputes were eventually transferred back to such a school no matter what the outcome of their cases. Apparently, parents initially attracted to the private education market retained this attraction, providing some justification for the oft-heard complaint among school personnel that no educational plan could have induced such parents to use the public schools. However, these cases constitute a very small proportion of the appeals load; in our study, only five out of 71 cases.

Summary

Parents who lost appeals were somewhat more likely to return children to public schools than parents who won, primarily because of the continuing financial burden. But about a third of the winning Private School parents did eventually return their children to public school, either for social reasons or because they could not find appropriate private secondary programs. The rapid turnover among special education administrators also enabled parents to establish new, more amicable relationships with school staff.

However, most children in Private School cases never returned to public school, regardless of the outcome of their dispute. Parents who lost were bitter about their experiences and refused to consider public programs—but parents who won shared many of the same feelings. Although Staying-in-School and Leaving School parents did not engage in protracted litigation or withdraw their children from the schools, they seemed also to have been dissatisfied with the results of their appeals. The hearing procedure seems ultimately to have diminished support for public education among parents who had initially called themselves public school advocates, and whose other children continued to attend public school.

9

Parents Compare Public and Private Schools

The overwhelming majority of parents who appealed their child's educational plan requested private school placements. Clearly, many parents have grave doubts about the public schools' ability to provide special needs children with appropriate programs. This section will examine parents' views of how public and private special education differ, particularly for learning-disabled children. Both in interviews and at their hearings, parents repeatedly expressed their disillusionment with public schools.

Problems with Mainstreaming

In theory, mainstreaming is supposed to help children view themselves more positively by providing competent models rather than the less competent models found in a special class of handicapped students. But the parents of the learning-disabled children in our sample felt that, in practice, mainstreaming had other results. At private nonmainstreamed day schools, they found their children attending very small classes geared wholly to their special learning and emotional needs. The entire environment, even ancillary services like Outward Bound-type physical education, was designed to improve the child's self-esteem. By contrast, even when public school programs could offer a

159

broader range of services, such as speech therapy or adaptive physical education, these services were embedded in substantial periods of large-group mainstreamed instruction. The frequent switching back and forth between regular and special education classrooms posed difficult problems for the child already frustrated by academics and suspicious of school learning. Such a child was further required to develop work relationships with an array of different teachers and specialists, an added strain.

When we asked parents requesting private schools whether they had any strong preferences for a particular type of class, the vast majority (31 of 46) preferred "segregated" classrooms. Twenty-two of these 31 parents selected the following statement to represent their feelings: *"I feel my child should be in a special class so s/he can get all of the individual attention and help s/he needs."* This sentiment was confirmed when we asked parents to respond to the statement, *"I feel that children with the types of problems my child has should be in a special class or a special school and not mainstreamed in regular classes."* Fifty-seven percent agreed and 27% disagreed, with 16% choosing not to respond.

Poor Coordination of Their Child's Programming

Private School parents, as well as many teachers, sensed that though children were being offered a rich mix of services through the public schools, the delivery of these services was poorly organized. No one seemed to have been clearly assigned the day-to-day responsibility to coordinate the child's special activities. Parents in our study were told by clinical professionals that the entire day's programs should be coordinated around their child's special needs. They saw this approach in private schools and failed to see it in public schools, whose programs seemed to lack cohesiveness. Thus, even when the amount and variety of special services offered in public school exceeded those in private school, parents were willing to forego the added services to get personalized, coordinated contacts between teacher(s) and their child.

This is how parents discussed both the mainstreaming and the coordination issues:

> The first year, the law was so new, I just trusted [the public schools] and hoped they would give [my son] enough. But they didn't give him anything. They promised to give him one-to-one time but they kept cutting back, or the teacher would cut out, or it was a woman who came once a week and it wasn't every day. It was half-hearted. But even if they gave everything they said they would, it still wouldn't be enough. They don't have regular teachers in the

classroom who understand the problems when the kid comes back from getting one-to-one. They refuse to see it. Right to my face they told me there was no such thing as a learning disability; that was a new gimmick to get free things. So whatever they were doing in the one-to-one, and she was a very nice woman, it was just wasted the rest of the day.

* * *

It's not integrated into the school at all. There is no coordination between the resource room staff and staff of the rest of the school. The resource room staff are not on staff. They are hourly paid people—no benefits, no vacations; they're sort of second class citizens.

* * *

They said [at the child evaluation meeting] that [their program] was a small class that was maintained throughout the day. But when I visited it, I found it was a resource room, just like [our daughter] had before where she couldn't deal with the integrated parts of the program.

* * *

[Our son] kept complaining that his teacher got mad at him when it was time to go to the resource room.

* * *

The first time they gave him a program, he was out of class one hour a day, and it wasn't enough. It wasn't helping at all because when he was gone, he missed what they had for that hour and he couldn't make it up.

* * *

The plan didn't specify any follow-up between what would happen in the resource room and what would happen out. And we went to the school to talk to some of these people. I forget what the terms [for teaching reading] are, one is "the phonetic" and the other is something else, but the resource room teacher was teaching reading in one way and the other was teaching it the other way. According to independent testing, one of the ways is not good for him. He doesn't pick up aurally, and that was one way that they were teaching. So there was a real lack of follow-up [on] what happens when he gets back in the classroom.

* * *

The hearing officer kind of pooh-poohed the [problem] that [the city] did not provide a plan that was clear. There was no provision for communication between the classroom teacher and the special team people. No statement as to how the classroom teacher would carry over into the classroom the kinds of things [the resource room teacher] was doing. It was sort of, "Oh well, we get along fine together." But the fact is that 75% of the kids in that classroom were expected to get four papers done by noon and how was our son going to do that if he was out doing tutoring, and how is the teacher going to work that out? Those kinds of things are really important.

* * *

Before, [our daughter] was basically a happy, jolly little person. But [after her special programming started] she did not want to go to school. She said her teacher ignored her. And I think that was probably true because she went to special classes so much that the home room teacher did not have the same relationship with the child.

* * *

I feel that children with learning disabilities should be isolated because no matter how you handle it, they're pointed at in a regular school. It hurts their learning process. At a special school, they see children come in very maimed by this thing but they see that they can improve. In the public schools, they would always think in their heart that they were stupid.

* * *

Our child was an emotional basket case; it was ruled [by the hearing officer] that he was very borderline learning disabled, and, looking back, if it had been handled correctly I don't think it ever would have been blown to the proportions it was. His fingers were bitten down to the bone. He would say things like "I'm dumb" and he was in the top math group and I would say, "[Son], you can't be dumb." But they put him in a resource room at [a teachers college]. The [local] school didn't have enough staff and the college needed students and they would bus him over there. I'm sure the intentions were all very good. [Our son] is a quiet child, but the other children would refer to them as the dumb children because they were going out. It was a bad experience for him.

* * *

For [our son], the important thing was to pull him out of the resource room and all of the social rejection and pejorative things that go with that. So he went to [the private school] and it was really good for him. . . . Here is a child who, by disability, legally, probably belongs [only] in a 502.2 [up to 25% special services]. But he had already been through that program and it was destructive to him. [Private school] suited him very well because he was no longer competing with kids in the regular classroom program. He was able to go into a program where he wasn't any different than anyone else and that made him feel good. I bet there are a lot of kids who fit into that category, who are not heavily dyslexic and would just do better in a situation where they can relax. Resource rooms don't allow that because they have to continue to compete with peers the rest of the time.

The Public Schools' Failure to Implement Programs

While parents' fear of schools failing to implement programs was obviously related to general issues of trust in the schools, some parents also felt they had suffered a series of actual deceptions as well. Assessing a school's trustworthiness is very difficult to do at a hearing. School staffs have learned to produce generally acceptable educational plans, and parents found it hard to document their belief that the proposed program was more good intentions or wishful thinking than reality.

At our first hearing, I made a statement that I thought the plan was adequate, but I didn't think they would carry it out. They claim

that is what lost the case for me. Now again, I thought that was very
unfair. Who am I to say whether the plan is adequate? I'm not a
teacher. I'm an eighth-grade drop-out myself. I can't read a thing
and don't know beans whether the plan is suitable. All I know is
that they never did anything they said they were going to do. What
happened in elementary school is that [our daughter] had a tutor in
the resource room and she would leave, and they would get another
one and another one. They never once finished anything they
started.

* * *

There were a lot of people telling us, "Don't believe it. [That
administrator] is famous for making statements and plans and not
delivering on them." That we don't know for a fact, that was just
rumor.

* * *

I don't want [my son] back in the public school system until he can
at least compete with the students or be further ahead. Even though
the school system says they have this help, what they say and what
is actually practiced isn't necessarily true. I have found that out.

* * *

They said he would get one-to-one tutoring. It was tutoring in
groups of six. They said he would get 45 minutes a day. He got it
three times a week, but lots of weeks no one would show up for the
sessions. Over the years, they have promised endless amounts of
service, and according to the tests, he just kept falling further and
further behind. Now they promised me some more. What is on
their educational plan and what he would get in that school are
two entirely different matters.

Clearly, a past history of broken arrangments would predispose parents to
mistrust the programs promised by the schools under the new legislation.
Eleven of our 49 Private School parents had in fact accepted a public school
educational plan during the first year of the new law's implementation. But
by the second year, they rejected the plan, or withdrew their child before a
second plan could be offered; they had found that the services promised in the
educational plan were simply not provided. The disorganization evident in

the child evaluation process during those early years further reinforced parental doubts about the school's proposals.

Past relationships with school personnel were perceived as deceptive in other ways:

> [My son] was getting tutoring for three years before I took him out. We would go to the school, and they would say how pleasant he is, that he is well-liked among the other children. What they didn't tell us was that the tutoring wasn't getting anywhere, that he wasn't improving. It wasn't enough, but they didn't tell me that it wasn't enough. That's their ego. They feel that if they can't teach a child, that's a personal embarrassment to them.

* * *

> I was a model parent. I baked cakes. I went on the field trips. I thought these were friends of mine. But all that time I didn't raise the important questions about how [our daughter] was doing. I thought if there were problems they couldn't handle, they would tell me. When we finally started asking the questions, we were shocked at how they turned on us.

With such a past history of broken agreements and limited communication with school personnel, it is not surprising that many parents were reluctant to trust these new programs:

> They set up a new resource program and they were going to put him in it. Well, my child has been in two or three new programs in [that school system], and nothing has come of them. I didn't want him in another new program. They had botched his education, and I felt it was time we sent him somewhere where they had experience with these things and knew what they were doing. I couldn't risk it anymore. Their new programs would probably turn out as badly as their old programs, and each time it's my child who's suffering.

Parent Perceptions of Private Special Needs Schools

During our first interview, when their children were already enrolled in private school, parents were asked if they were satisfied with the private program. All but a few parents had very positive responses. Of the 49 Private School parents, 37 reported being "very satisfied" and seven "somewhat satisfied." A few parents did complain that private schools tended to be weaker at higher grade levels and about a third of the parents reported their children were having "problems in making or keeping friends in the neighborhood." But, overall, the level of satisfaction with the programming provided was exceedingly high.

Parents found private-sector school personnel willing to communicate with them in a more forthright manner than their public school colleagues. They found them interested and knowledgeable about their children's needs and strengths. They saw real changes in their children's reactions to school, in their willingness to go, and in their achievements. These are anecdotal reports, but they reflect the impressions not only of parents but also of the clinical professionals who independently evaluated these children. These positive feelings were communicated enthusiastically in the recommendations which parents then made to other parents.

Here is a sample of the way parents described their experiences with their child's private school (see Note 1):

> [Our private school] attacks the actual and real problems head on. For instance, our kid came out of a sustained streak of failure. The first year, they set about making school a non-threatening, fun place again, and they worked on the fear factor. Among other things, while at the [private] school, [our boy] became a very skilled rock climber, the point being if you can jump off a 20-foot cliff, you can read. Another thing is that it is a truly individualized teaching program, and therefore expensive. But of course, that's what 766 says: If that's what your kid needs, that's what he should get. We would go over to conferences with those teachers and those teachers knew [our son] cold . . . they knew his whole psychodynamic structure, knew all his little defenses and gimmicks to get approval. They knew his strengths and how to work with them.

> Another thing that worked well is that it seems to be a very happy place. They play with the kids and they talked with them. It was more of a community. It's incredible. These kids come from all over the place—45, 50 minutes away. You don't see the stuff you see in schools—the acting out, the anger, the malicious teasing. None of that. It was weird. Somehow or other, they've made it into a happy place.

These are bright, mostly better-than-bright kids. There is nothing wrong with them except a technical problem. They are so relieved to be in a place where they don't have to explain things to anyone. They don't get humiliated daily. They get peer support, faculty support, administrative support.

* * *

He loves it. I don't know how we'll ever get him out of there. The first day I spoke to the teacher and she said, "Mrs. _____ , [your son] has got to succeed every day and that is my goal." Within three, four days, he was home and he said, "Hey, Ma, you know there is something else I'm good in." And we had been telling him this all along, but it wasn't being reinforced at [public] school. In his class [at the private school] that first year was a child who, I think, was basically a little genius. And on Halloween, [our son] said, "Ma, do you know what one of the other kids said to _____ ? He said, 'You don't need a costume. I could just stick a pin in you and you could go as a crybaby.'" And I thought, that's so unkind. Why should he say that? And he said, "Mom, don't you know that he cries in school every day, but that's the area he's not good in." And I thought, boy, they have really gotten to this kid.

* * *

His attitude is a whole lot better. He's not as worried about himself and he understands what the strictures are—what the limitations are—and he manages. We went and we looked at our local [public] school, just down the street from us, and it's a pretty darned good school. We went and spent a day there, went through the classes and talked to the headmaster and we felt that they were not geared or really interested, I think, in a kid like [our son]. Essentially, I think it would have been hard for him there. He wouldn't have been in charge of his own learning. [The private school] said, essentially, we know what these kids need. You have to take charge of yourself and know what your limitations are.

* * *

[The private school] saved his life. I don't know how, but I know that they saved his life.

* * *

First year, his classes were just two or three children in a class. They
were able to pinpoint his problems. They know this child inside
out. Maybe too well. Maybe [even] his parents shouldn't know that
about their child. The teachers were superb, incredibly sensitive.
He was reading on a second grade level [in the sixth grade] and in
one year they brought him up to grade level. It was really a miracle.
It's just incredible. He's at [a private school for normal children]
now, working without any remediation.

* * *

When he went to the school, he was very frightened, had a very
negative attitude towards school. It took probably six months until
he got to the point of enjoying school, making friends. At that
time, I would say that the academic learning took ground.

* * *

A standard dyslexic defense is that they learn to cope with the adult
society without doing what the adults want them to. [Our son] is a
very attractive boy, physically. So he learned to be a mascot to
adults, to please them right and left, and he learned how to fake
answers. He was great at it. [His private school] worked on
pushing the kid, they pushed the kid to acknowledge failure, to
admit that it was hard. It was a very sensitive environment.

* * *

There's a great caring involved.

* * *

He needed to be in a small classroom, we felt, where he would
receive the individualized attention he needed. We also felt that he
needed to be with his own peers, that is, children who had the same
problem as he did. I was quite satisfied. It gave him the skills he
needed. [Our son] is dysgraphic [writes very poorly] as well as
dyslexic. He still has manifestations of the problem. But now he
has the self-confidence, the wherewithal to overcome or to accept
the fact that he's not so good on some things but good in other

things. He can tackle anything he can put his mind to and he's not a defeated kid at all, even though he does have difficulties in certain areas. All of that he got from [the private school] as well as [being able to] read and write and spell, all reasonably well.

* * *

[The public schools] only had two things to offer. An L.D. [learning disabilities] room and an E.D. [emotionally disturbed] room. . . . The weakest part of their case substantively, was that they insisted on saying [the problem is either] one or the other. We kept saying, you can't deal with him that way. And [the private school] doesn't; [it] assumes there is a kid there with a lot of things going on and you've got to look at all of them.

* * *

They dealt marvelously with us as parents and as people, not as bad people who are somehow responsible for our child's problems. That was the attitude of the public schools—that he was emotionally disturbed and it was somehow our fault, for which a string of very fancy doctors that I've paid for have never found a shred of evidence. But at [the private school], he was a child who had a learning problem, and we were no longer the villains.

Parents do not measure private schools' superiority by specific remediation techniques so much as by the social, personality, and achievement changes evident in their children after the move to these schools. Parents emphasize their child's increase in positive attitudes and behaviors after the years of failure, dejection, and frustration. They see in their child a greater willingness to work with academic materials, and view this interest as evidence of increased academic capabilities.

The irony is that even when public schools can provide a broad array of services by qualified specialists, the parents we interviewed preferred the private schools' coordinated delivery of services over the public schools' wider range of choices within a mainstreamed setting. They felt their child coped more effectively in a more restricted and more managed set of adult relationships, and that the segregated programming also gave their child a sense of protection from the competition and the real or imagined ridicule of their more ably achieving peers. By contrast, parents felt the large mainstreamed class was uncomfortable for their child, forcing him/her to focus on failure, and reinforcing a sense of incompetence, an inability to cope, and a feeling of futility that the child tended to apply generally to out-of-school activities.

Many of these parents also had difficult relationships with public school staff. By contrast, they felt private school employees invested considerable energy in regular contacts with parents, to gain parents' understanding of and support for the private programming. Parents appreciated the sense of care and understanding conveyed by these private school staffs and contrasted it with the public school's evident lack of awareness of their child's needs. They felt that private school staff members had helped them understand their child's needs, the nature of the school's efforts, and the role that they as parents could play in enhancing future growth. Although public school administrators dismiss these practices as self-serving attempts to retain the paying parent's child, this client-oriented attitude does seem to have achieved the kind of relationship mandated by the special education reform, in these parents' eyes at least. By contrast, parents were bitter about the public school's failure to relate to them as clients, much less as collaborators.

Parents' Expectations for Their Children

The last time we interviewed parents, four years after their first hearing, we found another important effect of the child's private school experience: many parents had now developed more realistic expectations for their child. Many public school administrators believed parents confronted schools because they could not accept their child's handicap. Seemingly, as a child began to show some improvement, parents seemed able to cope more easily with the real and possibly persisting weaknesses of their child. What public school personnel seemed to forget is that they must also help parents understand their feelings about their child's handicap(s), while also developing realistic perceptions for their child, a process as important as the actual work with the child.

Some parents talked about their child's experience at special schools as an unalloyed success; for example, a child who "couldn't read a word now reads practically a book a day. We are thrilled." Or a child "getting A's in everything. He's on the honor roll. He's like a different child." Approximately 15 to 20% of our Private School cases yield this kind of extremely positive report, with no indication from the parent of any continuing difficulties.

At the other extreme are parents who have had to come to terms with their child's continuing and severe difficulties. For example, one child re-entered a local high school after two years at a learning-disability school. Both his performance and behavior deteriorated after his return. In part, the parents blame the school system, which is "waiting for him to drop out," but in greater measure they feel he has simply failed to make progress, no matter where he has been placed, and they are at a loss to explain why. Some parents moved their child from one special school to another, trying to find a better alternative. For example, a child who spent five years at a learning disability day school was finally moved to a special needs residential school, with the parents and the school system splitting the cost. Another child moved from a residential program to a day school after one year, and then back to a residential program after two years. In these cases, parents began by blaming the child's school but eventually had to accept the child's own difficulties in learning, which seemed to be resistant to remediation by any educational program. Mercifully, only about a fifth of the cases in our study involved these conspicious failures to progress.

More generally, parents reported their child's private school experience to be positive, but also revealed their growing recognition that their child's difficulties would likely continue for some time to come.

> He's at grade level in everything. We were afraid that if we put him into big classes in the public school he might fall behind again so we put him in the [non-special needs school]. He is doing just wonderfully. He will always have problems, of course. His reading is very good, but he still has difficulty with math. But he is not a defeated child any more and his teachers are aware of his problems and try to accommodate them. We are just so pleased.

* * *

> He is still slow in reading and [the public schools] are giving him some help. It's not really remedial help, it's help to keep him up-to-date with his classes. Otherwise he is doing it on his own. I would not say they cured him completely at the [private school], but he is much better off and psychologically he is better off. He knows his limitations; he's never going to be the star in the class, but he knows he can do his work and he can adjust to his problems. They are now allowing him to use a tape recorder to take notes, which is one of the things I asked about a long time ago, and they said it was impossible. So they've changed to some extent, and he's changed.

* * *

> When I investigated where he should go, [the public school] told me themselves that it would be unwise to put him in the high

school because there is no program in the high school. So I sent
him to [a regular private school], where he is working without any
remediation. The things difficult for him will always be that way;
English will always be difficult for him; but his self-image is so
improved. You just can't beat what happens at [the private special
needs school] in that.

While such comments can be viewed as reflecting the effect of private
schooling on the child's academic performance and self-esteem, a more
important effect may be on the parent's expectations. For example, one parent
told us her son now gets honors grades each quarter, is the captain of three
sports teams, and has succeeded "beyond our wildest dreams." She then
mentioned that "Of course, reading is still difficult for him. [The special
school] helped him to deal with the problem, but they couldn't eliminate it."
This child has certainly changed since our first interview, but his parent's
perceptions and beliefs have changed as dramatically. During our first
interview, this parent talked about learning disabled children as "super
bright": "If they're in a school that understands their deficits, they can use
different ways of teaching them and really bring them up to par, above par."
Once her son began showing some improvement, this parent could more
accurately focus on her child's strengths and his continuing problems, and was
able to give up her insistence on the superiority of the learning disabled. Her
more realistic acceptance of her son's problems seemed easier as he showed
some improvement, but the private school staff also worked to help her
understand her son's strengths and weaknessses. They were able to help her
because they understood and accepted that she felt confused, and perhaps
guilty as well.

In our interviews, parents emphasized the close parent-teacher contact
encouraged by special schools. Again and again, they told us these schools
bolster confidence by saying that a child may be limited in some areas but
successful in others, a message that parents may have needed as much as their
children. When these schools involved parents in the child's education,
parents could understand and eventually accept their child's problems.

We did not collect data on achievement and do not know how much the
children in our sample have actually improved. We do know that most of our
Private School parents were enthusiastic about their child's progress, even as
they admitted the child's continuing difficulties.

This suggests to us that public school education could achieve much of the
same effect with parents if they would learn to see parents as clients. Besides
their natural focus on formal academic training for the child, school staffs
must attend to the parents' needs for support and understanding. Seeing
parents as clients is a pressing issue, and public schools must come to

understand the implications of a client relationship to parents and their children. One intent of the mandate for parent involvement in special education was to help parents come to terms with their child's strengths and weaknesses. Our study suggests strongly that this intent was not clearly understood by public school staff, and has not been reflected in their practice.

Notes

1. These comments do not reflect parental experience with a broad set of private schools, nor can they be used to support the argument that private schools are generally better than public ones. Only three major private schools are discussed here, all of which serve children with learning disabilities or emotional problems. These three may not represent the mass of other private schools serving learning disabled or otherwise handicapped children.

Section III.

School Administrators View Going to Hearings

10

How the Schools
Approached Their Hearings

School personnel have different interests, different responsibilities, and a
different base of information than parents when they approach the special
education hearing system. While a parent normally attends only one hearing,
special education administrators attend many hearings, and they are thus in a
unique position to observe the consistency of the decisions rendered by
different hearing officers. While a parent is primarily concerned with the
disposition of an individual case, school personnel must look at the
cumulative impact of hearings on special educational practices in their
communities. School personnel have a special contribution to make to our
study of the hearing process. This section presents their perspective.

Who Speaks for the Schools?

School personnel have no single viewpoint on either the given child's needs or
the most appropriate educational program for a special needs child, especially
early in the parent-school contact. Different kinds of school personnel differ
in how they perceive the child and his/her needs, and have different kinds of
contacts with parents. Although school personnel in different positions hold
different perspectives, these perspectives change as a case moves closer to a

hearing. No wonder, then, that as parents come in contact with many different school personnel while developing their child's educational plan, they report receiving different messages from different staff.

The differences in communications from the different types of school personnel during this process may account for widespread parental reports that school personnel made different statements at hearings than they had made prior to or during the development of the educational plan. The school staff's disparate views evolve during the educational planning process. Especially when the case goes to a hearing, the disparate staff views tend to coalesce into a more consistent view of the child and his/her programming needs. This switch is important to keep in mind when considering the materials presented in this report.

Staff personally familiar with the child's daily functioning will view him/her differently than those who know the child from reports and test scores. Teachers, for example, can see a child's daily response to a special needs program and are more likely to tell parents about the program's weaknesses for the child. Parents reported that special education teachers who worked with their child might indicate that the child was not progressing because the program was inadequate and might therefore recommend a different placement, usually outside the district.

Evaluation personnel are caught in a more difficult position, torn between a teacher's concern with learning and an administrator's concern with costs. School-based evaluation personnel are likely to have had considerable direct contact with the child or the child's teachers. They become personally familiar with the child and understand the poor response to the current programming. They may feel caught most keenly between what they feel are the child's unmet needs and their loyalty to the programs available within the system. When evaluators are not based in the child's school, they have little or no personal contact with the child and rely on test scores and similar assessments to develop their recommendations. We observed that the further removed s/he was from the child, the more likely the evaluator was to recommend the less costly public programs, whether appropriate for the child or not. This occurred because it represented the policy of the district as espoused by the special education administrator. Even evaluators personally familiar with the child did not feel comfortable expressing their views of the child's needs by the time of the educational planning meeting if they saw the need for added services or an out of district placement. Not surprisingly, parents often saw evaluators as equivocating—sometimes communicating their sense of the child's continuing difficulties, sometimes emphasizing the adequacy of the school's proposed program.

Administrators did not personally work with children or have experience of the child's frustrations with the program. They were most likely to stress the value of existing school programs and were less willing than teachers to add services or to place the child outside the school district. Sensitive to issues of costs, which were of great importance during this period of rapid expansion of services, they sought a rationale to justify recommending a placement within the existing services available within the district.

Due to the newness of the concept and the shortage of programs, learning-disabled children bore the brunt of this concern for costs. Few parents of moderately or severely physically handicapped children sought hearings, though their children were often unserved or underserved before Chapter 766. School districts dramatically expanded their programming for these children after the law was passed. The public schools were also willing to provide these children with out-of-district placements when their programs were inappropriate. By contrast, the public schools displayed a strong reluctance to offer special services to learning-disabled children, even within the public schools. This study is in some ways a testament to the struggle by parents to obtain more appropriate programming for their learning-disabled children. The public schools' reluctance to serve them forced many parents to appeal for private school placements.

In preparation for the hearing, school staff tend to adopt a common viewpoint toward the case, usually the one espoused by the administrator. Thus, while teachers and evaluators might once have told parents during the evaluation process that their child could best be served in a private school, by the time of the hearing their position has shifted to reflect that of the school department. While school personnel might privately admit to the parents their errors in processing a case, for example, losing a child's school records, they will hardly admit errors before superiors at a hearing. Instead, they emphasized their effective performance and good intentions.

Given this complexity, our limited resources presented us with a difficult choice. While we wished to document the viewpoints of the different types of school staff, resource limitations forced us to narrow our focus. We chose to present the perceptions of the school system from the vantage point of the special education administrators, since they are ultimately responsible for implementing the district's policies on special education and for their presentation at hearings.

The Special Education Director

Chapter 766 requires the special education administrator to approve all the educational plans for children who have been seen by the Child Evaluation Team (CET). This team must include a social worker/guidance counselor, teacher, psychologist, physician or nurse, and the child's parent(s). They conduct assessments; hold educational planning meetings to identify the child's needs; propose short- and long-term objectives for the child; and suggest which services the child requires to meet those objectives. Once the evaluation team's recommendations are in, it is the director of special education who must specify the child's actual program: the services to be delivered, the frequency and duration of these services, and the site at which delivery will occur. This is the educational plan submitted for parents' approval. The director is thus the key figure responsible for the school system's program for the child.

The special education administrator also most frequently represents the school system at appeals hearings, with the pupil services director as the next most likely representative. This finding, represented in Table 10-1, derives from the analysis of a 50% sample of the decisions written during the first three years of appeals. In 87 of the 135 decisions which included attendance listings, the special education administrator was present at the hearing. The pupil services director attended 51 hearings and the superintendent of schools attended 28. In only five hearings were none of these administrators present.

Table 10-1.
School Representation at Appeals Hearings

	Hearings Attended	
Administrator	Percent	Number
Special education director only	39.3%	53
Director of pupil services only	26.7%	36
School superintendent only	4.4%	6
Special education director and director of pupil services	9.6%	13
Special education director and superintendent	14.8%	20
Director of pupil services and Superintendent	0.07%	1
Special education director, director of pupil services, and superintendent	0.07%	1
None of the above	3.7%	5
Total	98.6%	135

In some communities, the director of pupil services also serves as the director of special education. A few small communities had neither position and the superintendent represented the school district at the hearing. Since hearings were new procedures, directors of pupil services and superintendents sometimes attended all hearings in their district during this period, just to learn more about the process. This probably happened less frequently in later years.

How the interviews were conducted

We tried to interview the special education directors for 49 of the hearings we attended. These 49 cases involved 29 communities; but only 23 special education directors were interviewed, representing 41 of the 49 cases. Two special education directors who initially agreed to be interviewed withdrew from the study on the advice of counsel, who thought it inappropriate to be questioned about an issue still in litigation, indicating the formality associated with the hearing process. A variety of problems account for the other missing respondents.[1]

Goals of the interview.
These interviews were conducted in the spring of 1977, towards the end of the third year of appeals. As initially conceived, the interviews were to seek a detailed description of directors' experiences with particular cases about which we interviewed parents. This information proved difficult to obtain. Sometimes, the case was an early one and could barely be recollected by the respondent by the time the interview was conducted. In other instances, our study included so many observed cases in one community that we could not get the details of each case in the time available.

High turnover of school staff.
An unanticipated problem was the high turnover rate of special education directors. Only 10 of the 23 directors we interviewed had been in that or a similar position since the inception of Chapter 766. In three communities, there had been a new department head each year. In 10 communities, there had been only one change: three after the first year of implementation; four after a year and a half; and three after two years of implementation. Thus, in more than half the districts in this small sample there had been at least one change in the administrator of special education since the effective date of the law.

This high turnover rate is one indication of the difficulties school systems were experiencing in trying to meet the requirements of Chapter 766.[2] Several administrators suggested this turnover reflects their employers' dissatisfaction with special education reform, leading school boards and superintendents to take out their frustrations on the administrator responsible for enforcing the law. There also seems to be a high "burn-out" rate among special education directors, many of whom become convinced that Chapter 766 could not be humanely implemented. For example, in one community, the special education director initiated many private school placements, convinced that appropriate school district programs were not available. Her contract was not renewed. In at least one other community, a special education director for many years returned to the classroom to teach severely handicapped children.

This high turnover of special education directors has meant that many respondents had little familiarity with the details of a specific case, least of all with the circumstances resulting in parents' decision to appeal. In general, respondents were better able to discuss the events immediately preceding a hearing and the hearing itself than earlier stages of the process. In some instances, when the respondent knew little about the particular case(s) of interest, we discussed their experiences with other cases and their general perceptions of the appeals process.

Length of the interview.

The length of these interviews varied considerably. One lasted for 35 minutes; six were approximately an hour long; eight lasted about an hour and a half; eight were more than two hours long. The longest interview was three and a quarter hours. This variation reflects the different administrative styles and personalities of the respondents, the extent to which the appeals hearing involved the particular respondent, and differences in rapport between the interviewer and the respondent. All but two respondents allowed their interviews to be tape-recorded.

The variation in the length of our interviews is a key indicator that these were "focused" interviews, to use the term popularized by Merton, Fiske and Kendal (1956), where the "main function of the interviewer is to focus attention upon a given experience and its effects," and the interviewer has the "freedom to explore reasons and motives, to probe further in directions that were unanticipated." A major difficulty with the focused interview is that it "results in a lack of comparability of one interview with another," making the analysis more problematic. Much of our interview material is consequently qualitative and suggestive, rather than quantifiable and objective.

Another problem stems from the differing levels of rapport which our interviewer achieved with respondents, all of whom were interviewed by the same person. Longer interviews may have involved greater rapport which led to greater honesty on the part of the administrator. For example, there was a marked tendency for longer interviews to include more material on the district's errors in processing a child's case.

The Communities Represented

The 23 communities included in this study do not represent a cross-section of Massachusetts school districts. Wealthier parents were more likely to use the appeals system and, consequently, well-to-do communities were more likely to be represented among the hearings that we observed.

Larger school systems have more potential for appeals cases, and so were also overrepresented in our sample. According to the State Department of Education, nearly half of Massachusetts school systems have fewer than 2,000 children. Yet this was true of only one-fifth of our sample. Fewer than five percent of Massachusetts communities have more than 11,000 enrolled students, while this was true for nearly one-quarter of our sample. Given the exploratory nature of these interviews, however, this sample did expose us to variations that might be associated with size—ten systems were below 4,000 in enrollment; seven were between 5,000 and 11,000; six were above 11,000.

According to the United States Census, the 1970 median family income in Massachusetts was $10,835. The communities in our sample could be roughly divided into three groups: nine blue-collar communities (1970 median incomes below $11,000); four middle-class communities (median incomes between $11,000 and $14,000); and ten upper-middle-class communities (median incomes above $14,000). Of the ten smaller communities (population less than 4,000), six were upper-middle-class and three were blue-collar. Thus, our sample underrepresented poorer small communities, and overrepresented richer small communities, including many of the state's elite suburban school systems.

The Issues in the Case

Before considering the appeals process from the perspective of the special education administrators, we will identify the types of issues which brought cases to a hearing.

Staying in School cases.

There were six Staying in School cases in this sample, raising such questions as: Should a child be mainstreamed or put in a substantially separate program for emotionally disturbed children? Should a child be given learning-disability tutoring during school hours, or after school? Should a retarded child's school program be changed because s/he was a behavior problem at home, even if s/he behaved well at school?

The directors did not focus on these issues; rather, they argued that these parents had had long-standing conflicts with school staff prior to the law, and that they tended to have difficulties accepting their child's handicap. They saw the parents' appeal as just another battleground onto which parents could project these conflicts. These parents had come to be seen by school staff as "troublemakers."

In the four of the six Staying in School cases parent-school relationships were described as "severely strained," and the directors reported a long history of conflict which predated the new law and its appeals process:

> [That mother] has been fighting with that principal for years; so when 766 came along, she was one of the first in line.

* * *

> In my opinion, Mrs. _____ is a sick woman who needs handicapped children to maintain her own sense of self-esteem. This has been going on for years. It's not that all her suggestions are bad—some are good, I admit that—but it's her manner. She walks into a school, and no staff member wants to face her because they know that if you disagree with anything she says, there's no controlling her . . . Frankly, I'm glad we went to appeal. Whether I'm right or she's right, at least it's settled for a while. Anything to get her off my back.

In two instances, the directors suggested that, given the complexity of the educational plan, the disagreements which brought the parties to a hearing were minor, and that these parents were using the appeals proceeding to avenge a long history of perceived grievances. In both cases, they felt the hearings and decisions had settled little and were simply part of a continuing adversarial relationship between parents and school.

In all six Staying in School cases, the directors felt the parents had considerable difficulty accepting their child's handicap and were using the appeals process as a substitute for such acceptance. Consequently, their requests for altered services in the public schools tended to be discussed in terms of the family's problems rather than as realistic concern with the school's plan.

Leaving School cases.
There were nine Leaving School cases, in which children were attending

public school while awaiting a decision on parents' request for a private placement. The most interesting of these were three cases in which parents requested residential school placements. These cases were distinctive because the families had multiple problems and required a broad range of human services in addition to educational assistance. In fact, by the time of the hearing, the families were already known to a variety of human-service agencies. The school administrators felt the families as a whole would have benefited from a range of human services—counselling, respite care, home training for the parents to help in management of the child, perhaps a foster placement—and that these would have obviated the need for enrollment in a residential school. That is, they argued that a residential placement was being requested on other than educational grounds. In all three cases, the schools won and the children were kept in public school.

These cases dramatically illustrate a major failure of the special education reform. Before the reform, parents had found it hard to sort through the uncoordinated variety of human service agencies as they tried to find appropriate programs for their children. The reform therefore made the schools responsible for coordinating all services.

The law did not charge the school with providing services, only with coordinating them. But human service agencies, unused to working together and strapped for funds, had their own interpretation of the law. Instead of coordinating their services, they simply withdrew them from children covered by Chapter 766. This withdrawal of services left schools to fill the vacuum, sharply increasing the burden on limited school budgets already suffering from other special education increases. The schools had no incentive to act as case coordinators, and were cast instead into the role of direct service providers. Instead of developing the outreach skills intended by the reform, to assure these children the range of services they and their families required, the schools sought to minimize their own responsiblity, defining children's needs in the narrowest possible way. Children who might have been helped by state service agencies were often denied all services except those directly related to their educational needs.

Special education directors seemed keenly aware of this dilemma because Chapter 766 made them newly responsible for services which had been previously provided with state dollars. The major issue raised by school personnel about residential placements in particular was the extent to which the schools were being asked to pay for socialization training and a "more positive home environment." A major issue that resists definition is the distinction between educational and non-educational services, a distinction crucial to apportionment of fiscal responsibility between human service agencies and the schools.

Private School cases.

Special education directors were most involved with parents who sought a private day school placement, usually for learning-disabled children, because of the high potential costs of the tuitions involved. Private day and residential school tuitions have become a substantial segment of the special education budget. Losing an appeal and having to pay private tuition is viewed by administrators as a serious defeat. As one special education director put it: "There is no upbeat way—no amusing way—to tell the school board that you are overdrawn in your out-of-district [placement] account." He continued:

> Despite the fact that the law has accelerated the increase of kids in programs outside the system—for whatever reasons, and I'm mystified by that—let's hope that it's leveling off, because [the cost of such placements] went from zero before 766 to half a million dollars next year. The School Committee has reached a limit for how much they'll pay for that sort of thing. It's become supply creating demand. It's now an option. It was never an option before. It was illegal before 766 for the [school] system to pay for a kid to go outside the system. So either the parents paid, or the state paid sometimes. But [in the school] system, we just limped along. If [a child] got old enough, they excluded him from the [school] system, or he was ground up by the curriculum machine, or pushed out of school and called a dropout. Let's face it. That happens everywhere, and here too. So despite that—despite the increase in the number of kids—let's hope that there is a certain basic number that can best be provided a program outside. I'm afraid of backlash. It's the same everywhere. Cherry sheets [state reimbursements] are down; special education demands are up; and parents of regular education children are beginning to wonder, "Are my kids getting less and less?"

Other respondents were similarly explicit about the financial pressures on their positions and how this created an adversarial atmosphere at hearings:

> I find lately that I've become personally involved in the budget. If I have to sign a bill that someone gets therapy or goes to the [private] school, it's like it's my money, because that's the kind of flak I get. And if I don't watch the treasury, it's my neck that's in a noose. So I become paranoid about the money almost. And so when things get going [at an appeals hearing], it's like "gotta win." I gotta protect that coffer. And if I win, it shows. The program is that much better.

It becomes a very personal extension of ourselves. As an administrator, you become the program and vice versa. And it's my dough and hands off. So it becomes very much of a we-they situation. It's "schools" versus "other," and we have to sit that way too. Even the way they sit at an appeal is at one side of the table or the other, instead of just mixing us up as people trying to resolve a common problem, a task. The task becomes to win—to win a battle, as opposed to coming up with what's best for the child—somehow, we've lost that in the process.

A third respondent described how hearings were being used to "stem the tide" of private school requests:

One of the things that we have felt quite strongly about is that people in our community—some people in our community—have felt that a good option for their kid has been a private school placement. We felt that we had to take a stand and say that what we have been trying to do in terms of core evaluations and special education programming was being carefully done. In spite of the fact that I tell you about the holes in that stuff, we were doing it carefully; we have a pretty sharp staff and ought to be able to do a pretty good job. We have been pretty resistant, as a matter of fact, to any kind of compromise in these hearings . . . I guess my feeling is that we have had to make it clear to the [town] citizens that we have a program here and they should use it.

Most directors claimed their school system could have provided appropriate programming for the children whose parents withdrew them from the public schools, regardless of the issue of cost. However, any sensible analysis must recognize that there are strong fiscal and other pressures throughout school systems to control the number of outside placements.

How Consistently Were Cases Judged?

Directors of special education were often very critical of the way that cases involving private day schools have been judged. Their most important observation was that the continuing turnover of hearing officers and consequent changes of approach had made the appeals system unpredictable. It offered no consistent pattern to show them whether to meet "excessive," but legal, parent demands or to fight a costly, but winning, battle.

This wish to know how the system operated was so great that a number of administrators asked our interviewer whether he knew of a publication analyzing decisions and defining precedents. One school system, a frequent user of the appeals process, undertook their own analysis of the 11 decisions rendered for children from that community. The report based on this analysis concluded:

> After having looked at each decision described herein, no patterns emerge that would link the cases won or the cases lost. There is but one consistent trend which can be identified: that of the parents' placement of their children in private schools as an alternative rather than seeking out other possible options within the school system first. In relation to the private school placements, it is also evident that keen support is given by the staff of private schools in terms of the child receiving services there. (A great interest in keeping students at the private schools is apparent.)
>
> It is difficult to give any formula for winning a case for these reasons: Every case and the variables in it are different; every hearing officer is different and from a different background; many Chapter 766 regulations are hard to fulfill without a diagnostic placement of the child to more carefully observe his/her problems; there is not an impartial expert in the field of the child's purported problems present at the hearing; and some cases are treated from an educational viewpoint and others from a legal viewpoint.
>
> Recently, it appears that the hearing officers arbitrarily pick one side or the other in deciding a case. Many reports given, particularly those by medical people (M.D.'s and private psychologists) are accepted at face value without question. However, the School Department is questioned often, as shown in the decisions.

Our interviews elicited similar perceptions, particularly from administrators who had attended many hearings. These comments make clear that written decisions were not communicating any consistent set of implicit standards by which Private School disputes were being judged.

> One of the things that I take issue with when I think of the hearings is that in no case—whether we've won or lost—has the hearing officer really done a good job of stating his or her rationale that brings them to the conclusion that they have at the end.

* * *

We feel in each case we've presented a pretty good case and I can't tell you why we lost one and won another one . . . And it's extremely variable as far as the hearing officer is concerned. In every case . . . I've seen a wide variation in hearing officers . . . [In] the case I described a little while ago, I think the hearing officer . . . probably did a pretty good job of documenting and reviewing all the evidence . . . not just accepting one side or the other, but really bringing it up to some standard. In that case they did a good job. I would say in that case also, the hearing officer did a very good job in managing the case. That other [case]—the one that's going to the school board next week—my feeling was the hearing officer did a very good job in managing the case but did a lousy job of writing it.

The Role of the Expert Witness

Directors repeatedly complained that hearing officers rely far too much on the testimony of expert witnesses. In a typical Private School hearing, the child has usually been attending private school for some time. Thus, teachers there can testify to the child's good progress in this placement. Private school employees may also act as advocates for the parents at the hearing or present the results of their own evaluation of the child. To school administrators, these witnesses, expert though they may be, clearly have their own interests to protect. Many of these children have also been tested by university-affiliated hospitals and clinics, or various private practitioners, so that the hearing pits expert witnesses and written evaluations from these prestigious institutions on the parents' side against the child evaluators from the school system.

They bring in fancy doctors from _____ Hospital, and we're just the local school system. Who'll believe us?

* * *

We had six witnesses from the school system. Now you look at the summary of evidence in that decision and you wouldn't know that we were there or that we had a point to make.

* * *

I'll tell you one that really burned me. About three months ago, the hearing officer let them go on for three hours—three hours, mind you—criticizing our educational plan; the people from the private school he was going to. Who knows what their program is like? Let them write out an educational plan and I could filibuster on it for the next week.

* * *

We were up against some sharp advocate from the [private] school. They knew the regs [regulations] better than [our] lawyers, and [the hearing officer] just bought their side of the case.

Besides the status differentials that seem to work in favor of the parents, school personnel related anecdotes of parents who "shop around" for a diagnosis, even finding sophisticated help in locating an "expert" who will support their position:

So the hearing was scheduled and along about that time, again we learned second hand—the Bureau of Special Education Appeals was very apologetic to me—because I called them up about a week before the hearing was set and I said, "Hey, what's the story with the hearing?"

"Oh, that's been postponed because Mrs. _____ has requested a second independent evaluation." That was the first I ever heard of that.

She went back to _____ Medical Center again. I was left out of that decision completely. I think in the regulations I have some input into [going for an independent evaluation], which doesn't really bother me. I think she just wanted more evidence for her case. When people want something, they can find a way to justify it.

* * *

I had another case, an emotionally disturbed kid. We wanted him in a separate class, but these were not the kind of parents who would accept anything to do with emotional problems. So they got hold of one of the child advocates, who contacted a friend and got them the name of some psychologist who always recommends mainstreaming, no matter what. And they were going to take me to appeal. Finally, we compromised on a learning-disability resource room, [for] something around 30% [of his school day]. Now he's unmanageable in there and I'm getting complaints from the other parents, and I may have to go to appeal on some of those.

School personnel claim that parents sophisticated enough to search for an appropriate diagnosis can easily find particular hospitals and particular clinics that consistently produce diagnoses supportive of day school placements, and that hearing officers do not take these diagnostic proclivities into account.

> I can show you the last ten cases I sent over to _____ Hospital. Every one of them came back as "the worst dyslexic kid they've seen in a decade."

* * *

> Everyone in the business knows that _____ Hospital is a feed-in to the _____ School.

An additional complaint is that many "experts" do not restrict themselves to a diagnosis of the child's problems, but also make recommendations concerning placement, often without knowing much about public school options for the child.

> One of the doctors at [a private hospital] came out with a recommendation that [a boy] should go to a particular program at the _____ School—that [the school] could present a "total environmental approach," whatever that means . . . Another thing, too, they had a counselor from a counselling clinic over here support them in their belief that [this child] should go to a private school, although he had only seen [the boy] three times, had never seen our intermediate school, knew nothing about it, never seen the educational plan—which was all brought out at the hearing [which was nonetheless lost].

Are expert witnesses impartial?

Many administrators in our sample have had the experience of hearing "prestigious" professionals from university-affiliated institutions supporting the parents' position. They raised important questions about what standards should be used in judging such evidence:

> If they want an independent evaluation, fine. It's a good idea. But let's make sure it's independent, and let's get some standards for what's independent. Not some doctor who's on the board of directors of the private school, or some psychologist who'll charge

a steep fee and say what the parents want him to say, or someone
who hasn't stepped foot in a public school since the forties.

Our respondents do not claim that school systems were never believed, but
they felt the self-interest of the private sector was not adequately taken into
account and that this self-interest was a key factor promoting parent-school
controversies:

I've heard of other towns running into parents placing a child of
theirs in a summer [private school] program [whose staff says] to
the parent, "This is the most disabled kid we've ever had. Should be
in our program." Causing a great amount of anxiety to the parent,
[who then goes] to the school system requesting a full core. The
system does the full core; they come up with the finding, "no
special needs whatsoever." Now, I mean, what the heck's going on
[for two sets of professionals to end up] at those opposite ends of
the spectrum? [And then you go] to a hearing and the hearing
officer finding in favor of the private school . . . That's an actual
case and I think that's terrible.

These administrators also claim there was unpredictable variation in
hearing officers' willingness to entertain "expert" testimony as opposed to
public school testimony:

Did the independent evaluation settle anything?
It hardly ever does. We read into it a slightly different focus for our
services. They read into it a case for the _____ School. So it
comes down to who was debating, and did the hearing officer trust
the public schools.

In sum, administrators questioned the possible effect of the private sector's
self-interest on its testimony (two respondents described cases in which they
felt that test scores had actually been falsified by private school personnel).
They were also concerned about the differing diagnostic tendencies of public
versus private evaluators, and the ability of hearing officers to evaluate these
differences. Many also asked how schools were expected to challenge outside
evaluations if these were presented as written reports, with the evaluator not
there to be cross-examined.

How Should Programs Be Evaluated?

These concerns led administrators to question the focus of hearings; that is, whether hearings could or should compare public and private programs. Public programs for learning-disabled students usually combine time in a resource room with time in a regular classroom, plus a considerable array of specialist services. Private programs usually offer small self-contained classrooms with few or no specialists. The administrators in our study felt that parents, independent evaluators, and hearing officers all presume private school programs to be superior. (For parents' views, see Chapter 9.) Administrators, of course, do not agree. But since school personnel have no experience and few resources to develop the kinds of data that private professionals can offer, they often find themselves at a loss to defend their programming at a hearing. They themselves feel strongly that their programs are "adequate" under the law to meet the needs of the child, but not as impressive as the extremely expensive programming to which they are being compared. The issue of how and whether hearing officers distinguish between "adequate," "appropriate," and "optimal" was raised most forcefully in two interviews:

> The [law states as its] purpose a concentration on the educational plan for the child. In fact, most of the discussion does not talk about that at all—instead there is discussion of the procedural violations, errors in processing the child—and what I call the "versus" situation; that is, we get into the public school versus the private school, to which our lawyer keeps saying, "But the focus should be whether the public school program in and of itself is adequate." We have not found this [focus]. It's always been a comparison between our [educational] plan and services from the [private] school . . . The public school is put into the defensive posture of having to prove its program.

> We have asked on occasion that the hearing officer come and see our schools or [allow us] to submit evidence about the fact that we have a superior school system [offers which were not accepted] . . . Being the public school, the onus seems to be on us to prove ourselves. For example, we have tried to present the special education budget, to show the good faith in which we are working and the types of things we are trying to do, and we were not allowed to present that. We often go into the background of our teachers, which seems to be only reluctantly accepted in these appeals . . . What instead seems to come up is that the milieu isn't right. On

our latest appeal, our services were not questioned, but the fact that the child had a bad experience here and perceived it that way [became a milieu question which] led to an outside placement . . . It would be very helpful if the appeals proceeding dealt with the base line of how badly off is this child to begin with, and what types of academic services are required to remediate the child. It would be helpful, too, if hearing officers could distinguish between what is essential for the child and what is desirable.

In another interview the administrator mentioned that at the hearing "an inordinate amount of time was spent on the child's good progress at the [private] school," which he did not find germane to evaluating the public school's proposed educational plan. He also raised the issue of whether the appeals system was fair, given what other children with similar problems receive:

I'll tell you where the unfairness comes, in my estimation . . . if I place a kid out-of-district in a private school, I rely entirely— almost entirely [on] the current functioning report and how the kid's making out there and the recommendations of the staff at that private school for continuation. When a parent places her child out there and they do very well, the case they can present becomes a bit stronger. They can say, "Hey, look, he was doing lousy in the schools but he's doing super now," and so that's a good case. O.K. One of the things that I think is grossly unfair is . . . that the kids who can have the advantage of a private education . . . are those kids who have parents who have the money and are aggressive enough to be willing to pursue the system—buy a lawyer, pay an advocate . . . With a lot of these cases . . . I look around and say, "If that kid needs a private day school, then I got another 20, 25, or 30 that should be in line before that kid." I see that as taking unfair advantage of the other people who don't have the funds or the aggressiveness to say, "Hey, I'm going to lift my kid."

The Concern with Procedural Compliance

Finally, another area of variation between hearings involves the emphasis on procedural violations, which some hearing officers stress while others de-emphasize.

[In two cases] I wrote a plan that the parents said was really acceptable, and they were quite happy with it. . . In one case, the hearing officer chose to deal with procedure and [in] the other one, they did not—they dealt with the adequacy of the plan. But that's the problem—you don't know what the rules of the game are. They change from hearing officer to hearing officer. [Only] one out of three [hearings attended] have focused on the plan.

* * *

The last case I had . . . I had heard . . . from my sources, that [the main criterion] was now adequacy of educational plan. Well, hell, we had a good educational plan. But the hearing officer came in and said, "We're going to talk about procedure." I said, "Hell, why talk any more? Just close up the books and we'll pay the bill." And the decision, the five-page decision, addressed the procedures, 85% of it—30 days, notifying parents, not ever sending a statement of rights. The law was in operation a full year at that point and there was no excuse. The first case I had there was a little more tolerance [for mistakes because the law] was new. It was just such an inundation at the start. But I was very much surprised that after two years, we were not going to address the adequacy of the educational plan.

* * *

In one case, the hearing officer seemed to accept that we had not dotted all the i's on the educational plan but we had made a reasonable attempt to follow the law. What was not shown in writing, we had told the parents. In another case . . . I would say our procedural flaws were no more serious . . . If you read the decisions in the two cases, you would get very different impressions. In one, we are recalcitrant, violating these parents' rights. There is a long discussion of such problems. And in the other, we're nice guys with a questionable but probably all-right educational plan. Now I do not believe in those two cases that we gave essentially different service to those two parents. To some extent, it was the way the lawyers presented their cases, but to a large extent it was what the hearing officers were willing to listen to.

These critical comments were not meant to imply that no hearing decision was regarded as justifiable, competent, or humane. Rather, administrators were critical of the system's apparent unpredictability. The decisions, which varied considerably in the specificity of findings and conclusions, failed to communicate a consistent set of standards by which cases were to be judged.

Summary: How Should a Case be Judged?

From the perspective of these administrators, the school system's program seemed to be "on trial," with hearing officers accepting too readily the unproven assumption that private day schools were offering superior programs. School personnel have thus had difficulty determining what types of evidence about their own programming should be submitted at hearings, particularly in light of the time and money constraints on their preparation of such evidence. They saw the testimony of the school's witnesses as often questioned, while the testimony of other witnesses seemed to be accepted without regard for the selective process through which these witnesses were assembled, the conflicts of interest which might be inherent in their roles, or the diagnostic biases of the institutions they represented. Administrators saw privileged parents using the appeals process to demand services for their children which were not commensurate with the services given to other children whom they saw as needier. Hearings which compared public and private programming deflected attention from the real question of whether the public school's suggested plan was itself adequate and responsive to the child's special needs, making an unfair comparison with the possible benefits of other programs. Finally, during a period when school systems were deluged by children to be evaluated and programs to be developed, strict compliance with the timelines and procedures specified by Chapter 766 was often impossible, but hearing officers seemed to apply standards for compliance inconsistently.

The major question which still remains for the hearing system is: by what standards should Private School disputes be judged? The prognosis for a given child rests far more on the evaluator's judgment than on any objective criteria; nor is there objective evidence on the relative merits of mainstreamed versus self-contained programs. Despite the absence of objective criteria, or even a clear professional consensus on this issue, hearing officers are in effect forced to rule on the quality of programming, and program types. School personnel therefore complain that too many hearing officers have simply accepted the high status popularly attached to private schooling. The problem of special education which professionals have been unable to resolve has now been put to the hearing officers: what standards can be used to make judgments of "adequacy" or "appropriateness" of programs for children with special needs?

Notes

1. One potential respondent was hospitalized. Another had been on the job a very short time, was unfamiliar with the case, and declined the interview. In one community, the interview was not approved by the superintendent. We were unable to reach another potential respondent. Finally, while an interview was completed with Boston's director of special education, the problems in this community are so distinctive that they deserve separate treatment.

2. While we have not kept a systematic check of the communities studied during the interviews, two more of them were subject to additional turnover between the spring of 1977 and the opening of the 1977-78 school year.

3. Further discussion of this problem can be found in Chapter 14, in which we present an analysis of the structure and content of decisions written during the first two and one-half years of the system, and our own proposals for a model decision.

11

The School Systems
View Hearings

The Hearings as Trauma

Not only parents, but also administrators, viewed hearings as unpleasant and threatening experiences:

> I don't remember one of those things where we even took a break for lunch. You come out after a whole day nervous, irritable. You're tense for the whole day. You come out drained. I'll tell you, we really try and avoid these things like the plague.

Their treatment at hearings seemed to hurt the self-image of special educators. Chapter 766 placed unprecedented demands on schools to evaluate and provide services to a greatly expanded range of handicapped children. To the extent that the law has been effective, it is largely because special education personnel have worked long hours, a kind of dedication which many special education directors saw as well beyond the call of duty. As one respondent put it, "Go to a school at 4:00, 4:30. It's my people that are still there. One of the biggest problems we have is that people are burning out from doing too much." In addition, special education personnel often see

themselves as advocates within their school systems for more humane
treatment of children, advocates who must often overcome resistance from
regular education personnel. "We like to think of ourselves as advocates for
the child. It's upsetting to go to a hearing and find how differently we are
sometimes perceived." For people with great personal and ideological
commitments to making the law work, the frequent implication at hearings
that their work was incompetently, sloppily, or callously done is extremely
discomforting. Perhaps the most disturbing aspect of a hearing is having
one's professional judgment questioned:

> We've had people really ripped to shreds by the attorneys. Good
> people doing an honest job. And the minute we get back to town, of
> course, it spreads throughout the whole system and I tell them,
> "Do an honest job and we'll try and protect you." But I mean, their
> honesty is questioned, their competence is questioned. You get
> some of the Perry Mason types, and they think that Jack the Ripper
> is on the stand. Now, of course, we give it back to them. We've had
> some of these private school people on the stand and our lawyer has
> really caught them in outright lies, really outright lies. We give as
> good as we get. That's why our lawyer has insisted that these
> witnesses have to be at the hearing, not just some paper evaluation.
> But these Perry Mason types, I don't know who they think they're
> questioning.

* * *

> *Is the staff anxious about going to hearings?*
>
> I think they have appropriate anxiety.
> *Does that mean high anxiety?*
> Yes.

The use of lawyers to represent the school system has increased. Some
communities have used lawyers at every hearing. Four administrators
indicated that the outcome of their first hearing led them to use a lawyer at
subsequent hearings. This was justified in terms of the protection an attorney
could offer:

> We didn't feel it was necessary to use a lawyer. It was our first case
> and we went into it rather naively perhaps; we thought we had the
> information. But I think the outcome of that case said to us, we

really do need legal assistance. On the next case, we didn't have a lawyer because the other side didn't. But on [our third] case, we did.

What was the outcome of the first case?

They ruled in favor of the school system.

Why did that lead you to think that you needed a lawyer the next time?

Well, we didn't know we'd won . . . until almost four months later and during that time we felt that—the process was really very traumatic for the staff.

Why?

It's an adversarial situation. Being asked questions that one's not used to being asked. We're not trained as legal people and it's a strange process. The staff feels threatened, challenged. They feel it's time better spent with children. It's too confronting a process. They don't like that kind of confrontation. They don't want to see parents across the table and arguing. That first case really got out of hand. You know it shouldn't. But it becomes adversarial. People start condemning each other and it becomes adversarial. And then you get to the hearing and they have a lawyer who believes everything they say—that's his job. And you need a lawyer too.

How did an attorney help? For example, did he help organize the case?

I did that. I think his greatest value to us was being able to deal with the procedures at the hearing. I can remember specifically—and I don't know anything about being an attorney—but I know when I was being questioned by the attorney for the [parents], they went through a ten-minute sentence one time with about fifteen different issues in it and said to me: "What do you think?" And not being very perceptive about court proceedings or whatever, I didn't know what the hell to do. So [our lawyer] stepped in and said, "What are you asking the guy?" And that was very helpful. [The parents' attorney] referred to about seven different items and about 100 pages of documents and so on and really had me going. If they have an attorney, you really need one.

Two administrators described cases in which they had urged parents not to use an attorney. "If you can maintain open communication with the parents, you can try to keep the thing as informal as possible, and that's the way it should be." A number of directors claimed they would use an attorney only when parents were similarly represented, though others felt they also needed legal help when the parents were represented by an advocate:

> My feeling is that without lawyers—including our own—hearings would be over in a lot less time. They would be much shorter. We've come up against the same attorney [for the parents] in three cases and the same advocate in three others. These people are doing this thing a lot more than I am. They're doing it professionally. They know what they're looking for when a particular kind of issue comes up, they have standard ways to deal with it. Maybe I could get enough skill to do that, but it would cost me some money along the way. This way, I find . . . that I don't have to be concerned with all of the aspects of managing the case and presenting witnesses and cross-examining or procedural kinds of things. All I have to worry about is my testimony.

In describing the value of legal representation, these administrators emphasized two themes. First, hearings often revolve around procedural issues, with which lawyers are better able to cope. For example, one respondent described how parents at one hearing introduced written evaluations which the school system had not previously seen. The school's lawyer was able to delay the hearing until the evaluator could be present for cross-examination. The director doubted he would have been able to win this delay on his own.

A second reason for the use of lawyers is the protection they afford in the face of an advocate or lawyer representing the parents. In what is viewed as an adversarial situation, one does not come unarmed: the financial stakes are high; one's honesty and competence are being questioned; and the people testifying for the other side are viewed as having prestigious affiliations which make their testimony more credible than one's own.

The increasing use of lawyers testifies to the fact that hearings are perceived as difficult and threatening situations. These are the same reasons parents give for using lawyers. It seems to be inherent in the nature of a formal, adversarial hearing process that both parties feel so threatened by the situation they feel they cannot act on their own.

The Costs of a Hearing

The administrators we interviewed agreed that hearings are very costly to school systems in terms of staff time. Special education departments are severely overworked, and the time spent preparing for an appeal often means neglect of other aspects of the school system's special needs program:

> I think the preparation [for a hearing] begins at the onset of a referral. But specifically once a rejection is made, I find it very, very difficult to prepare the case for the school system. We've got so many other things to do for so many other kids. We had just one meeting with our attorney prior to going to the hearing and that was a very short meeting. I spent a great deal of time summarizing, putting the case together, sending it over to the attorney for his review. [To prepare for an appeal] I would say, nonstop, it would take me a full week, getting the thing together, identifying the issues, putting it in an organized way that people can deal with.

* * *

> There is a wide variation between appeals cases in how much time I spend, and I spend more than anyone else. In terms of preparation, from the time the plan is rejected, I probably spend a couple of hours on the telephone with mediators, advocates, parents. Reviewing the materials [takes] another couple of hours. A lot of the stuff in the files is really superfluous, a lot of junk and you have to pick out what's relevant. Up to 4 or 5 hours on the phone with the attorney. If there's mediation, that's another few hours. Any time there's a hearing, that's a full day. I think the longest we've had was three or four days, I don't remember. In [one] case, there was the re-write of an educational plan. If you're talking about my time, and thinking about all the telephoning, overall, [it takes] a full day of preparation, two full days at the hearing. I hope that's not exaggerating. It could be anywhere from 40 to 60 [hours].

* * *

> *How much staff time does it take to prepare for an appeal?*
> In man-hours, hundreds. We're talking about a number of steps involving groups of people, meetings with attorneys, meetings with witnesses. It means re-evaluating the information because by

the time an appeal comes up, the situation is old. You have to go
back and rethink and reconstruct.

The lowest estimate of the time spent preparing for a hearing was ten hours
on an unusual case in which the special education director neither consulted
with the attorney hired by the school board nor presented any written
documentation of his own; instead he relied solely on inconsistencies in the
evaluations presented by the parents. Higher estimates are much more
common, although there was significant variation among the directors in
how much they consulted with their attorneys and how much time was
available to meet with potential witnesses. Many administrators felt they had
too little time to prepare adequately. Among those using an attorney,
variation in degree of use ranged from those who prepared the case on their
own to those who claimed that "It's not my case. It's the attorney's case and he
prepares it."

Other school personnel besides the special education director are often
brought to testify at a hearing either by the school system or at the request of
the parents. In one extreme case, 14 school employees attended a three-day
hearing; at the other extreme, only three school personnel attended a one-day
hearing.

Several respondents saw hearings as a major disruption of school
programming. Lowered morale and loss of staff time were cited as the most
important costs to the school system of participation in the hearings. The
direct dollar costs vary considerably. Some systems hired private lawyers for
some or all cases; many used counsel already employed by the town or city
government.

How a Case Reaches Appeal

Given the anxieties and costs involved, we wanted to know what school
systems did to prevent Private School cases from escalating to the point of an
appeal. We asked our respondents: *"Do you think there was anything you
could have done to prevent an appeal?"* In most cases, the answer was "No."
Administrators felt that the school system was usually willing to negotiate
with parents over in-school services, but in Private School cases, the child had
already been placed in a day school. In many of these cases, the administrators
believed that the parents had never seriously entertained the idea of keeping
their child in public schools, because they had lost confidence in the school
system's programming. We were told that no matter how much one

negotiated with such parents, they would no longer accept a public school placement.

Parents lose trust in the school.

Asked why parents had lost confidence in the school system, there were four frequent types of replies. One theme was that the child had a history of not progressing very rapidly, so parents would not trust any further attempt at remediation, no matter how adequate:

> I would guess that [the parents] had some reservations about whether or not we were able to meet their child's needs as early as grades three or four. I think that they had seen some [previous] failure, some resistance on the part of their child to special education services in the school. I think there [had been] some communication breakdowns [in the past]. I certainly would not assign blame at this late point. But that did happen and it happened throughout this [evaluation] process. And I guess the feeling that I would have was that they were feeling that we could not provide an adequate service for their child.

* * *

> In all three of our cases, you have a self-help action taken by the parents. The arguments are almost identical: We've given the system two, three—in the [one] case I think they said maybe even five years—of our time, our child's life and we're not willing to risk it anymore. Trust is not going to be the name of the game at this point. You said you were going to do certain things in the past; [you] have or have not come through—in most instances, [you] haven't. The child, on the basis of standardized testing—achievement testing—has not progressed significantly. Ergo, we don't trust you. Literally, we don't trust you.

Previous parent-school conflict.

Second, specific conflicts were sometimes mentioned which contributed to the parents' distrust. For example, an older sibling in a family had had a bad experience at the junior high school that the special needs child would attend; a mother felt that the special needs personnel at an elementary school "didn't understand [my son's] problems"; a tutor reacted defensively toward the parents when they complained about their child's apparent lack of progress.

Processing errors.

Third, serious errors had been made in processing evaluations which lowered parent trust. For example, a school system during an administrative change lost the child's referral for five months; another school system could not get appropriate information from a private school in order to conduct an evaluation; and a third school system was so inundated by requests for evaluation that the process moved at a snail's pace, taking over eight months.

The influence of private institutions.

Finally, some directors felt that evaluators at universities and hospitals were encouraging parents to enroll their children in private day schools and that private school staff and lawyers were likewise encouraging appeals:

> Our work with parents has usually been very productive. When other people get involved in the case, we have found that communication diminishes.
> *What kinds of other people?*
>
> The advocates they bring. [The headmaster of a private school] has been the advocate for one of these parents. Two people on his staff have been the advocates for the others.

* * *

> We had a mediation session and I almost sold [the parent] on the plan. I think she was going to buy it. But she had this lawyer there, drumming up business, and he said, "Let's caucus" and she came back and wasn't buying. I worked so damn hard on that one. And there was nothing wrong with what we were offering her. I can do as good a job with that kid as [any private school].

Whatever the combination of factors which led a parent to become acutely dissatisfied with the school system, most of our respondents say negotiation with parents could not have prevented an appeal once a private placement had been requested.

The School's Concern with Costs

In a few instances, the directors did present case histories much more damaging to the school's position as a willing and honest negotiator than those above. The differences in rapport achieved in different interviews make it impossible to establish how frequently such practices occur, but, by their own admission, at least some schools had failed to act in good faith.

For example, we were told that a strong concern with the costs of some special needs programs occasionally damaged the school's ability to negotiate. In two such instances, directors told us that their professional judgment dictated that a child be placed out of district, but that they were forced to deny this judgment in the hearing because the superintendent or school board did not wish to pay the tuition costs.

Other directors implied that cost considerations had more subtly affected the school's decisions for a child. For example, after an educational planning meeting, a special education director wrote himself a note, which he included in his files, that the child warranted an out-of-district placement. However, the parent had agreed to an in-school program and, therefore, this was recommended. Shortly thereafter, the parent changed her mind and wanted the evaluation to be reopened. By this time, a new special education director had been installed, whom we interviewed. The new director found the parent very antagonistic from their first meeting. With the support of his superintendent, he stuck with the original in-school recommendation, which led to the appeal. Financial pressures were acknowledged to be a major consideration at the original and subsequent evaluations. Being new to his position, the second director felt he was in no political position to argue with the superintendent's strongly-held position that outside placements must be curbed. The original evaluation—which tried to "sell" the parent on an in-school placement—had very likely poisoned the negotiating climate between the parent and school and prevented any further negotiation over services the child might have been offered in public school. The school system lost the hearing when the files of the former special education director were presented as evidence.

Most directors admitted that there were strong pressures to contain costs inherent in their positions and recognized that these pressures had also been communicated to school staff members. However, many communities had actually volunteered outside placements to learning-disabled children when they felt their own resources were insufficient, and respondents felt that the professionalism of their staffs would lead to outside placement recommendations when warranted. Very few directors openly stated that costs had been a paramount consideration in planning for a child, despite the frequency of such claims from parents. Even when special education directors claimed that their decision was based on staff recommendations to meet a child's needs, the question must be raised as to the extent to which these recommendations were shaped by the general concern with costs. Parents report costs were frequently discussed by personnel at all levels of the school system, suggesting that the educational planning process had been insufficiently insulated from these pressures.

Poor Parent-School Communication

A school's position as a willing and honest negotiator is damaged when special education departments are so overwhelmed by the number of referrals that they can pay little attention to individual parents, thus communicating a lack of interest in the specific child. A candid director comments on a rejected educational plan:

> When I look at the plan that was actually rejected at the time . . . I felt and continue to feel that there were enough gaps in that plan so that the parents should have asked questions about it . . . Someone did a lousy job in writing the plan . . . And that has been part of a learning process. It was a tough plan and it wasn't unique. There were other tough plans, too.
>
> *Did the plan that was written have a reasonable chance of being implemented?*
> Oh, yes. As a matter of fact, a better plan . . . could have been written [and] implemented [but] it wasn't, because it wasn't written. [The actual plan] was revised somewhat as part of the appeals process. But it wasn't done during that period of time when they had [the original] plan in their hands.

Consider now the long history of this dispute, which exemplifies many of the problems of parent-school communication:

> If we were to go back through the child evaluation procedure and the way that it was followed, I would be pretty certain that the whole procedure . . . was somewhat muddled. We are talking about the first 766 year. I'm not sure we were more overwhelmed by referrals [then] than we are now. We [actually] sat down before 766 ever came into being [to discuss] this child. Of course, this child has been receiving some kind of services since probably the third grade. There was a procedure before 766 when, yes, an educational plan was written and sent home; the parents were there at the meeting. They received a copy of the assessments before and the plan after. Then there was a step when—and again, I'm doing this without

notes or anything—when 766 came in, there was a request of the principal and myself to talk about what kinds of services the child was receiving and needed. We sat down with the parents. What I proposed at that time to the mother—at that point she was saying, "I want an [evaluation] under 766." I said, "There's already been the assessments done. I think what you really want is to sit down together and review the educational plan based on current functioning and revise that to provide certain kinds of services."

In fact, the parents at that time, when it first came up in this kind of review thing, they were asking for some tutoring services outside of the school. And our decision was that we could provide the tutoring and were willing to do so within the school. We never initiated that because we never got an acceptance of the educational plan. . . . That may have been due to confusion on the part of the parents. We did another re-evaluation the following spring. We got the parents involved again. We sent the plan home, say April, May. We did not have any response [to the educational plan] until September. Before that time we heard that the child had been placed in a private school.

The lack of follow-up.

Here we get a sense of the difficulties of parent-school communication. When on two occasions parents failed to return a signed educational plan, the school system had no procedures to routinely call parents to find out why. In one instance, the lack of follow-up resulted in the child not receiving a service the school saw as reasonable; the parents maintained they were never asked to sign an educational plan that included this service and were angered that their son had not received it. The special education director felt the evaluation team chairperson was too new at the job and too overworked to communicate adequately with the parents. Throughout this period, the parents saw their child failing to progress at his current level of special education services. Finally, the parents were given a "spotty" educational plan. The plan was so incomplete that the special education director decided to present a modified plan at the hearing, which he felt more accurately reflected the high quality of services available in his system.

Follow-up on non-response by parents would not only have reassured parents of the school's interest in the child. It would also have provided a chance for the parents to voice their concerns and for school staff to respond by adjusting the child's program or speaking to the parents' feelings of frustration. In this case, the only offer to negotiate a better educational plan was made too late, as the special education director told us:

Somebody from the state—a mediator—talked to me on the telephone, talked to the parents on the telephone and came to a decision that there was going to be no further benefit from mediation. I said . . . if you think I can change my mind and say I'll pay for a private school placement, I can't do that. But I said, if mediation can do other things, then I'm interested in it. The parents said something similar and the mediator made the decision based on what one of us had said. We found that out at the hearing and, in fact, I'm not sure there was any worthwhile purpose to mediation.

Overworked staff.

This school system had relied upon evaluation staff attached to local schools to develop educational plans. However, some of these people were only aware of services in their own school and did not know of other services elsewhere in the system. The educational plan developed for a child was highly dependent upon the evaluation team chairperson; his/her expertise and time determined the plan's quality. The school district as a whole had no quality control over a plan unless it was reviewed by the special education director, who was usually not involved unless dissatisfied parents had already requested a hearing.

Because of the district's lack of active response, the parents in this case came to believe the public schools were not interested in their child and could not program effectively for him. The continued lack of contact and their child's lack of sufficient progress impelled them to seek the private school placement.

The role of negotiations.

As this story suggests, the argument of administrators that negotiations were "futile" needs to be questioned. These "futile" negotiations usually occurred very late in the evaluation process, when the educational plan had already been rejected, and/or the parents had found a private placement for the child. At that point, negotiation was indeed futile, a classic case of "too little, too late." But school staffs frequently seem to have ignored opportunities to negotiate while an evaluation was still being conducted, when parents claim to have had a more flexible position. More responsiveness earlier in the process might have prevented several appeals.

Earlier, we cited a report from one school department which claimed the appeals process was capricious. It found "but one consistent trend . . . that of the parents' placement of their children in private schools as an alternative rather than seeking out other possible options within the school system first." While parents may occasionally remove their children too soon, the reports of school personnel themselves indicate a variety of possible reasons for such behavior: most often, the schools' disorganized response to the requirements of Chapter 766, and their failure to maintain continuing consultations with parents.

Lack of coordination in the evaluation process.

In the case we have just discussed, the director assigned fault to a particular staff member, the evaluation team leader who did not maintain adequate communication with the parents. But the system itself had no organized procedure for maintaining such contact. Nor did the team chairperson have access to resources or expertise from outside his individual school when his own school's resources seemed insufficient for the particular child. The director had no organized system to monitor the activities of team leaders, while parents had no avenues to express their concerns if they saw a particular team leader as unresponsive. The school system had in effect relied upon a single, overworked staff member to communicate with parents, organize and run a child evaluation meeting, prepare an educational plan, and handle parent grievances. Even within his individual school, this staff member had little cooperation from regular education personnel or support from his principal; the district as a whole was even less equipped to help. With such a lack of supporting structure, it is not surprising he functioned less effectively than he might have. The special education director's recognition of these problems led him to experiment repeatedly with the whole ·evaluation process, using such tactics as developing a central, system-wide evaluation team for more troublesome cases and using this team at local meetings to provide extra support to local staff. In this and many other communities there have been continuing modifications of the evaluation, educational planning, and programming systems to minimize these breakdowns of communication with parents and to provide support to school staff.

How Special Education Systems are Changing

Most of this study has focused on conflicts over specific special education programs. However, the appeals system has also pushed school districts to change their overall procedures and to expand the range, intensity, and effectiveness of the programs available. Impelled by the traumatic loss of a hearing, and the attendant problems of staff morale, credibility in the community, and the cost of private programs, systems have begun to provide services which were previously not available, particularly to the learning-disabled child.

Re-educating staff.

This potential impact is illustrated by one interview tracing the evolution of a completely altered attitude toward special education programming, which our respondent claimed was due to previous appeals losses. The director of pupil personnel services in one suburban community was appointed the fall that Chapter 766 became effective. He realized early that the communication between parents and schools was very poor, and that there was only a narrow range of special education services available within the community. During the first year the law was in effect, this district lost four hearings, creating considerable negative publicity. Parents were seeking outside services representing noteworthy sums of money, because they claimed the schools lacked suitable programming. This director used these losses to mobilize support for a considerable infusion of new monies to develop such programs, and began to work with his staff to develop more effective communication, both with parents and among themselves. The results, as reported during our interview, were better defined educational plans; parents' openly expressed satisfaction that they were being listened to by school personnel; a broader range of available programs; and no subsequent appeals by parents. In addition, two of the appeals children were voluntarily returned by the parents after a year at a private school.

A spur to reform.

This administrator saw the impact of the appeals process as quite positive. The bad publicity of the hearings mobilized reallocation of resources far more rapidly than would have otherwise been possible, even with the new legislation. The acrimony of the hearings so upset his staff that they were amenable to reconsidering their prior style of operation.

Similar reports came from a second community which had participated in three very bitter hearings, leading the school board to dismiss the former special education director. The new administrator told us:

> When I got here, nearly two years ago, the community was up in arms. They felt they weren't being treated fairly. They were being lied to; the educational planning conferences were being bagged...

> *Meaning?*

> Meaning that the plans were already written before the educational planning conferences were held. The principals would hold little meetings with their specialists to figure out how to sell plans to the parents, real hard-sell. If a parent complained, it was the fault of the child, or "give him more time." Never that the program might be bad. Now, take one of the appeals cases they had. They were busing students for a half day to the program at [a college] and

these kids were in the first [or] second grade—we had four of them—and they all became objects of ridicule among their peers. And this one child reacted very poorly; from the mother's description, the child was a wreck. Well, she came to school to find out what was going on, and they never told her about educational planning conferences or ed plans or anything. They had never held a planning conference—just sent the parents a letter and shipped [the child] off to [the college program]. Now I had to go to that appeal, and we lost, as we should have. And the next month, I sat down with the parents and said, "Here's what we have and we can provide a program for the child." The parents decided to keep him in [the private school] for this year. But they are paying for it. I told them we did have a program and when they realized we did, they couldn't see fighting us on it. But I think that we will get that child back. I have a good relationship with the parents. Hell, we're friends. But that's the kind of stuff that was going down.

When I got here, I started attending every educational planning conference at every school. It's been a very long process of training the staffs on how to run these things, getting rid of the old patterns of how they dealt with parents. Now I could do it. We only have four schools, and two of them, I let them run the educational planning conferences on their own. But it was a lot of work. Four lousy schools. I thought when I came here, it would be a piece of cake. One of my schools is running as well as any school in the state, I bet. But I still have troubles in the others. The teachers playing all sorts of games. Who's responsible for the child? Does he really need services or does the teacher just want him out of the room? [The school district where I was previously employed] had 16 schools. When I came here, I thought, "Four schools—a piece of cake."

System-wide change.

By acting to secure appropriate programs for individual children, the appeals process may thus shape the school district's response to the needs of many other children. Repeated costly losses force a district to examine its programs and reform them. This pressure will certainly increase as the retrenchments of the 1980's reduce already scarce resources. In our opinion, the hearing system will be most effective in changing special education practices as long as there are better alternative services outside of the school system. The high cost of assigning children to private schools is a direct incentive for public schools to reconsider their own programming.

Even among those special education directors who support the hearings system, there is considerable regret over the cost to the district of private placements. Many directors simply resent a system that has cost them so much. The following interviews from two directors illustrate this range of feeling:

> I have a lot of respect for the hearing system. It's a civilized way to settle disputes. I have a lot of respect for the parents who have taken us to appeal. We make mistakes and parents have a right, an obligation really, to make sure that their child gets what he or she needs. I have great respect for the _____ s, for example. Super people. I don't know that their child's problems are going to be solved by [the private school] but if I was in their position, I hope I would have protected my child's interests by taking the school system to appeal. The one comment I would make is that I think overall, in my system, I don't know about the state, but I would say the money it's cost us has hindered our programs here, in the system. You spend so much money on outside placements, you wish you had the money in the system to serve more children. If the hearings were being run so that you couldn't pay for outside placements but had to use the money for the child in the system, we would be further along. But I have no quarrel with the hearing system. We've won and we've lost. But I have no quarrel with it.

* * *

> These are people who are ripping off the city. It is nothing more than that. We have poor parents in our system who don't know enough to return their plans, so we can't service their kids. And I don't have enough staff to chase after them because we're spending all our time on rich parents who are using the law to take us for a ride. They don't want their children in the public schools. Their other children aren't going to our schools. My town counsel is no match for the lawyers they bring in. We're just the public schools. No one believes that we can do a good job. And the hearing officers believe that too. We're really being taken for a ride.

Summary

It is instructive to compare the responses of school personnel with parent responses. Whereas parents often pictured school administrators as overly concerned with budgets and insufficiently concerned with the child's needs, school personnel often pictured parents as either emotionally troubled or motivated by a greedy desire to use Chapter 766 to finance private schooling. While parents complained that school personnel were unable to communicate with them honestly and openly, school personnel often portrayed parents as so intent on an outside placement that no amount of negotiation could dissuade them. Where parents saw the large number of school witnesses brought to a hearing as lending weight to the schools' position, school personnel felt that the parents' prestigious witnesses and evaluation documents were more readily accepted than their own testimony. Both sides complained about dishonest testimony. Both felt that hearings put them "on trial," giving the other side the benefit of the doubt. Both sides feared being attacked by opposing lawyers and justified their own use of lawyers as necessary for their protection. Both sides found hearings to be costly and emotionally straining.

Such comparisons suggest that as conflict escalates, both parents and school personnel develop perceptions to legitimate their own positions while defining the actions of the other party as self-serving. This mutual distrust appears to be the inevitable product of the adversarial postures which the hearing system has forced these parties to adopt.

We believe, however, that an active appeals system does provide an accountability mechanism, however flawed. It forces changes in local school practice, especially when private educational arrangements are available to threaten schools with an even more costly alternative than modified programming. The hearing process may be extremely painful to both parents and school personnel, and it may not be the best way to resolve individual disputes. Nevertheless, by tracing individual cases we have come across several instances of system-wide change that administrators trace directly to appeals losses. The possibilities for such change and the way an appeals system can be structured to promote such change require further study.

Section IV.

The Hearings and the Views of Hearing Officers

12

When One Goes to a Hearing:
An Overview

A hearing is a legal proceeding. The biggest surprise for parents and school staff who were involved in hearings was that hearings are formal proceedings that require careful preparation, documentation, organized presentations, and a controlled willingness to contend with the other side so as to achieve one's goals. The hearing is clearly an adversarial proceeding. There are winners and losers; the abstract ideals of "right" and "justice" do not prevail unless "you do your homework."[1]

Both parent and school personnel must understand the nature of an adversarial proceeding in order to present an effective case. Yet this adversarial nature has been the most difficult feature of the hearing process for participants to accept. The requisite confrontational approach is foreign to schools, and to most of us; furthermore, both sides come to the hearing under considerable emotional strain. Parents feel they must justify their concern for their child's future, even though the child has clearly failed to progress in public school. School personnel feel barraged by the implied insult to their professional competence, the strain added to their already heavy work load, and the tension of having their professional judgment questioned in cross-examination before their supervisors. If their personal judgment differs from the district's position, they are under the additional stress of arguing for a position not their own.

As the previous chapters amply demonstrate, hearings are universally regarded as avenues of last resort to resolve disputes. This chapter seeks to demystify the hearing process by relating step by step what happened at the hearings our own staff observed, along with commenting on issues related to the nature of hearings. Again, we will focus on the personal rather than the legal dimensions of these proceedings, except to reiterate that these proceedings are markedly more flexible in form than courtroom proceedings, and allow hearing officers considerably more latitude than a judge in a courtroom.

When a Hearing Takes Place, What Can a Parent Expect?

By the time a hearing takes place, the hearing officer should have reviewed the exhibits sent by parents and schools to the Bureau of Special Education Appeals. At the start of the hearing, parents and school personnel are usually seated on opposite sides of a rectangular table, with the hearing officer seated at the head, operating a tape recorder. The hearing is tape-recorded through a microphone in the center of the table. Some cases in our sample actually had to be re-heard because the poor quality of the recording made it impossible to produce a transcript upon request for court review.

The hearing officer begins by reviewing the parents' rights. S/he explains the procedures to be followed at the hearing, and asks both parties if they have seen the other party's exhibits. If evidence is presented by either party that the other has not previously seen, that party may either examine it during an adjournment or ask for a "continuance," that is, a delay. Parents are told they may also postpone the hearing to obtain representation, or if they are unprepared.

Usually, the parents present their case first, with the schools able to cross-examine each witness. The parents or their counsel may then elicit further testimony from the witness in light of the cross-examination, followed by additional cross-examination from the schools. The school's presentation, which follows, uses a similar format. Hearing officers may interrupt at any time to clarify issues being presented. Each side makes a closing statement at the hearing's end, either orally or in writing.

Variations on this form have been mentioned by the hearing officers we interviewed, or were reported by our observers. After the opening statement, some hearing officers might describe the outstanding issues as defined by the case materials (exhibits), and then ask the parties if they agree with that definition of the issues. If the parties do not agree, the hearing begins with the attempt to define the central issues, in order to focus the hearing from its outset.

Before a hearing formally begins, hearing officers may sometimes ask if any of the outstanding issues can be negotiated informally. Occasionally such negotiation has been successful, making a hearing unnecessary. More often, only some issues can be negotiated, but the hearing proceeds more smoothly because of the clarification of the parties' actual differences. Whether such negotiations cover all or only some of the issues, their results can be written into agreements which both parties sign. Implementation of the agreed-upon program can proceed immediately. Agreements, however, do not have the same binding status as "decisions," which formally embody the findings and conclusions of a hearing officer after a hearing. To protect both parties, agreements should be incorporated into a decision.

This order of presentation evolved over the first year of conducting hearings. Its formality gives both parties the opportunity to present evidence in an orderly manner and increases the likelihood that relevant evidence will be elicited. According to the hearing officers, the formality also helps both parties keep their angry feelings in check.

The guidelines for the conduct of a hearing are stated more specifically in a manual which prescribes procedures for the conduct of the hearing ("Chapter 766: Special Education Appeals Guidelines," Massachusetts Department of Education, 1977). However, as noted, hearing officers have considerable leeway in actual practice.

Some Characteristics of Hearings

This section summarizes the ratings made by our observers, who attended 60 hearings. These ratings indicate some features of the hearings and convey a general flavor of their content. Since most of the hearings we attended involved parents we later interviewed, these data may echo observations quoted earlier from parents. However, at the time this material was prepared, parents had not yet been interviewed, so these comments represent opinions arrived at independently.

The major issues.
Our observers were asked to review their notes on the testimony and documents presented at hearings, and to tally the parties' views on various aspects of the hearing. Table 12-1 presents our version of how parents and schools perceived the central issues at their hearings, based on their testimony. Interestingly, both parties usually agreed on what their disagreement was

Table 12-1.
The Major Issues: Viewed by Parents and Schools in 60 Hearings

Issues Identified	By Parents	By Schools
Diagnosis of a child's special needs	25	20
Educational plan content	44	46
Program quality	32	26
Transportation	10	4
Exclusion from special education programs	3	4
Placement in private school	35	16
Other	18	9

about: most commonly, over the child's diagnosis (for example, was s/he learning-disabled or emotionally disturbed?) and the contents of the educational plan. Parents also tended to doubt the school's ability to actually deliver an acceptable program, even if they approved of the plan on paper; the majority of parents therefore wanted their child to be placed in private school, an action which the public schools, of course, opposed.

To provide a check against later parent reports, our observers made their own assessments of educational plans, using a number of criteria. As reported in Table 12-2, they found that the evaluations on which the plans were based

Table 12-2.
Characteristics of the Evaluation and Educational Plan

	Yes	No
Was the school's evaluation broad — for example, did it include a broad enough spectrum of tests to discover special needs?	35	22
Did the school prepare an educational plan which followed from its evaluations?	36	20
Did the school propose a program which followed from the educational plan, that is, was it adequate to meet the objectives stated therein?	31	24
Did the school's educational plan comply with Chapter 766 regulations?	24	31
Was the school's educational plan flexible and individualized — that is, treated to meet the stated needs of the child rather than constructed from what was available?	22	32

were usually adequate; that is, they had employed a range of tests broad enough to discover any special needs. They also thought the goals and services outlined in the plan seemed appropriate to the results of the evaluation. However, they felt that the plans were often not sufficiently tailored to the individual needs of each child.

Table 12-3 indicates the child's placement at the time of the hearing, as opposed to the placements desired by the parents and the school. Most of the children whose hearings we observed were attending private day placements (35), where their parents wanted them to stay, and from which the schools wanted them to leave.

Of this sample of 60 special needs children, parents initiated evaluations for 54. The principal (2), regular education teacher (2), special education teacher (1), and counselor (1) initiated far fewer evaluations. However, the proportion of parent-initiated cases in this sample was unusually high and reflects the parents' activist concerns for their child well before the schools had become fully aware of the Act. In this sample, parents and the school evaluation personnel had met before the educational planning meeting to discuss the evaluations informally in 27 cases; the parents were present at the educational planning meeting in all but one instance, and 41 of these 60 parents had chosen to obtain independent evaluations. Although these outside reports were all submitted to the school system, in only nine instances was the school's educational plan revised to include them, based on our examination of the

Table 12-3.
Child's Placement at Time of Hearing
And Those Desired by Parents and Schools

Placement	Present placement	Parent choice	School choice
Regular education with modification (<25% time in special education)	4	4	6
Regular education, 25% - 60% time in special programs	4	3	14
Regular education with 60% time in special programs	1	0	12
Substantially separate public school program	7	8	25
Day school program	35	44	0
Residential school program	3	5	2
Home or hospital program	1	1	1
Other	5	0	0
Total	60	60	60

documents in the case. Twenty-three parents indicated at the hearing they had initially accepted the educational plan and tried it with their child, before subsequently rejecting it and requesting the hearing.

Table 12-4 lists the types of persons parents consulted to prepare for the hearing, as indicated by the testimony at the hearing and the documents submitted.

Table 12-4.
Persons Consulted by Parents Prior to Hearing

Person Consulted	Provided Advice	Evaluated Child
Representative of private school	19	15
Independent educator	16	14
Attorney	14	10
Advocate	10	8
Medical doctor	11	20
Child's psychotherapist	6	11
Licensed psychologist	7	7
Family friend	5	3
Family relative	6	2
Representative of the office for children	10	0
Regional representative of department of education	23	0

Table 12-5 lists the types of evidence the parents and schools submitted at the hearing. The "other" category comprises a diverse array of reports that were not easily categorized.

Who was there.
Table 12-6 lists the types of witnesses the parents brought to the hearings, and Table 12-7 presents a similar listing for the schools. As one can see, the hearings could on occasion become rather crowded, especially with school personnel. An average of 4.2 persons attended on behalf of the schools, with 1.2 parent witnesses in addition to the parents themselves. Parents sometimes complained that the number of persons present to testify for the schools served to overwhelm the parents, who found their numbers intimidating.

Table 12-5.
Evidence Submitted by the Parents and the Schools

Evidence Submitted	By Parents	By Schools
Correspondence	28	21
Psychological report	25	20
Medical examination	24	13
Examples of child's work	11	7
Report card	9	8
Child's school file	-	13
Family information on child	-	11
Other	37	36

Representation.

In 46 cases, parents had some form of representation (25 had lawyers and 31, advocates). In 32 cases, the schools also had a lawyer. The observers rated the quality of the advocacy for parents as good to excellent in 30 cases and fair to poor in six cases. They rated the quality of the representation for the school as good to excellent in 21 cases, and fair to poor in 35 cases. As we shall see below, representation adds a critical dimension to the case, since the quality of the school's representation was found to be a major determining factor in the outcome.

Table 12-6.
Witnesses Testifying for Parents: Number who Appeared at a Hearing

Witness	Number of Persons/Category		
	1	2	3
Attorney	21	1	-
Advocate	20	1	-
Teacher	16	3	1
Psychologist or psychiatrist responsible for independent evaluation	10	2	-
Private school administrator	9	4	-
Independent educator	5	4	-
Medical doctor (other than psychiatrist)	3	1	-
Other professional	10	1	-

Table 12-7.
Witnesses Testifying for School: Number who Appeared at a Hearing

Witness	Number of Persons/Category			
	1	2	3	4
Director of special education, pupil personnel	45	2	-	-
Other administrators	28	11	-	-
Attorney	27	1	-	-
Chairperson of educational planning team	35	-	-	-
School psychologist	27	1	-	-
Teacher	25	11	2	-
School psychiatrist	0	1	-	-
Other professional	22	1	2	2

The role of the hearing officer.
Our observers paid particular attention to the manner in which the hearing officer conducted the hearings. Hearing officers seemed to encourage careful cross-examination by both sides, and were rated as being generally neutral. Our observers reported that in 41 of 60 cases, the hearing officers would tend to help either parents or school staff if they seemed confused. The hearing officers' behavior in these circumstances was observed to be controlling, but reasonable and neutral.

Quality of presentation by parents and schools.
Our observers made overall ratings of the quality of parents' and schools' presentations at the hearing. The basis for these ratings is specifically described in Table 12-8.[2] The number of cases assigned each rating is indicated in parentheses after the description.

Nearly two-thirds, or 39, of these parent presentations were rated as well organized and well supported (ratings 4, 5, and 6); approximately one-third, or 20, of the parent presentations were found to have serious defects (ratings 1, 2, and 3). The schools' ratings, on the other hand, ran only half and half: 28 strong versus 28 weak presentations. These ratings support the widespread perception among both parents and administrators that during this early period of implementation, parents were better prepared at hearings than were schools, particularly because parents utilized the active support of private schools and lawyers in preparing their presentations.

Table 12-8.
Quality of Presentation at Hearing

	Parents	Schools
1. No Presentation	1	4
2. Presentation Poor; Subjectively Based	9	16
3. Presentation Adequate But Not Objectively Supported	11	9
4. Presentation Objectively Based, Supported, Not Well Organized	14	19
5. Presentation Objectively Based, Supported, Well Organized and Argued	21	10
6. Presentation Well Organized with Social Issues Addressed	4	1
Totals	60	59

Cross-examinations.

A major aspect of a hearing that often determines the overall impression made by a side is the conduct of and response to cross-examination. Global ratings were made of how each side challenged the other's witnesses to develop and support their position. Here again, parents were rated as better than schools: 27 parent cases were judged to have presented strong cross-examinations (ratings 4, 5, and 6); 27 cases, weakly or poorly organized cross-examinations (ratings 1, 2, and 3). By contrast, only 18 school cases were judged to have displayed well-organized cross-examinations, while in 41 cases, their questioning was judged as poor.

Analyzing the presentations.

To understand the relative importance of each element in each side's presentation, we subjected these data to "factor analysis," a statistical technique that allows us to see how various components of a process relate to one another and to gauge the relative importance of each variable within the identified cluster. We identified three groups of items which were clearly related to one another while seemingly unaffected by other aspects of the hearing process. These groups or "factors" are listed in Table 12-10, with the

Table 12-9.
Ratings of the Parents' (Counsel)
And Schools' (Counsel) Cross Examination

	Parents	School
1 = Does not question or questions in a self-defeating manner.	6	10
2 = Questions, but does not challenge the opponent's witnesses, evidence, or presentation. The parent/school may suggest the evaluation or classification is wrong through the use of random questions, but there is no organized basis to the process and the thrust is primarily subjective.	14	14
3 = Questioning challenges the witnesses, evidence or presentation, but without any apparent reference to a coherent, orderly framework in which the particular challenges develop an organized thrust. Parent/school is verging on true cross-examination but does not consistently achieve it.	9	17
4 = Cross-examination challenges opponent's presentation within a coherent, narrow framework. The thrust of the cross-examination is used as support for the parent's/school's case. Parents/schools at this point usually begin to question content of the school's proposal/parents' request as they address the issue of classification.	12	4
5 = Cross-examination challenges opponent's presentation with a coherent, broad framework. Parent/school challenges opponent's facts, classification, program content, and the quality of the proposed program. Cross-examination is coherently presented as an adjunct to the original presentation and greatly enhances the case.	12	4
6 = In addition to the criteria established in category 5, the cross-examination is used to challenge the whole approach of the opponent on the basis of the broader theoretical issues of special education which are relevant to the particular case.	6	2

Table 12-10.
Factors Identified from Hearing Observation Form
and Loadings of Items Within Each Factor

Factor	Factor Loading
I. Strength of Parent Presentation	
1. Quality of parent presentation	.86
2. Quality of advocacy for parent	.81
3. Quality of parent cross-examination	.78
4. Number of witnesses	.39
II. Strength of School Presentation	
1. Quality of advocacy for school	.77
2. Quality of school presentation	.70
3. Quality of school's cross-examination	.61
4. Number of witnesses	.29
III. Extent to Which School Adequately Meets the Educational Plan Requirements of Chapter 766	
1. Did the school propose a program that followed its educational plan?	.85
2. Did the school's educational plan follow from their evaluation?	.82
3. Was the school's educational plan flexible and individualized?	.71
4. Did the plan comply with Chapter 766?	.50

items that compose them. The numbers under "Factor Loading" refer to the relative strength of each component in making up the factor—the closer the number approaches to 1.00, the greater the component's strength.

Factor 1, Strength of Parent Presentation, is most affected by the quality of the parent's presentation (.86), representation (.81), and cross-examination (.78).

Factor 2, Strength of School Presentation, identifies the same three variables as similarly important for the schools, though the quality of the school's advocacy was somewhat more important to its case than the parents' representatives were to theirs. We did not find that the number of witnesses attending the hearing weighed as a significant factor for either parents or schools. This is interesting, since parents often complained bitterly about their inability to bring witnesses, whom they had to pay, while the schools had "free" witnesses at their disposal. Parents and hearing officers both told us that schools often brought any staff even remotely connected with the child, trying to impress by the sheer numbers of witnesses. However, neither our observations nor our subsequent interviews with hearing officers suggested that witnesses were important for their own sake, though many hearing officers did feel that experts' reports were clarified by being presented orally. An oral presentation also gave them the chance to explore the programmatic implications of the experts' findings. Nonetheless, the hearing officers felt that the schools' witnesses, however numerous, more often tended to hurt the school's cases with their disorganized presentations.

The third factor important to a hearing's outcome is the extent to which the school adequately met the educational plan requirements of Chapter 766. As indicated in Table 12-10, the variables weighing most heavily were the extent to which the plan was individualized (.71) and followed from the assessment findings (.82), as well as the extent to which the program actually proposed followed from the educational plan (.85).

Our Observers' Impressions of the Hearings

Formal ratings do not convey the richness of our observations, especially in an area of study that was new and ill understood at the time the rating schedule was being developed. We constructed the rating system described above to enable us to attend systematically to the identifiable features of the hearing. However, as the system was limited to easily quantifiable elements, we asked each observer also to record relevant anecdotes or observations, which provided considerable and often surprising insight into the hearing process.

Setting and atmosphere.
The state guidelines (Massachusetts Department of Education, 1977) require a "neutral" room in the state education region in which the family resides. The few times we observed hearings held in local school buildings, particularly in the school the child had attended, tension in the atmosphere increased distinctly. In one instance, the hearing was held in a room whose broken windows were attributed to the students of the school, supporting the generally bad feeling about the school which the parents described. Clearly, the location of the hearing can have a definite effect on the feelings of the parties.

In all hearings the hearing officer sat either at the head of a long, narrow table, with the parties on each side facing each other, or in the middle of a table with the parties sitting to either side. A tape recorder operated continuously to create a permanent record of the hearings. Thus, those testifying were constantly being reminded to speak clearly, one at a time, and the microphone had to be moved to face each witness. Parties were consequently quite aware they were being recorded, which may have made them more self-conscious. The hearing began with the formalities of tape recording, administering the oath, and reminding parties about the requirements of the law, which emphasized the procedure's legal aspects. The positioning of parties on opposite sides of a table underlined its adversarial nature. Thus, the setting conveyed an atmosphere of formalized controversy. Hearing officers told us they found the hearings' adversarial air appropriate to their concept of the hearing process, although they varied in the degree to which they maintained this formal atmosphere. But generally at least some degree of restraint and discomfort was evident on both sides.

The atmosphere was also affected by the number of people in attendance. When only one or two parents and one or two school persons participated, hearings were usually more informal, with participants behaving less self-consciously and communication occurring more directly—often with open discussion among the parties. One hearing involved only four persons, all of whom knew each other socially and were on a first name basis. The issue in debate was only a detail of the educational plan, and the hearing was short and amicable. This hearing would probably not take place today, but would be resolved at the mediation stage.

The larger hearings involved 10 to 15 people and these were particularly formal. School departments usually brought child evaluation team members, school psychologists, special education teachers, speech therapists, administrators, and many other such professionals as witnesses. Often school principals came, and usually special education directors. In some cases one sensed that the school brought anyone who had had any contact with the child, on the assumption that the more witnesses they had, the better their case would be. In some cases not all the witnesses testified, though the presence of these people meant increased expense for the school and probably increased intimidation for the parents. In one instance, a special education director stated that the hearing had cost his school thousands of dollars. This particular hearing took two days, and the final result was an agreement between parties outside the hearing room. Another hearing lasted five days, involved 15 witnesses, and resulted in a decision in favor of the parents, although the school had employed a highly experienced lawyer, while the parents had only a voluntary advocate. This hearing was characterized by endless rounds of presentation and cross-examination, with witnesses subpoenaed, dismissed, and again recalled. This unnecessarily long and legalistic hearing seemed to continue largely because the particular hearing officer did not try actively to manage it.

Hearing officers usually called periodic recesses for various reasons. In many cases, parties had not been given time to read new evidence submitted by the other side and requested a recess to do so. Other recesses were called to allow further discussion betwen counsel and clients, to allow parties to recover their equilibrium, or to allow all parties to have a break. The hearing officer manual suggests that one hour-long break for every four hours of testimony is reasonable during a hearing, and this guideline was usually followed. In addition, short five- to ten-minute breaks were allowed during the four-hour period. Breaks seemed very important, as much of the testimony was complex and difficult to follow. Concentration was difficult to maintain continuously for five or six hours of the hearing. Testimony which is complex and often conflicting must be listened to in circumstances which encourage concentration; our observers found such circumstances were usually well established by the hearing officer.

Most hearings ended at five p.m., but frequently continued for a second day. A few went to three days, and one to five days. The shortest hearing attended was two hours.

Emotional climate.
All of the hearings we observed were concerned with important decisions about children. Much of the discussion during the hearing was predictably emotional in content and delivery. When the parties had no representation, the hearings were often more emotional. Parents had particular difficulty discussing their child's problems and history in a calm and orderly way. The facts usually concerned their child's failure in school, a tragic handicap or deformity, and their own disappointments and hopes for these children. In the face of these kinds of emotional issues, parents understandably may not present a calm and detached view at the hearing. Even when an advocate or attorney represented the parents, the child's history was almost always presented by a parent, usually the mother. This account would usually be emotional and, as a result, confused and rambling.

School witnesses had a different kind of emotional investment in the hearing. Many saw the hearing as a personal challenge to their competency and expertise. Under cross-examination from a parent's attorney, one teacher refused to answer further questions.

Many hearings seemed to involve hidden agendas, such as parents punishing the school for their lack of concern, or schools airing hostility toward the parents. Parents often made bitter remarks about the school's indifference to their child's problem. In some cases it was apparent that schools saw the parents as "nuisances" who lacked any real understanding of their child's abilities, expecting either too little or too much—usually the latter. A few parents became so enraged by their treatment by school staff that they pursued hearings out of sheer anger, even when both parties substantively agreed on the child's educational plan. Cases resulting from bad communication and hostility, with no substantive disagreements, would probably be resolved today through mediation.

Sometimes, however, emotional testimony clarified, rather than confused the issues. One hearing concerned an orphaned 16-year-old girl with severe emotional problems, who insisted on being present at the hearing and demanded an opportunity to testify. At the time of the hearing she was living with foster parents, who represented her at the hearing. All of the parties present were dubious about her attending the hearing, but they allowed her to remain. Evidence was presented at the hearing about her behavior problems and her difficulty in accepting any home environment. The girl finally testified and spoke for ten minutes. She was very articulate and expressed gratitude and love towards her foster parents, with a clear and moving account of her needs and problems. During her testimony the room was silent and people were visibly moved. In this case, the hearing's tenor was undoubtedly emotional and appropriately so.

Another hearing with useful emotional testimony concerned a severely retarded child with Down's Syndrome. A psychologist, a witness for the parents, spoke about the human sadness in cases of this kind and the process of denial and rejection which parents often go through when they know their child is seriously retarded. He spoke of the severe emotional problems suffered by parents of such children, and articulated many things which are often left unsaid during public discussions of handicapped children. No one had expected to hear this kind of testimony, and there was an atmosphere of shock and embarrassment in the hearing room. In fact, this testimony had the effect of focusing those present on the issues of the child's and parents' problems rather than on the politics of dispute, which is too often the focus of hearings.

The role of the attorney or advocate.

The presence of attorneys and/or advocates in a hearing tended to heighten the degree of formality. Lawyers in particular seemed to function more comfortably in a more formal environment, which to them was predictable and familiar. They would often employ legal terminology and such traditional courtroom techniques as trying to trip witnesses up by objecting to details of their testimony, techniques which seemed inappropriate for hearings whose basic function was to clarify the special needs of the children and the appropriate services, not to determine who would "win" or "lose." Lawyers would likewise use cross-examination in a hostile way, or launch into lengthy discussions of the legal requirements and interpretations of the statute. However, when lawyers were involved in hearings, the information process did seem to be more orderly and clear, and often the lawyer's presence defused an emotionally charged atmosphere.

Advocates are non-lawyer representatives, either unpaid volunteers, paid by parents, or working for state or private advocacy organizations. Although they acted more formally than parents alone, advocates did not present cases as formally as lawyers and were often confused and undirected. While often seeming more "human" and approachable to parents, in many cases they did not do an adequate job of presenting evidence, especially in organizing the evidence for the parents or in the examination of witnesses. They seemed to be at a particular disadvantage when confronted with a lawyer for the other side. Hearing officers were highly critical of both lawyers and advocates, characterizing them as "unprepared," "confused," and "long-winded." (See Chapter 13 for more on hearing officers' views of representation.)

The involvement of lawyers in special education hearings is increasing, and this is probably both useful and inevitable. The comfortable attitude that "we are good people, and we can solve this with good will" may be appropriate to informal situations, but not to an adversarial process like a hearing. Even in informal mediation sessions, parents reported feeling coerced to "bargain" and to be "reasonable" so as to attain an agreement; thus, even there, they may need legal help to withstand these pressures.

Most parents probably require some type of representation to help them organize their materials into a coherent and reasoned presentation, and to help them manage this presentation at the hearing. We found few lawyers who were sufficiently familiar with the parents' rights or with the substantive issues involved in their disputes. Nor were many lawyers familiar with the procedures appropriate to an administrative hearing, rather than a trial. Advocates, while often familiar with the law, varied in their understanding of the substantive issues involved in the particular disputes, and often failed to help the parents organize or present their cases in a coherent and temperate manner. The parent's counsel must often help the parent maintain some emotional "cool" in a highly charged situation. Advocates frequently had difficulty in this restraining role.

Unfortunately, while informed representation at a hearing has become more readily available, it has also become more expensive. An attorney who represents parents told us in 1981 that he only accepts one out of three parents who come to him for representation because most cannot afford to present their cases adequately. A usual fee seems to be $2,000, with parents also paying for expert witnesses, independent evaluations, and other supporting material.

Entering evidence.
In the hearings we attended, the formalities such as labelling exhibits, stating

the law, and administering oaths were handled first. Both parties are requested to submit evidence prior to the hearing, which at the start of the hearing is labelled by the hearing officer and read into the record. The Massachusetts Administrative Procedures Act allows documents to be presented at the hearing itself, and even after the hearing has started, but hearing officers made sure that the opposing party had time to examine the documents submitted.

Most objections by lawyers or advocates were formal statements of objection with no substantive argument or reasons offered. But occasionally parties might object to documents which they considered unreliable or out of date. Hearing officers usually dealt with such objections by asking the other party for its comments and then overruling the objection, but stating that all documents would receive only the weight and credibility they deserved. Most documents were accepted into evidence by hearing officers, but with the proviso that inconsistencies would be kept in mind and noted in the decision.

The process of identifying and labelling documents took place off the record, was time-consuming and often messy. Procedures could certainly be developed to expedite this process of entering evidence before the hearing, while still allowing flexibility for last-minute evidence to be submitted and avoiding penalty to parties unfamiliar with a legal process. For example, the hearing officer now usually makes available a complete typed and numbered listing of documents submitted at the hearing's start, instead of conducting this time-consuming clerical chore while the parties are present. Only newly submitted documents need be entered at the actual hearing, although time must then be made available for the opposing parties to review them.

Presentations by each side.

In most cases, the parents presented their case first, although the hearing officer usually asked if either party had witnesses to present early, for instance, expert witnesses who had to leave for appointments. Usually, a witness was sworn in, testified, and was then cross-examined by the opposing side or its representative. The witness might then testify a second time to present additional evidence and/or to rebut statements made in cross-examination. This cycle of multiple testimony by a single witness could be repeated many times. Both parents and schools were largely unused to presenting their argument in this way.

Our observers often found the testimony of parents to be long and somewhat confused, understandably, given their emotional involvement. Each parent witness was cross-examined by the school's attorney or special education director. In many cases the school superintendent or some other senior administrator was present but did not participate actively in the proceedings. We assume they simply wanted to understand the hearing process, which was then still new.

Many lawyers would engage in repetitive exchanges with each witness. They often reserved the right to recall witnesses at any time and were reluctant to give up a witness. Hearing officers continually had to intervene to curtail repetitious questioning.

Many lawyers would utilize traditional courtroom techniques, for example, casting doubt on the credibility of a witness by focusing on his/her "expertise," qualifications, experience, and the specific details of his/her testimony. The hearing officers agreed that a witness' expertise was an important factor in considering evidence, but found lawyers' preoccupation with it inappropriate and unpleasant. Many witnesses became defensive and reacted as though they were being accused of being dishonest or incompetent. This lowered the quality of testimony and impeded the hearing's real purpose—to get information about the child.

Some lawyers became aggressive during the hearing. In one case, the lawyer paced around the room as though he were in a courtroom, making for a tense and difficult atmosphere. In another hearing, a school witness became very distressed under cross-examination, and a recess was called by the hearing officer to allow all parties to calm down.

When the public school was being asked to pay for an expensive private placement, they invariably employed an attorney. These cases usually involved more witnesses on both sides.

Closing statements by each party or its representatives ended the hearing. The parties sometimes were allowed to mail written closing statements to the hearing officer by a specific time.

Evidence presented.

The same kinds of evidence were submitted at all hearings. Both parties submitted written documents, usually evaluations: medical, psychological, educational, and social. Correspondence was frequently submitted by both parties, much of it seemingly irrelevant.

Witnesses called by parents usually included psychologists or professionals who had conducted an independent evaluation, and teachers from independent schools. They occasionally brought physicians or psychiatrists, speech therapists, or friends of the family. In one case, parents brought representatives from the Departments of Youth Services (for delinquent youth) and Public Welfare.

Testimony on the parents' side was a mixture of fact, opinion, and hypothesis. Much of it concerned testing results, about which there was much debate between the parties. Personality testing in particular was the subject of much contention, as parties argued over how to interpret these test results.

Much evidence was presented by psychologists who had had little direct contact with the child, making for generally speculative theories. One hearing involved testimony from a school learning-disabilities specialist which challenged the whole basis of the parents' test results and developed into a two-hour lecture on testing theory. In this context it was difficult to determine the important facts about this particular child while restricting the less relevant aspects of the theoretical discussion.

The kinds of evidence presented by schools were fairly predictable. Members of the child evaluation team spoke about their evaluations, the child's needs, and the educational plan which they had developed in response to those needs. Teachers gave background information on the child, and educational administrators gave background information on the school's policy and special education services. Much evidence seemed repetitious. School psychologists' evidence was usually important, particularly for learning-disabled children, a high percentage of our sample. In a few hearings the psychologist did not appear, so their reports were presented and interpreted by another member of the sttaff. This was usually an unsatisfactory process because the psychologist's findings could not be discussed further nor his/her conclusions clarified.

Witnesses attended hearings not only to present new evidence but also to answer questions about the written evidence already submitted. Most hearing officers said they found the physical presence of witnesses extremely useful so they could question them in person about their evaluations.

The quality of evidence varied considerably. Some evidence was comprehensive, well presented, and clear, while other evidence was insubstantial, confused, and vague. Most hearings were a mixture of poor and good presentation. Many witnesses clearly did not know what was expected of them during the hearing and were ill prepared and confused. Even in cases where attorneys represented the parties, they had often not prepared their clients for the hearing. On one occasion, a witness appeared on the second day of a hearing to replace a witness who was ill. Her testimony was in direct contradiction to the testimony offered by the original witness at the prior session.

The issues in the hearings.
In most hearings, the formal legal issue as stated in the decision was "whether the educational plan was . . . adequate and appropriate" for the child. However, there were always other issues. A major issue in Private School cases was who would pay for tuition and transportation. Other disputes concerned the location of the program, responsibility for transportation, program elements desired by the parents, and the diagnosis of the child. Often the parents were implicitly challenging the school's ability to deliver the program

it had promised. While the educational plan might be agreeable "on paper," parents doubted that the school could implement the plan. These cases were particularly marked by an undercurrent of hostility since a school's competence is hard to assess, with many intangibles difficult to convey to the hearing officer.

Most of the hearings we observed concerned children with learning disabilities, very often called "dyslexia" by parents or schools. However, interpretations of what is considered dyslexia vary widely. In some cases, the meaning of dyslexia appeared to be the issue in debate, and arguments on both sides were largely theoretical discussions of dyslexia, complete with photocopies of newspaper and journal articles, while the actual needs of the child were often ignored.

Emotional problems are often associated with learning disabilities in a complex nexus which rarely permits observers to say which are cause and which are effect. However, a common interpretation of Chapter 766 requires parents to establish that emotional problems directly affect the child's ability to learn, that is, are directly related to the school learning problems.

Schools sometimes argued that a child's problem was primarily emotional, and thus not within the province of the school's programming. In one case, the school argued they should not be responsible for residential care because the child's problems were primarily caused by an unhappy home situation. This case was made even more difficult by the complete refusal of the state mental health system to share responsibility with schools for such children, a particular problem for those portions of residential placements that do not involve direct educational services. Two similar hearings involved disputes over whether the school district or a state agency was financially responsible for the child. The children were clearly the real losers in these cases, as their educational problems will probably not be addressed until the jurisdictional dispute is resolved.

School's response.

Observing school personnel during the hearing is no accurate indication of their general response to the law. Most school personnel presented a case at the hearing which essentially argued they had done their best for the child and that this "best" was in fact adequate. In three hearings, school personnel did admit they had not been in compliance with the law, but these were usually only minor breaches, most often a failure to meet specific time requirements. More serious instances of noncompliance to which schools did not admit included failure to involve the parents in the writing of the educational plan or to invite them to the planning meeting. A few schools were obviously in gross noncompliance with both the letter and spirit of the law: little had been done for the child and it was difficult to imagine that anything would be done without a decision from the hearing officer. Although these schools presented themselves as acting in good faith, the parents' case was made stronger by the schools' evident malfeasance.

School departments often presented a defensive and hostile face during the hearings, especially for Private School cases. Staff clearly felt threatened, and they dealt with the perception of threat by challenging the parents, the process, even the law. In one hearing, a school administrator commented to the observer, "It's a ripoff"—meaning the parents' request for a private placement.

In most hearings, however, both school personnel and the parents' witnesses presented themselves credibly. Public school teachers had usually had more contact with the child than any professional in the room, and they usually conveyed a sense of sympathy, understanding of the child's problem, and concerned involvement with the child. In many cases, they seemed to be doing their best with little support. Even when there were feelings of obvious hostility between the parties, the teachers were often friendly and uninvolved in the "battle," usually seeming on friendly terms with the parents. By contrast, the school administrators appeared detached and unsympathetic.

Relationships between experts testifying for opposing sides—psychologists, speech therapists, and teachers—were often strained. In cases where there was no attorney or advocate, cross-examination of the parents' expert would often be conducted by a public school specialist. Testimony then became theoretical debate. For example, in one hearing, two teachers spent considerable time arguing about the effectiveness of the Gillingham method of teaching reading, a discussion unrelated to the actual needs of the child concerned.

Summary

The opportunity to attend hearings, even during this early period (1975-1977), provided us with a basis for thinking realistically about how the hearing process functions and about the conflict between the formal legal requirements and the human nature of these proceedings.

Massachusetts has had considerably more experience in this area than any other state. At the time of this research, the state was still developing rules and guidelines, and re-evaluating the appeals system. It is clear that each state, when complying with the federal statute P.L. 94-142, will develop hearing procedures that reflect its own particular philosophy and interpretation of the law. Some states, for example, provide parents a chance to appeal to the local school board before taking their dispute to a hearing at the state level. This kind of variation will obviously affect the kind of cases which get to a full hearing and the kind of hearing forum that will develop. Some states prefer to have more than one hearing officer, as California does—a trio representing the schools, the parents, and the public weal. Some states may opt to employ hearing officers who are not primarily lawyers. There are arguments for all of these options, and their implications have been presented elsewhere (Budoff, 1979).

Barry Mintzer, an attorney who has represented a considerable number of parents at special education hearings, concluded in 1978:

> The special education hearing has shown itself to be a legal process more than an educational process. This is not necessarily bad, but it is somewhat different from the notion of those who originally conceived of a hearing as a relaxed, informal arena where parents and educators could reason together toward the common goal of educating a child.

Mintzer proceeds to discuss the role of the attorney.

> The lawyer's principal responsiblity is to gather all the available records and information, to assess the strengths and weaknesses of the case, and to ultimately advise parents whether the case has enough merit to pursue. Lawyers must help parents recognize that they may not be successful in their appeal, regardless of how "correct" they may feel about it. No case can be won without sufficient supporting evidence or a basis in law, and parents should be introduced to the reality that their case must be proved. They should also understand the test used by a hearing officer in evaluating the parent's case: A child is entitled only to an educational plan which is adequate and appropriate to the child's needs. Only with a thorough understanding of these elements can parents effectively participate in strategy development.

He concludes this discussion of the role and responsibilities of the lawyer with some general observations about the hearings procedures.

> There are several problems with hearings as they are currently conducted. Among these is the length of time, and therefore the cost, involved with each hearing. A well-prepared, well-controlled hearing can be done in one day, in many cases, and should rarely go beyond two days. Nevertheless, they frequently do, and no one is quite sure why. One reason may be that both sides tend to utilize

too many witnesses. There is no need for a witness (and, again, it is counterproductive to use a witness) who has said everything he has to say in a written report. There are several possible remedies to the increasing length of time hearings take. The parties may wish to meet before the hearing to separate out the areas of agreement from disagreement, and to prepare stipulations to be entered into evidence. Another possible remedy would be to require each side to submit a written synopsis of its case for the hearing officer to read prior to the hearing.

Clearly, the flexibility involved in the administrative hearing allows one considerable latitude to solve these problems. Given the basic requirement of an adversarial system, a number of instruments might still be used to streamline it. Despite the danger of these mechanisms being used to restrict a hearing's fairness, an overly complex and legalistic process may be experienced by potential appellants as too difficult and costly to consider. Parents who feel their child is not receiving the educational program appropriate to his/her needs will not appeal the plan because of these perceived barriers. The flexibility permitted in a hearing allows state bureaucrats to construct a system that combines procedural fairness with a clear focus on the issues, in a minimally legalistic setting that assures an equitable, speedy, and directed proceeding. Hearing officers' bias must be tilted toward assuring that the child's needs are met. They must pursue an active role in eliciting the evidence they require to make these judgments. This represents a challenge, but, with suitable safeguards, one that can probably be met.

Notes

1. The adversarial nature of hearings was even misunderstood by the Massachusetts Department of Education. The bureau charged with overseeing appeals was first named the "Bureau of Child Advocacy" and a social worker was hired as head. Once hearings began, the name was changed to the "Bureau of Special Education Appeals" to reflect a more neutral stance in the legal contests between parents and schools, and lawyers were hired as hearing officers and director.

2. The three rating scales were developed by and reported in Kuriloff, P., Kirp, D., and Buss, W., *When Handicapped Children Go To Court: Assessing the Impact of the Legal Reform of Special Education in Pennsylvania* (National Institute of Education, 1979).

13

Hearing Officers
Talk about Hearings

A major actor in the appeals process is the hearing officer, the person charged with judging the merits of the school's and parents' cases and rendering a decision. Administrative hearings allow the hearing officer considerable leeway. The "state-of-the-art" evidence presented in special education disputes and the uncertainty regarding the standards for judging a handicapped child's proposed program place a considerable burden on hearing officers. This uncertainty also offers them considerable latitude in judging each case. Thus, such factors as hearing officers' education, training, and prior experience; their beliefs about justice and their personal values; their perceptions of their role; and the degree to which they are active at a hearing, are likely to have important effects on the hearing process and its outcome. We interviewed Massachusetts hearing officers to see how their perceptions of their role and their style of operation affected the appeals process.

This chapter illustrates that despite the many factors which might have pushed them into commonly held opinions, there is considerable diversity among the views and styles of hearing officers. The small cadre of state-employed, full-time hearing officers worked closely together in the early years of the new law. They were an idealistic group who saw themselves in a key position to shape this special education reform. They collaborated as a staff to develop guidelines for hearings at a time when such procedures were largely unexplored. Although each hearing was held in the educational region of the state where the dispute had occurred, hearing officers were based at a single central office of the Massachusetts Department of Education. They attended day-long staff meetings every two weeks and associated informally in their shared office space at other times. Despite these opportunities to share experiences and develop common views, we found persistent differences in their philosophies and approaches to their work which can only be ascribed to such causes as personal style and values.

This chapter presents the perspectives of the hearing officer cadre that was working in Massachusetts at the time this study was being completed in spring, 1977, when hearing procedures were just beginning to stabilize. The first section presents excerpts from the manual developed by the Bureau of Special Education describing the hearing officer's responsibilities. Subsequent sections describe the characteristics of the hearing officer cadre and their perceptions of their roles. It should be noted that the hearing officers interviewed in the present study are not necessarily representative of hearing officers per se, but only of those who were working in Massachusetts in the spring of 1977. Their opinions are presented less as a formal survey than to provide insight into the conduct of a hearings system.

The Function of the Hearing Officer[1]

Hearing officers are responsible for rendering decisions on cases appealed under Chapter 766. Basically, the hearing officer is responsible for determining the appropriateness of the educational program proposed for a child. S/he may therefore also pass judgment on any issues arising during a hearing that relate to that central issue.

The law identifies the qualities which the hearing officer should possess, including the ability to exercise sound judgment; a lack of prejudice about any of the hearing's issues; a complete knowledge of all law and policy of the Bureau of Special Education Appeals, and the ability to interpret the law fairly; the ability to preside over a hearing, and to articulate clearly what is going on to those present at the hearing; the ability to elicit and analyze testimony, and to determine the credibility of witnesses based on the quality of their testimony; and the ability to write clearly and concisely. The law stresses in several ways the overriding need for the hearing officer to be impartial, and also to be able to give the appearance of impartiality, so that both sides feel they have been treated fairly.

The officer is first assigned a case by the Director of the Bureau of Special Education Appeals or by his/her designee. The assigner later reviews the decision to ensure that law and policy were applied consistently; that the decision was supported by the evidence that came out at the hearing; and that the order seems appropriate to the conclusions.

After the officer is assigned the case, s/he begins to review the documents that have been forwarded to the Bureau, such as test results, professionals' assessments of the child, school records, etc., in order to have questions prepared for witnesses, and to allow the hearing time to be spent on live discussion rather than perusal of written documents.

The hearing officer begins the hearing by administering oaths and receiving whatever additional written evidence is offered by either side. A major function of the hearing officer is to keep the hearing running in an orderly, fair, and effective way; thus, s/he is the one who decides on both sides' procedural requests. The hearing officer is also charged with assuring that a complete record is made of the hearing.

But the hearing officer is not just an impartial administrator; s/he is also the arbiter who must ultimately decide on the suitability of an educational program for a handicapped child. In this capacity, s/he has the power to decide on the validity of evidence; to summon or interrogate witnesses; to ask for additional documents; or to take any other actions to produce the information needed to make an informed decision on the child's needs. This might include holding informal conferences between the two sides, to clarify or resolve disputed issues.

Ultimately, it is the hearing officer who is responsible for ensuring that all relevant information is presented at the hearing, and for safeguarding the rights of both sides. Because of the officer's impartial position, knowledge of the law, and access to information, s/he is presumed to be in the best position to rule on the appropriateness of a particular educational program for a handicapped child.

A Description of Massachusetts Hearing Officers

A structured interview was conducted by one interviewer with all officers employed full time during the spring of 1977, about two and one-half years after the hearing process was instituted. These interviews were tape recorded and lasted from two to four hours each. The officers discussed how they weighed various kinds of evidence, by what means they arrived at a decision, and what they saw as the strengths and weaknesses of the hearing procedure.

Seven full time employees constituted the hearing officer cadre at the time these interviews were conducted. Three officers were female; four were male. Their ages ranged from the late twenties through the thirties. All were either lawyers or had had some type of legal experience, for example, serving as a hearing officer with a rent control board. Several had had considerable legal experience, such as a trial lawyer, teacher in a law school, or employee of a private or public interest law firm. The two who were not lawyers had previously been public school teachers.

All had been employed as hearing officers for six months to one year at the time of the interview. Six had heard approximately 20 cases each, the seventh had heard about 40 cases. Two of the hearing officers interviewed were later promoted to Director and Assistant Director of the Appeals Bureau. Two had been employed as mediators of special education disputes prior to specializing in hearings. None of the seven had any formal training for the job before becoming hearing officers, but all had participated in discussion groups and in-service training programs organized by the Bureau and in a one-week course given by the American Arbitration Association.

All the hearing officers expressed interest in education and administrative law and one had a history of activist participation in town affairs. One officer became interested in special needs children because of family experience with such problems. Two were motivated by a specific interest in combining law and education.

Personal qualities of hearing officers.

When asked what personal qualities they felt were important to their jobs, they mentioned both administrative/legal and interpersonal skills. More specifically, they listed the abilities to direct and control situations and to make decisions; good analytic skills; the ability to seek out information and to communicate thoughts orally and in writing; and the ability to maintain the proper emotional distance from the human problems of the hearing. They also emphasized strongly their commitment to the purposes of Chapter 766 and to its implementation. Sensitivity to special needs children; an awareness of the educational system in Massachusetts; openness; integrity; receptivity to people; and the ability to be fair and impartial were other characteristics they saw as important.

Knowledge of special education.

All but one of the hearing officers felt that a knowledge of special education was not an important prerequisite for the job. As one hearing officer said, "Judges hear cases in real estate, for instance, with no special knowledge of real estate, but [they] can apply the standards that the law requires." However, some did feel that a general familiarity with education issues and, particularly, educational jargon, would be helpful in questioning witnesses and focusing on relevant issues.

Interestingly enough, two of the hearing officers felt strongly that a knowledge of special education was actually undesirable, as this might improperly influence their judgment of other experts' evidence at the hearing: "The hearing officer should not be in the position of a third and fourth evaluator."

Other areas of knowledge considered important by the hearing officers were child development, legal expertise, educational administration, sociology, biology, administrative law, and educational testing.

The concept of an "administrative hearing."

Hearing officers were asked their definition of an administrative hearing in general, whether inside or outside the field of special education. They described hearings as a kind of forum in which individuals who might be denied an important right could present evidence to see if this denial were legal and reasonable. They stressed the hearing's function as a place to "lay out all the evidence," with the hearing officer acting as "an impartial unbiased person" who can therefore end a dispute.

However, these officers found a significant difference between special education hearings and other such procedures. Since educational evidence is often subjective opinion for which there are no uniform standards of evaluation, "there is no right or wrong answer in most instances, unlike, for instance, a traffic violation."

All the hearing officers felt that participants' general ignorance of the legal process made it difficult for them to understand the hearing officer's role and the basic concept of a hearing. This inexperience, a legal process' inherent rigidity, and the newness of the concepts of parents' rights and school accountability often made for inefficient hearings.

The hearing officer must do more than make a standard ruling on how a given law applies; s/he must determine the most appropriate educational program for an individual child, a decision which will naturally depend on factors which the law cannot specify. Educational hearings therefore lack clear-cut standards for determining burden of proof, and for judging the relevance, weight, and credibility of evidence. Three officers who had worked with hearings at other state agencies were particularly sensitive to this lack.

Educational hearings are unique in other ways. One officer pointed out that "the party whose interest is most important, ...the child, is absent," making the hearing officer more than usually responsible for weighing the facts. Four officers mentioned the unusually personal nature of special education hearings: "the added burden on the hearing officer of dealing with a...person's...grief," and the sense that "a child's life is at stake."

Administrative Hearings in Special Education

Hearings versus mediations.

We asked hearing officers to compare hearings to mediation, because these are alternate systems of resolving special education disputes. Hearing officers saw mediations as quite different from hearings: mediations are more informal; have less concern with facts; emphasize areas of agreement rather than disagreement; and involve a lot of give-and-take between the parties, hopefully with a free exchange of information. Above all, the officers stressed that, unlike hearings, mediation has no third party to impose a final decision.

Hearings were seen as more adversarial—by some hearing officers, necessarily so—as more concerned with facts, and as emphasizing the differences rather than the similarities between the parties' points of view. The presence of the impartial third party imposing a decision was seen as the major defining element of a hearing.

The roles of the hearing officer and the mediator were likewise seen as being quite different. The mediator was described as sympathetic, allowing parties to vent their feelings; as flexible, able to suggest alternatives; and as bound to stress areas of agreement. Hearing officers were seen as more controlling, with less flexibility, providing a stronger leadership role, and less concerned with emotions. As one hearing officer said, "Mediators need to deal with everything a party comes to a session with: suspicions, emotions, and any hidden agendas, while the hearing officer needs to be more concerned with eliciting factual information."

The mechanics of a hearing.

All the hearing officers mentioned the importance of a neutral site for the hearings and were sympathetic to some parents' wishes not to have the hearing held in a school building, particularly in the school they were challenging. They also felt that a court building would be demoralizing to the participants. Three hearing officers emphasized the importance of maintaining the regional character of the hearings by scheduling them in the parties' region of the state.

A major problem cited was the length of the hearings. Some officers felt length was difficult to control, given both parties' frequent misperceptions of a hearing's nature. Thus they felt that hearings require active and efficient management by the hearing officer.

Some officers proposed a prehearing conference to make the actual hearing more efficient. Such a meeting could help both parties focus on the issues, while receiving guidance on what evidence was needed and by whom it should be presented. The rules of the hearing could be explained and the importance of presenting coherent arguments stressed. Such a conference would also offer another chance to resolve outstanding issues. Most importantly, the parties at this conference could define the issues in dispute, so that irrelevant matters would not intrude into the hearing.

Formal structure versus flexibility.

A major tension facing the hearing officer is the conflicting need for formal legal procedures on the one hand and a flexible response to events within the hearing on the other. The hearing officers we interviewed were split fairly evenly in their positions on this issue.

Three officers strongly favored retaining a formal legal structure for the hearings. As one said, "I have a fairly orderly mind. Therefore, it's better to get the information in sequence... The more formal the hearing structure, the better; it allows a more efficient process to get out all the facts."

Despite their differences of emphasis, all the hearing officers stressed the importance both of a formal structure and room for flexibility. They pointed out that an easily understood structure was necessary for parties to see what kind of evidence was required of them. Some formal structure was also needed so the officer could maintain control of the hearing and make sure that testimony was accurate and complete.

Given the need for formality, however, the officers also wanted to be as flexible as possible within this structure, particularly when parties did not have legal representation and might not have understood legal terminology and procedures. One hearing officer felt that especially in the early years of the law, when parties were generally unfamiliar with the hearing process, flexibility had been especially important "to guarantee a sense of fairness."

The hearing officer's role.

Most hearing officers saw their role as that of an impartial judge, a decision maker, and sometimes by necessity a fact finder and inquisitor as well. They thought they should keep tight control over the hearing to ensure fairness, while extracting the maximum amount of information relevant to the child. All interviewees thought the hearing officer should play an active role in the hearing, asking any questions necessary to clarify or elicit information. All were willing to interrupt testimony if they felt the issues "were going out of focus or if testimony was amorphous, irrelevant, or contradictory; or when testimony was becoming emotional, tensions were surfacing, and parties were interrupting the testimony of others." Calling a recess was seen as an excellent cooling-off tactic, so that the parties could then be brought back to focus on the relevant issues.

One hearing officer felt that an officer should always be aware of the emotional climate among these nonlawyer participants. S/he should "acknowledge that testimony is often a mixture of fact, opinion, and attitude, but...let this come out... This is important in allowing the parties to feel they have had a fair hearing... I would let parties go on and on so that they don't feel shortchanged...and have had their day in court."

"Off-the-record" conferences were often held during a hearing to solidify a possible agreement or to clarify any misunderstandings "like a bench conference in a court of law..." All the hearing officers thought they should act as mediators whenever possible, as all had done at one time or another. In one case, "the parties were under the gun and had nothing to lose." Another officer thought that sometimes "when parties [have heard] evidence they cannot rebut, [they] may be more in a position to compromise." The officers believed that parties who came to a cooperative solution rather than having a third-party solution imposed on them, were far more likely to implement the agreement.

The officers acknowledged that their impartiality might be threatened by mediation attempts. One hearing officer stressed that an officer should be aware of his/her power to compel a mediated settlement that might not be in the best interests of the child.

Most hearing officers felt that mediation could most easily succeed when the issues in dispute were relatively minor, such as the number of hours of special education the child should have, or over some part of the plan only. Mediation was seen as less likely to succeed if parents and the school had broken all communication or were openly hostile, such as when parents had already removed their child from public school. One hearing officer said, "Where a public versus private school program was at issue, there is no chance of mediating. This is a money issue, and the schools don't like to be in a position of giving in."

Changes in the hearing style.
All the hearing officers felt the basic format of the hearing had remained unchanged over the two and one-half year life of the system. However, they did perceive changes in the character of the hearings. Hearings had become more tightly structured, enabling officers to exercise more control. They dealt more with legal issues and technicalities; included objections that were more legalistic in content and conduct; and involved testimonies that were more professional and more complex, with more evidence presented, more witnesses involved, and with lawyers more frequently representing both clients. Officers also saw schools becoming more sophisticated in presenting their case at the hearings.

The Factors in a Hearing

Representation.
We asked hearing officers if they thought parents seemed to need

representation at the hearings they conducted. All agreed that parents face many special burdens in a hearing: for example, fear of the process, a high emotional investment in the outcome, lack of knowledge of formal proceedings and the law, and the greater financial burdens of having to pay personally for counsel, witnesses' time, production of documents, and time lost from work. They also felt that parents, who are usually not experts in education, might perceive the opposing school as more powerful, more experienced with hearings, and more knowledgeable than themselves.

"Parents have a tremendous burden and strain no matter how sophisticated they are," one hearing officer pointed out. "Going through a hearing is an ordeal, an uncomfortable process, and most have decided to go this route only as a last resort. Most parents are intimidated about challenging an institution with which they have been involved."

Under these circumstances, most hearing officers felt that representation by a lawyer or advocate could be useful. They thought lawyers and advocates could be helpful in interpreting the legal process, organizing information to prepare for the hearing, directing the presentation of the case, cross-examining witnesses, and generally helping their client to be controlled and rational at the hearing.

All the hearing officers emphasized that representation was helpful only when it was competent. They found most lawyers and advocates to be generally ill prepared on the facts of individual cases, as well as on the relevant law and regulations. Lawyers' lack of competence was thought to be due to their relative inexperience with administrative hearings and with special education. The hearing officers had the impression that lawyers needed to invest more preparation time than they were providing at the time of our study.[2]

Hearing officers had mixed feelings about the role of nonlawyer advocates. One hearing officer felt that a lay person was usually adequate except when complex legal issues were to be argued. Another cited a case in which inappropriate arguments were used by an advocate, resulting in a negative decision for the parents.

While lawyers tended to be overly legalistic, advocates often became too emotionally involved, a tendency which reduced their effectiveness. Like lawyers, they were often not well prepared or failed to understand the law and so did not serve as effective managers of the parents' case.

Schools, also, faced knotty problems at their hearings. Like parents, schools were often seen as presenting their cases subjectively, with a great deal of "ego investment" and defensiveness about their professional reputation and competence, which they saw as being under attack. "Their professional reputation is at stake during the hearing, and they have no ability to be objective about what is happening," one hearing officer remarked. Additional pressure was generated by the presence of superiors during school staff's testimony. Schools tended to present their case through a large number of witnesses, but these presentations were often poorly orchestrated. The hearing officers felt that the schools were frequently intimidated by the impressive credentials of the parents' expert witnesses.

Although schools and parents were seen to need lawyers for the same reasons, hearing officers generally felt that the schools were better able to represent themselves than parents. "They have the advantage of having been through the process before and having a town counsel available for advice," one officer pointed out.

Most hearing officers felt they would not be affected by the apparent inequity of one party being represented while the other was not. But they all felt the trend toward more representation for both sides was a good thing. In general, the officers felt that parents had coped very well in the hearings, with or without representation, but they noted that as of early 1977 the parents bringing cases were mainly well educated, affluent, suburban parents. They felt that as urban parents were not able to afford representation; they were more easily intimidated by the requirements of a hearing and thus far less able to assert their rights under the law.

Written evidence.

All the hearing officers agreed on the kinds of documents which should be submitted as evidence: educational, psychological, and medical tests and evaluations; the educational plans and programs from public and private school; parents' reports; independent evaluations of the child; school progress reports; and teachers' reports. The mass of correspondence with the schools which parents frequently submitted was described as generally irrelevant and unnecessary.

Clearly, the amount and kind of documents submitted vary with the child's problems. For example, a learning-disabled child's documents might include tests, educational and psychological evaluations, and educational documents, while those of a physically handicapped child would more likely emphasize medical evaluations. The more severe the child's problem, the greater the number of documents to be submitted. Some hearing officers felt that certain school districts consistently produced more documentation than necessary, submitting "anything they can lay their hands on." Lawyers' and advocates' involvement always produced more documentation. Most hearing officers felt there had been a definite trend toward submission of more documentation in general.

All the hearing officers said they would accept evidence handed in on the day of the hearing, if the documents were relevant. They usually dealt with objections to the documents by noting them on the record and then overruling them. But they did allow parties time to examine the documents during the hearing. One hearing officer said that if the parties were unrepresented, "almost anything would be accepted," but he would emphasize that he would attach to that evidence only the weight and credibility it deserved, giving little attention to out of date, vague, or unsupported reports. Another hearing officer noted that lawyers were trained to abide strictly by courtroom rules of evidence and often objected improperly to documents and so-called "heresay." "They find it difficult to reorient themselves to the fact that anything is admissible [at an educational hearing]."

Oral evidence.

The kinds of oral testimony seen as important by the hearing officers included the parents' history of the child, including personal anecdotes and stories, the school's elaboration and justification of the educational plan, and the school's evaluation. All the hearing officers stressed the importance of oral testimony if only for purposes of clarification. They found it extremely valuable to be able to question witnesses in person to establish their credibility and usually felt happier with evidence when they had been able to do so. Oral testimony seemed particularly important in cases where written evidence was vague or widely divergent. Interviewees' comments on the quality of oral testimony were mixed. Some hearing officers described such testimony as generally good, well structured, and coherent. But most felt they had heard a great deal of vague, irrelevant, out-of-focus, and speculative testimony, often not founded on objective evidence and occasionally degenerating into "banter."

Most hearing officers said that they did not value oral over written evidence or vice versa. When assessing the credibility of both types of evidence, they looked for the following:

- whether the tests and evaluations were recent, up-to-date, and comprehensive;
- how thorough they were;
- how long the particular witness had known the child;
- the credentials and expertise of a particular witness; and
- whether the opinion was supported or contested by other evidence.

Some hearing officers felt witnesses from a private school might have a "vested interest" in the case, which might color the hearing officer's view of their evidence. One hearing officer felt that a private psychologist or psychiatrist, with possibly higher qualifications than a school psychologist, often gave a more favorable impression. Generally, though, both school and independent experts were seen as having different but equally valuable contributions to make to the evidence. School experts often had the advantage of having known the child for a long time and hence having a broader perspective on the child, while independent experts were seen as having more experience with a particular problem and so being more sophisticated in their diagnosis. Although both parents and schools saw the other side as having an advantage, either because of the number or the quality of their witnesses, hearing officers seemed to think that these relative advantages balanced out, putting both sides on an equal footing.

Familiarity with the case.
Despite the state guidelines requiring officers to read case files before the hearing, four of our interviewees actively avoided becoming familiar with any written evidence other than routine documents and possibly the rejected educational plan. One said, "I like to come in fresh with no biased opinion and often only one party will have submitted things. I am a fact finder, and these must be judged on the day. Evidence in the file may be prejudicial."

Other hearing officers felt that it was important for them to have formed their own overview of a case beforehand, otherwise they risked being unduly influenced by the parent's initial testimony, which would be their first contact with the case. One hearing officer felt that familiarity with the file would help him flag areas which should be covered at the hearing and help formulate questions to be asked. "I would be less thrown at the hearing when handed 40 pages of documents." Two hearing officers said they routinely held a prehearing conference to become more familiar with documents and evidence.

The emotional climate of the hearings.
When asked about the emotional climate of their hearings, four officers described it as frequently turbulent, making the hearing difficult to manage. One attributed this to the usually long history of conflict between the parties, mentioning incidents such as a parent crying, a mother so distraught that she couldn't say anything, and a woman screaming and yelling during the school's testimony about her child. Other hearing officers described similar outbreaks with parties yelling or interrupting each other and even with bursts of temper between attorneys. Hearing officers said that if the atmosphere became too emotional they would either call a recess or remind the parties that the purpose of the hearing was to make a decision in the best interest of the child. Three other hearing officers, however, said they had not found their hearings particularly emotional.

All seven of the hearing officers had found hostility between the parties, though this was not always overt. "People seem concerned to put their best foot forward and don't want to appear overly emotional in the presence of the hearing officer," one told us. Another hearing officer felt that hostility caused the greatest problems when parties were not represented, because "by the time parties reach a hearing they have had each other up to the eyeballs," while lawyers or advocates can be more detached. Most of the hearing officers believed this hostility inhibited communication. One hearing officer thought the schools in particular aggravated the situation by their defensive attitudes and their ego investment in the process, diverting attention from the substantive issues at the hearing.

Significantly, all but one of the hearing officers felt that the adversarial format itself exacerbated any underlying hostility between the parties. Yet they felt strongly that the adversarial nature of the hearing was inevitable, given the formal structure of the event: seating the parties on opposite sides of the table, and using attorneys, whose major tactic was to raise doubts about witnesses' credibility and to damage the opposing side through cross-examination. The only way to make the appeals process less adversarial, these officers thought, was to avoid hearings wherever possible by the use of mediation.

But the seventh hearing officer argued that the adversarial format may actually lessen hostility. He felt that hostility was the result of the long-standing conflict already existing between parents and school, not necessarily exacerbated by a hearing. "The parties are in the presence of a third party, namely the hearing officer, who they do not wish to prejudice. The parties have been through this thing since the start of the evaluation, [so] I don't know that the hearing necessarily brings [their hostility] to a head."

It is difficult to prevent the hostility which may surface, regardless of its source. Some suggestions made to minimize confict included counselling parents ahead of time about the procedures and holding a prehearing conference. Such a conference would provide the opposing parties with information on the hearing procedures, rather than leaving them to speculate on their own. The low-key climate of a prehearing conference might also provide an opportunity for the hearing officer to mediate the outstanding issues.

Order of presentation of testimony.

Hearing officers' policy is to have parents present testimony first. As the appealing party, parents must indicate why they rejected the educational plan. However, this policy is within the hearing officer's discretion, and most did diverge from it at times, such as when experts had to leave the hearing to make appointments. One hearing officer would stop testimony if he needed clarification, which often entailed taking testimony from either party out of order. While one hearing officer thought the order of presentation made no difference, two others felt that the established order of presentation was a disadvantage to the parents. "Sometimes I never hear about the educational plan and the assessments. The present structure puts the parents in the role of being an appellant." They felt the results of the assessments and the educational plan should be presented early, with the issues in dispute clearly stated and agreed upon by the parties. Without this evidence, parents have a much harder time explaining the shortcomings of the school's approach, and, as professionals with well-prepared testimony, schools tend to get the benefit of the doubt.

Children at the hearing.

All of these hearing officers had conducted hearings or mediations where the child was present. Most had mixed feelings about the overall wisdom of this practice, particulary from the child's point of view. The experience could be damaging for a young child, and the child's presence might inhibit the testimony of some witnesses. But in the actual cases when a child had been present, most hearing officers had found that presence helpful. "It gave me more feel for what the child was like." In some cases, the child had actually testified, which was also felt to be useful. The hearing officers did believe that children over age fourteen should be present, and one hearing officer described a case where a useful and agreed-upon suggestion at the mediation had originally come from the child.

Writing the decision.

Although hearing officers had standard methodologies for writing their decisions, they varied in their methods of reviewing evidence, in how they actually wrote a decision, and in the length of time they took to complete a decision.

Most officers took copious notes during the hearing to highlight the important evidence. These notes provided the outline of the case which they later reviewed along with the documents. Most of the hearing officers did not listen to tapes of the hearing, unless they felt they had not determined the facts, or when there had been a procedural violation.

Most hearing officers began their writing process by composing a summary of the evidence, or as one hearing officer put it, "a statement of the case." For many hearing officers, this was the point at which the case started to "come together." Usually the officers had definite feelings about their decision well before they actually wrote it or reviewed the materials. One said, "In 50% to 75% of the cases, I know where I'm coming out [by] the end of the hearing, and [my] review of the evidence usually bears this out." On the other hand, the officer went on, "25% of the cases are so complex or so close, or have so much testimony, that I need to start from scratch reviewing issues, evidence, etc...

25% could easily go either way [and] an analysis of the facts is not going to give you the complete answer. Here is where the subjective stuff you sense, felt, or was intimated about the situation comes into play."

Sometimes hearing officers had a pretty good idea of what their decision would be before the hearing had even ended, mostly when legal issues were the main dispute. One officer said that only one or two of his cases had been so close that no decision could have been formulated right after the hearing. What is interesting about these remarks is their implication that decisions are based on the presentations made at the hearing, presentations which may or may not reflect the issues most germane to determining the most appropriate program for the child. Particularly since many officers do not look at documents until during or after the hearing, we think that their opinions may be unduly influenced by the quality of oral presentations.

Time taken to write the decision varied from two hours to two weeks, depending on the individual officer and the length of the case. One hearing officer made the interesting admission that it was harder to write a decision that favored a school: "I must justify retaining a child in a situation where the child has failed." Generally, cases with a great deal of testimony or conflicting testimony took the longest to decide and to write. Often these involved learning-disabled children and/or private school placements.

Hearing officers said they attached the most weight to the most recent reports, test scores, and independent expert testimony. One hearing officer mentioned the difficulty in dealing with the plethora of testing information that was sometimes submitted.

All the officers felt that the way the decision was written was very important. "It must be a legally defensible decision," we were told, "must show the parties that you have considered the evidence and made judgments on the evidence, show the reasoning and how your analysis went to get there, be clear about conclusions and implications of these."

One hearing officer emphasized the importance of writing for the layperson as well as the lawyer and avoiding the use of unnecessary legal jargon. "Decisions must clearly state the conclusions and the actions which must follow from those conclusions. Hence, it is important to frame the order to make clear to the parties what is expected of them."

Hearing officers did not advocate a single ideal form for all decisions but did agree that certain kinds of information should always be included:

1. **Summary of evidence.** This should be "a fair and honest rendition of the facts as presented and why they are or are not credible." Some hearing officers felt their own decisions usually included too much evidence in this section. Ideally, the summary should include only the

most pertinent evidence on which the ultimate decision was based and the reasoning behind the inclusion of that particular evidence.

2. **Clear statements of issues in dispute.**
3. **Clearly stated conclusions.** These should include the rationale for the decision and should refer to the evidence pertinent to each conclusion. One hearing officer commented that the conclusion should seem to proceed inevitably from the earlier sections of the decision.
4. **Specific statement of the order—what is required of both parties.** On the whole, all the hearing officers felt that decisions should not been seen as setting precedents except, perhaps, in a few cases where a particular regulation or procedure was the subject of the dispute. Usually, though, each case should be seen as unique and, therefore, should be judged entirely on its individual merits.

These officers disagreed somewhat over whether findings of fact should be included in their decisions and over how a "finding of fact" is defined. One officer felt that findings of fact were not even appropriate to this kind of issue, which concerns subjective opinions with no clear "ultimate truth." The officers also disagreed over whether they should include rulings of law. Some hearing officers said they would include them if they were specifically requested or if the resolution of the case depended on them. One hearing officer pointed out that the Massachusetts Administrative Procedures Act does not specifically require findings of fact.

Hearing Officers View Specific Issues

Interpretation of "appropriate" educational plan.
Most hearing officers thought that the crucial point in judging a plan was whether it had been written to answer the particular needs of the child. One officer believed that a plan could not be merely "sufficient"; it had to respond actively to the child's unique needs. Other interpretations were less generous: "sufficient, not the minimum, but not gravy"; "if the plan fits the child, and the child is making reasonable progress in the program, not necessarily spectacular progress but more than just minimal"; "not the best, not the least."

Most hearing officers said they had occasionally explained their interpretation of "appropriate" at the start of a hearing to make clear the standard by which they would judge the plan. That they felt a need to so define this term illustrates the striking lack of precise standards for judging this central issue.

Judging the child's progress.

All the hearing officers felt that this was a major factor in any decision, but that progress was very difficult to judge accurately. Too often, neither parents nor schools produced objective, empirical evidence, such as test results, in their presentations. Most hearing officers therefore had to rely on the reports of experts or persons who worked with the child, although they preferred test scores and objective measures when available.

The fiscal responsibility issue.

All hearing officers felt obliged to address the question of fiscal responsibility in their decisions. While they did not view this as their principal concern, they did wish to take it into account. But they insisted that fiscal concerns did not influence their decisions except as part of the issue of the "appropriateness" of the proposed programs. One officer said, "I resent the fact that these [fiscal issues] are there but, in many cases, this is the basis of the case." A particularly complex problem was determining at what point tuition reimbursements should begin, whether from the date when parents actually placed their child in a private school or only from when the educational plan was written. Factors complicating this question included how to assess the reasons for school delay in presenting a plan to the parents and how to assess parents' responsibility for speedily communicating with the school.

Attitudes toward the schools.

Some hearing officers felt that the schools were acting in good faith, with one officer in particular impressed by the improvement in educational plans since Chapter 766 had been implemented. However, these officers believe that just acting in good faith was not good enough, suspecting that schools often provided "kind treatment" in place of the individualized, highly skilled services required by the law.

Other hearing officers gave the schools even less credit. One said the schools only "marginally fulfilled their duty by being involved in the process rather than with the child." Another hearing officer felt the law was seemingly "repugnant to the schools." Even those who felt schools were acting in good faith thought that improvement had been patchy and insufficient at best.

Mediation information.

Some of the hearing officers we interviewed would allow information derived from mediation sessions to be discussed during the hearing, if both parties wished it and no objections were raised. One hearing officer wanted to know whether mediation had taken place but would accept only written evidence from the mediation, for example, a new educational plan or agreement that had not been implemented. He would not listen to hearsay evidence about what had happened. One hearing officer felt it was often impossible to keep that kind of information out and would accept it, but emphasized to the parties that it was only hearsay evidence.

Bureau policy requires a report of any mediation to be placed in the case file, to include when mediation was held and its result. The report must omit any substantive information about whether the parties came to agreement on specific issues, or continued their dispute. Thus hearing officers know whether or not mediation was attempted but do not have any specific information on what was discussed or how. One officer thought it would be better to withhold all evidence about mediation from hearing officers because "this might debilitate the mediation process, which should be without prejudice to both parties."

Informal discussion during the hearings.
Some hearing officers approved of informal discussions off the record, particularly when areas of agreement emerged during the hearing. These officers tried to encourage such discussions, to permit settlements during the hearing whenever possible.

The burden of proof.
All the hearing officers felt that both parties had a burden of proof to discharge. While the school had the burden of proving their educational plan was appropriate for the child, parents had to show the school's plan to be inappropriate, as opposed to their own alternative. Some hearing officers felt that casting the parents as complainants in this manner unintentionally increased their burden of proof. Some hearing officers preferred to discuss burden of proof during the hearing; others felt the concept was too complex and legalistic and would confuse rather than clarify matters for the parties.

Use of subpoenas.
Most of the hearing officers had had experience with subpoenas and had mixed feelings about their value. Some felt they were useful in compelling an unwilling witness to attend; some felt an unwilling witness was not worth having; and some felt the subpoenas "had no teeth" and didn't compel anyone.

Special education policy statements.
Most hearing officers felt policy statements could be important in guiding their decisions. While some such statements were phrased almost as if they were regulations, others were intended to provide only guidance and so were open to interpretation by the hearing officer. "We are not bound by them,"

our interviewer was told, "but generally go along with them, provided they are not interfering with the ability to provide a program which will largely benefit the child." One hearing officer felt that such statements were "more harmful than helpful."

Compliance hearings.
Hearing officers who had held compliance hearings, that is, hearings on parental complaints that a decision had not been implemented, said such hearings were usually shorter and focused more on factual determination: whether the decision had been implemented, and if not, why not. The hearing officers thought they could take a more active role and be more focused and directive in this type of hearing than in one to determine the appropriateness of a particular plan.

Summary

All the hearing officers with whom we spoke felt strongly that the adversarial hearings system is very important in special education decision making, though perhaps more as a way of achieving systemic change than as the best way of making individual decisions. As one hearing officer said, hearings are "a way to apply pressure on service agencies to be accountable to their consumers, most of whom are in some sense captives of the system, having no alternative but to go to the schools. There is no other way that these institutions can be held accountable, only by intervention of the law." All our interviewees strongly emphasized the need for schools to be accountable to parents and special needs children. One officer even felt that schools should be "made accountable" to "normal" children also.

Hearings were seen as a "more benign" way of putting pressure on an agency than class-action suits, which would cause greater disruption. One officer said flatly, "I don't think you can guarantee services without an appeals system." Most hearing officers felt the system was fair or "as fair as any legal process," but they pointed out that low-income parents were not being represented. This was attributed to the expense and intimidating nature of the process and what one hearing officer called its "legal mystification." The officers were concerned about the high cost to some parents of presenting their case but had no solutions to offer.

All the hearing officers acknowledged the high cost of the hearings system to the schools too but generally felt this was inevitable. One said that if the spill-over effect had been what they hoped, the system was not really so expensive, since resulting changes in school policy help make future hearings unnecessary. But most officers, while they hoped the hearings had brought about some improvement, were more skeptical about the extent to which they had improved services for other children in the district.

NOTES

1 Excerpted from Massachusetts Department of Education, 1977.

2. As of this writing, there is now a cadre of lawyers and advocates who have become sophisticatd and relatively expert in representing clients at hearings (see, for example, Mintzer, Appeal News, 1978).

14

The Decision

The actual product of the hearing process is the formally written decision. The decision contains the *order*, the statement explicitly outlining what the hearing officer requires both parties to do. The decision may also contain other sections explaining what evidence and what type of reasoning were used in coming to that conclusion.

When we examined a 50% sample of the decisions written during the first two and one-half years of the hearing system, we found wide variations in length, format, and quality of written decisions. Many seemed incomplete, failing to state clearly the evidence on which the decision was based. Some did not even contain a separate order section or were unclear about what actions were now required of each party. The Massachusetts Administrative Procedures Act specifies only that each written decision must include a "statement of reasons"; otherwise, hearing officers are not bound by law to any particular structure.

A definitive format for writing decisions would greatly benefit all parties to the hearing process. Hearing officers would be able to achieve greater consistency, both in the conduct of hearings and in the writing of decisions, if they had a consistent procedure to follow. Advocates, lawyers, and school officials would be better able to prepare their cases if they knew in advance what types of evidence would be considered in a decision and what type of reasoning would be employed. An easily understood decision format might help parties to focus their disputes more clearly, facilitating the hearing. Certainly, a clearly stated order section would help solve the problem of ambiguous decisions, which often require a second hearing for clarification.

Between the first implementation of Chapter 766 in September, 1974, and March, 1977, approximately 350 decisions were written. Relying on a 50% sample of these hearings—161 decisions—we will discuss the nature of these early decisions, their quality, and our proposals for a standard decision format. This analysis offers one way to see what Massachusetts hearing officers, operating without clearly stated guidelines, actually considered when rendering judgment.

The Nature of a Decision

A decision is the product of the hearing process. Its order section mandates the action intended to resolve the dispute. Since decisions are subject to judicial review, they are supposed to include sufficient evidence and reasoning to enable any further appeals board to make its own evaluation of the case. The decision should also be written so the lay people in the case can understand it.

Kirp, Buss, and Kuriloff (1974) explain that a decision marks the intersection of procedure and substance. The decision—the substance to come out of a hearing—must be based on reasonable and identifiable criteria, that is, it must have been made through a fair procedure. These "reasonable criteria" are supposed to ensure a consistent treatment of cases, minimizing any possible bias of the hearing officer. Only if clear criteria are mandated can an individual argue that a case was decided unfairly: that a decision did not consistently apply these criteria. However, they point out that a hearing officer must also have the flexibility to respond to particular circumstances. In analyzing these Massachusetts decisions, then, we must keep in mind the need for balance between consistency and flexibility.

Kirp, Buss, and Kuriloff (1974) further identify four types of facts that a written decision should contain:

1) facts concerning the special needs student;
2) facts concerning the school system's capacity to meet that student's educational needs;
3) facts concerning the possible disadvantages resulting from classification required to qualify for special education services;
4) peripheral facts bearing only indirectly on the decision.

The authors emphasize that decisions must refer specifically to the criteria on which they are based, whether from statutes, regulations, or prior opinions, and should separate the reasons for classifying a child as in need of special education in general from the reasons for placing him/her in a particular program. The opinion should make clear what distinguishes one case from an apparently similar previous case. Only if a case contains nothing new can the opinion forego such explanation and simply refer to a prior case. Again, we see the conflict between the need for consistency on the one hand and the difficulty of establishing precedent on the other, given the complexity of individual situations in special education.

According to Abeson, Bolick, and Hass (1975), a decision must be based solely on the evidence presented at the hearing, and should indicate both findings of fact and the hearing officer's reasoning. When an officer disapproves of a particular educational plan, they argue that the officer should explain what an appropriate educational plan would be. They also want decisions to explain how the parties can appeal and to include a list of agencies from which legal assistance may be obtained.

How We Analyzed the Decisions

This chapter examines the decisions written in Massachusetts between December, 1974, and March, 1977, with the intent of discerning their characteristics and quality. We asked four questions:

1) What kinds of orders had been made?
2) What rules had been applied by hearing officers, if any, in decision making, and what judicial or educational standards had been applied?
3) What was the structure of the decisions?
4) What kinds of information did the hearing officers find relevant to their decisions?

The information and the degree of structure in these decisions varied considerably. The early decisions of 1974-75 in particular were loosely structured, relatively vague, and often lacked consistency and an orderly argument.

Using a preliminary reading of 10 randomly chosen decisions, we formulated an instrument to code the issues in dispute, the evidence bearing on those issues, the hearing officer's findings, and the elements of the actual order. We then used this instrument on 40 decisions, revising it to use on the entire 50% sample. We looked at the following types of information typically included in the decisions:

- statements on the reasons for the hearing, with a list of the parties present and their relationship to the case;
- a comprehensive description of the child's needs;
- a summary of all written and oral evidence presented at the hearing;
- findings of fact and the reasoning behind these; and
- the actual order, with the reasoning behind it.

In addition, we were interested in the following issues:

- Whether what is meant by *adequate* or *appropriate* was discussed or referred to in the decision, and if so, how it was interpreted. The federal statute, P.L. 94-142, uses the word "appropriate," while Chapter 766 uses "adequate." How these words are interpreted reveals the standards the hearing officer used to judge the educational plan.
- How the hearing officer judged the *quality of the educational plan* and the proposed program, and how this was articulated in a written decision.
- Whether the question of *least restrictive placement* was addressed and how much emphasis was placed on this concept.
- Whether the issue of assigning the *burden of proof* was discussed in the decision and whether this appeared to be an important factor in the case. In Massachusetts the question of on whom the burden of proof rests has been a difficult problem.
- Whether the fiscal issues were addressed in the decision, and if so, what role they played.

How the study was conducted.

A 50% sample of the 350 decisions rendered between December, 1974, and March, 1977 was obtained by selecting each even-numbered decision from the state appeal agency's files. These decisions were coded, based on the instrument described. Five coders were trained on the same sample of 10 decisions; this procedure was also used to check each coder's reliability and to make sure each coder was making ratings in the same way. Two additional reliability checks were carried out during the process of the coding.

Of the 161 decisions in our sample, 143 were final decisions. The other 18 were statements of agreement (8), preliminary orders or a supplement thereof (3), interim decisions (4), decisions rendered without a hearing (2), or compliance decisions (1).[1] Because of their idiosyncratic nature, we did not include these in our coding.

Although Chapter 766 required that parties receive their decisions within 30 days of the hearing, many decisions did not contain any record of the dates of either the hearing or the decision. Hence, our data were incomplete for this variable. However, those data which were available showed a definite decrease in the length of time taken to render decisions over the three years of this sample: from 2.6 months in the first year to 1.4 months in the third year. We can thus infer that decisions were written and issued more efficiently as the law became more familiar.

The format of the decisions.
We analyzed the 143 final decisions to find the relative length of each section, based on subheadings contained therein. Table 14-1 summarizes these data. Knowing a decision's average total length of 3.9 single-spaced pages, one can gauge the weight generally accorded each section by looking at its average length.

Analyzing the decisions by outcome, those favoring the parents averaged 3.83 pages long, those favoring the school averaged 3.65 pages, and those coded as compromise decisions averaged 3.95 pages. Thus there was no significant difference in length by outcome.

Analysis of the Content of Decisions

As we analyzed this sample, we found decisions on the whole to be poorly written and unclear. We present a detailed look at each section of a decision,

Table 14-1.
Format of the 143 Decisions

Defined Sections	No. of decisions containing this section	Average length of section (in pages)
Introduction		.49
List of those present	134	
Formal reason for hearing	132	
Issues	120	.29
Summary of Evidence	119	1.30
Findings of Fact	85	.58
Conclusions	140	.76
The Order	55	.01
Average Total Length:		3.90 pages

followed by a discussion of the shortcomings we discovered and by our own proposal for a decision structure.

Statement of Issues

Most decisions (120) contained a formal statement of the issues by the hearing officer. Some officers felt a statement of the issues should be restricted to a simple statement of whether the educational plan was appropriate to the child; others felt this should be a detailed statement of all the issues raised during the hearing.

The issues stated formally in the decision can be generally classified as related to one or more of the following:

- educational plan content;
- special needs and services required by the child (diagnosis);
- quality of public school program;
- placement;
- compliance;
- fiscal issues.

Educational plan content.
Massachusetts' Chapter 766, as we have said, uses the word *adequate* in describing the educational plan, whereas the federal law, P.L. 94-142, uses the word *appropriate*. Both terms began to be used by hearing officers during this period to describe their standards for judging an educational plan. Some 41% of these decisions formally stated that the hearing's issue was whether the educational plan was *adequate* to the needs of the child, 38% used *adequate* and *appropriate*, and 18% used the term *appropriate*.

It is difficult to assess whether these different usages reflect different interpretations, as interpretations are rarely defined explicitly in decisions. Hearing officers seemed to interpret *appropriate* as something more than *adequate*. The use of both words together suggested a still higher standard than either word alone. However, without a further detailed analysis of the reasoning and criteria used in the decisions, it is difficult to draw any conclusions. It is also likely the parties and hearing officers may have overused formulaic statements such as the "adequacy and appropriateness of the plan" and thereby have not indicated the substantive elements of the dispute.

Seven decisions (5%) referred to the adequacy or appropriateness of the educational plan submitted by a private school.

Only four decisions formally referred to the issue of "least restrictive placement," suggesting that this was not seen as a major concern, though many of the decisions did refer to this issue informally.

The child's special needs and the services s/he required.
Fifteen decisions (10.5%) included the formally stated issue of whether or not the child was even eligible for special education services. This may have been an issue in other cases, but was not so stated.

Ten decisions (17%) indicated a dispute over the kinds of services the child needed, although parents and schools had agreed on the child's diagnosis. Only two decisions (1.4%) identified the actual diagnosis of the child as an issue, and only three decisions (2%) mentioned the service site as a disputed issue. These issues may have been in dispute in more cases, but they were not formally stated as such in the decisions.

Quality of the school's program.
Ten decisions (7%) said the issue was whether the public school had the capacity to implement the proposed educational plan. While our parent interviews showed this to be a frequent source of objection to the school's plan, the decisions we analyzed mentioned it only rarely. Parent interviews, as well as those with the hearing officers, also referred to schools' frequent defensiveness at the presumed challenge to their professional competence, yet only nine decisions (6%) specifically referred to staff competence as an issue. Although in their interviews with us, hearing officers identified schools' competence as a significant issue, they were evidently reluctant to confront it openly in a decision.

Placement issues.
Some 43 decisions (30%) identified placement as a major issue. But considering that 84.5% of our interview sample concerned private school requests, this issue was clearly not being fully addressed in the wording of decisions. Only 16 (11%) decisions formally stated that the dispute was over the child's placement in a private school; another 11 (7.7%) formally described the issue as whether the child currently attending a private school should be returned to a public school setting. Based on our interviews with parents and school officials, placement issues loomed much larger than these decisions suggest.

Compliance.
Thirty-six decisions (25%) referred to issues of compliance; all but one involved failure to comply with regulations. Hearing officers seemed to feel that procedural violations were not really material to the case unless they were

serious. The one remaining decision indicated failure to comply with a previous hearing decision. It is likely that later decisions involved more failures to comply with prior decisions than these earlier ones.

Fiscal issues.
Twenty-four decisions (17%) formally stated that fiscal responsibility issues were in dispute, that is, these hearings involved payment of private school tuitions by public schools. Four other decisions (3%) identified the "grandfathering question" as an issue: the child had been supported by another human services agency before Chapter 766, and the school wanted this situation to continue, but the agency refused further support. Seven decisions (5%) identified other fiscal issues, such as payment for after-school tutoring. Hearing officers had told us they felt obliged to address questions of fiscal responsibility in their decisions, although some were reluctant to do so. Given the early confusion among hearing officers about who should bear fiscal responsibility and under what conditions, it is probable that many more decisions were concerned with this issue than specifically addressed it. Fiscal responsibility may well be at the unspoken heart of many disputes, particularly in cases involving private school placements.

Summary of Evidence

When we compared this section with the length of the average decision, we could see what an important part of the decision it was. Hearing officers told us that the summary of evidence might well be the decision's most important section. As one hearing officer said, "this is where it all starts coming together." This section is important because it puts in a public written form all the evidence relied on by the hearing officer, and provides the basis for the subsequent sections of the decision.

Of the 143 decisions, 119 (83%) contained summaries of evidence. Hearing officers told us they included only the evidence they felt was relevant to the decision at hand, rather than summarizing all the evidence presented. Clearly, a decision must contain enough evidence and reasoning to inform all parties of the basis for each conclusion.

The kinds of information contained in the summaries of evidence included the following items, suggesting the kind of evidence to which hearing officers were responsive:

- the past educational history of the child (114, or 80%);
- the child's present educational placement (113, or 78%);
- the parent's reasons for rejecting the educational plan (92, or 64%);

- the history of the child evaluation procedures (82, or 57%);
- the child's educational progress (82, or 57%);
- the current child assessments (43, or 30%);
- other educational assessments of the child (72, or 50%)—any private educational testing carried out by the parents outside the public schools;
- independent evaluations carried out at the parents' request (66, or 46%) (Over the three years of decisions, there was a definite increase in the proportion of cases in which such evaluations were conducted [29%, 43% and 53% for years 1, 2 and 3, respectively]. This trend could reflect the increased awareness of the parents of their rights under the law, as well as the increased support available as private schools and professionals also became more aware of the law.);
- the public school's justification for the educational plan (69, or 48%);
- the substance of the plan submitted by the schools (66, or 46%);
- psychological evidence given by someone other than a school psychologist (42, or 29%);
- medical evidence (20, or 14%) (The small number of cases with such evidence could reflect the small proportion of medically impaired children whose parents requested hearings in Massachusetts.);
- information about the educational plan submitted by a private school (20, or 14%) (Either this evidence is not sumitted often, or hearing officers do not consider it relevant to the decision. This is significant since a large proportion of these decisions were concerned with private school placements.);
- evidence from a social worker's report (19, or 13%) (This is often associated with psychiatric evidence or with severe family problems, which were relatively infrequent.);
- psychiatric evidence (15, or 10.5%) (The low incidence of this evidence is consistent with the relatively small number of special needs defined as serious psysychiatric problems. Less serious emotional problems were frequently mentioned in the decisions.)

Findings of Fact

A detailed discussion of the importance of findings of fact is found in Chapter 13. We should only note here that there is confusion among hearing officers about defining a finding of fact, as well as disagreement about the appropriateness of including such statements in the decision. However, findings of fact were included in virtually all decisions. Findings of fact included:

Findings on diagnosis.
- The child's eligibility for special services (90; 63%).
- The nature (70; 49%) and extent (32; 22%) of the child's needs.
- The appropriate placement for the child (37; 26%).
- The child's educational progress (34; 24%) and the child's progress in other areas (12; 8%).

Findings on services needed by the child.
- The nature of the services required (39; 27%).
- The extent of the services required (19; 13%).

Findings on placement.
- The present (44; 31%) and past (22; 15%) educational placements.
- The appropriate placement for implementing the current educational plan (35; 25%).
- That a public (23; 16%) or private (21; 15%) placement was most appropriate.
- That a public (7; 5%) or private (6; 4%) placement was the least restrictive option.

Findings on compliance.
- The public school had not complied with procedural requirements of the law (24; 17%).
- The public school had made a good faith effort to comply with the procedural requirements of the law (12; 8%).
- The public schools had not complied with the substantive requirements of the law (11; 8%).
- The proposed private placement was not at a state-approved facility (6; 4%).

Findings on fiscal responsibility.
- That the public schools had agreed to finance a transition period from private school to the public school (5; 3.5%).
- That the parents wanted the school to pay retroactive as well as current costs of private school placements (5; 3.5%).
- Whether a state agency or the school was fiscally responsible for the child—a "grandfathering" issue (4; 3%).
- That the public school had financed private tuition in the past (1; 0.7%).

The small number of these findings does not accurately reflect the wider significance of financial issues. Many cases in this sample involved the private placement of learning-disabled children, but hearing officers seemed reluctant to address directly the fiscal issues in their decisions.

Other findings of fact.
- The quality of the educational plan submitted (28; 20%).
- That the public school showed a willingness to be flexible (6; 4%).

Ten decisions (7%) included summaries of witness evidence. Two stated that insufficient evidence had been submitted to prove the educational plan met the child's needs.

Findings of fact as they appeared in the decisions we read did little to clarify the information presented and often became confused with conclusions, summaries of evidence, and the hearing officer's actual order. Since these findings lay the groundwork for the conclusion, we recommend considerable clarification of what is to be included in this section, in order that future decisions be clear and easily understood.

The Conclusions.

The average length of this section shows it was a more significant part of the decision than the section outlining findings of fact, and it was more consistently used. This section also proved to be more consistently written and more informative than the findings of fact. Because the conclusions embody the hearing officer's judgment in the case and prepare the ground for the order, they must be clearly stated and easily understood by the parties. Parents and school officials complained that, when conclusions were too generally stated, the decisions failed to indicate clearly what the schools were required to do, because most decisions in this sample did not contain a separate section detailing the order. The actions required of the parties had therefore to be inferred from the hearing officer's conclusions.

The contents of this section varied considerably. Some officers used this section to restate the evidence and the requirements of the law. Others gave their opinions of the schools' or parents' intent, followed by recommendations which were clearly part of the order. The frequently vague nature of this section probably contributed to the confusion over what the parties were actually required to do. We distinguished the content of this section under the following headings:

Conclusions relating to evidence.
- The diagnosis of the child (88 cases; 62%).
- A description of the educational plan presented (32; 22%).
- The educational history of the child (29; 20%).
- A description of the education the child was receiving at the time of the hearing (1; 0.7%).

- The psychiatric history of the child (6; 4%).
- Information about the medical history of the child (4; 3%).

Clearly, the information included here overlaps with the summary of evidence. Hearing officers stressed in their interviews with us that conclusions should be obvious from the reasoning in the summary of evidence and should follow consistently the reasoning used throughout the decision. Ideally, therefore, one could simply refer to previously described evidence to derive the conclusions, and these, in turn, would dictate the contents of the order. But the conclusions were not always thus apparent in the less well-structured decisions.

Conclusions related to interpretation of law.
- The requirements of the law (54; 38%).
- The intent of Chapter 766 (26; 18%).
- The intent of Chapter 766 to place the child in the least restrictive alternative (32; 22%).
- The school's failure to comply with the requirements of the educational plan, either procedurally or substantially (18; 13%).

These statements reflected the hearing officers' desire to clarify the law to the parties concerned. Forty-two decisions included a statement which legally defined the assignment of fiscal responsibility.

Conclusions related to opinions and recommendations.
One hundred thirty-six decisions included the reasoning behind the decision in this section. This is an important category, since it included:

- Assertions that the schools evidently understood the needs of the child and had the capacity to address them (31; 22%).
- Recommendations for cooperation between the parties in the future (29; 20%).
- Claims that both parties were acting in good faith (12; 8%).
- Assertions about the school's attitude, either relating to this case or in general (17; 12%).
- Statements that the public school had not been able to meet the child's needs in the past (18; 12%). Based on their comments in the interviews, hearing officers may have believed this more often than it was specified in the decision.
- The recommendation that the child evaluation team obtain further training (1; 0.7%).

- The personal opinions of the hearing officer about the evidence presented at the hearing (15; 12%). These included statements about the quality or the manner of either side's representation. Hearing officers told us that evidence was often poorly presented but that this was to some extent inevitable at this early stage of the process.

Some statements can be described as directive conclusions, instructing parties on what is expected of them. For example, recommendations:

- for modifications of the plan submitted by the public school, as part of a changed plan of services (41; 29%);
- for further development of the educational plan (29; 20%);
- for re-evaluation of the child (22; 15%);
- for a transfer to a private school (8; 6%);
- for the immediate implementation of the educational plan (6; 4%);
- for family counselling or therapy (4; 3%).

In six decisions, the hearing officer concluded that the evidence presented was insufficient to make a decision. This is a small number, particularly in light of the comments made about the poor quality of much of the evidence presented and the disorganization of the early hearings.

The burden of proof.
This issue was discussed in only six decisions. Hearing officers' views about this issue are discussed in Chapter 13. We note here only the hearing officers' expressed belief that the concept of burden of proof was too complex and legalistic to be explained at a hearing, that it would confuse rather than clarify the issues. In two of these six decisions, hearing officers placed the burden of proof on the parents; in four decisions they placed it on the school.

The Orders, or Outcomes of the Hearings.

Most decisions did not contain a separate section for the order, which was usually part of either the conclusions or the general body of the decision. While hearing officers said they felt the order should be framed as clearly as possible, our raters reported that in fact orders were frequently unclear, particularly in the early decisions. In general, all parts of the decisions became much clearer as time passed. We had difficulty coding these early decisions for outcome, since many did not explictly indicate the contested issues or the hearing officer's specific orders. Based on the statements in the order, the coders were instructed to code "favored parent" or "favored school" only when evident in the decision, and to code "compromise" when the decision did not clearly favor either party. Of our sample, 28% (45) of the decisions favored the parent, 25% (39) the school, 6% (10) favored the parent with modifications proposed, 16% (26) the school with modifications proposed, and 18% (29) were coded as compromise.

Table 14-2 shows a significant increase in the schools' "success" rate in years 2 and 3 in contrast to year 1. Perhaps the first year of Chapter 766 found schools ill-prepared to provide the necessary services for special needs children and/or to present a reasonable case in this quasi-judicial hearing. By year 2 (1975-76), they had evidently improved their special needs services, developed their techniques at hearings, or had become more skilled at writing acceptable educational plans. Hearing officers told us schools seemed to have become more sophisticated in their technique at hearings; one commented that schools were using more "strategy." A pessimistic view often expressed by parents was that the schools had become more practiced at writing convincing educational plans and presenting these plans at hearings but no better at actually providing needed services.

Table 14-2.
Outcomes of Decisions Rendered
in Massachusetts by Year from 9/74 to 3/77

	Total	Pro-Parent		Pro-School		Compromise		No Score	
		No.	%	No.	%	No.	%	No.	%
9/74 - 7/75	42	20	48%	11	26%	9	21%	2	5%
9/75 - 8/76	77	18	23%	37	48%	15	20%	7	9%
9/76 - 3/77*	42	18	43%	17	41%	6	14%	1	2%
	161								

*Year 3 was incomplete, including only those decisions received by 3/1/77.

Summary

The major shortcoming we found in the typical Massachusetts decision was the weak section on findings of fact. This section should lay out those facts presented at the hearing which the hearing officer found relevant to his/her decision. For example, this section might include the child's diagnosis (for example, learning-disabled versus emotionally disturbed), the child's educational history, and the testimony of expert witnesses on the most appropriate education for a child with such a diagnosis and history. Clearly, these are all matters over which parties to a dispute may disagree. Parties must therefore know the basis on which a decision was made, so they can direct their appeals accordingly. (For example, if the hearing officer made a finding that a child was emotionally disturbed, an appellant could specifically take issue with that diagnosis, citing relevant testimony to that effect.)

Hearing officers agreed that a decision should discuss the relevant evidence fully, and should specify the reasons for relying on such evidence. But they disagreed noticeably over whether the decision should include findings of fact. In this sample of decisions, therefore, findings of fact were often left out, or were presented in an unclear manner. Hearing officers seemed unsure of the meaning of the term "finding of fact," as well as of the appropriateness of including such findings in these decisions. Their confusion reflects the difficulty of determining objective "fact" in a special education hearing, where much of the evidence offered is necessarily based on incomplete knowledge, personal opinion, subjective judgment, and hearsay. Under the Massachusetts State Administrative Procedures Act, all such evidence is admissible at a hearing. Any structure for decisions must recognize the difficulty of establishing factual evidence in special education cases.

We found similar shortcomings in the conclusions. This section should show how the facts determined by the hearing officer lead logically to the particular school program mandated by the order. Again, parties need plainly stated conclusions to determine the basis for possible later appeal (for example, "We disagree with the hearing officer's conclusion that a learning-disabled child requires a segregated program.").

Finally, as we have mentioned, the section containing the orders was sometimes unclear, or even omitted entirely. This ambiguity could easily result in an order not being carried out or in another hearing being called to clarify the officer's order. Orders must be clearly stated so both parties can understand what each party is required to do.

It is critical that decisions be written clearly. As a legal procedure, a hearing is subject to judicial review but as educational proceedings, hearings take place without the clearly stated rules that characterize such judicial actions as a trial. The early decisions were particularly unstructured, given the general confusion over what exactly the new law required.

When hearing officers wrote that the major issue was the "inadequacy" or "inappropriateness" of a particular plan, they inadvertently masked many of the component issues in dispute. While some issues may not be easily articulated—for example, concerns about the school's ability to deliver a quality program—such articulation may nonetheless be a very useful first task at a hearing. If the hearing officer began by having the parties specify the disputed issues, either at the hearing itself or at a pre-hearing conference, the hearing could then more clearly focus on the issues in dispute. Greater clarity about the issues in dispute might lead hearing officers to greater clarity in their final orders; with agreement at least on the areas in dispute, both parties might be more disposed to accept the decision, or at least to understand it.

The lack of a clearly stated decision can exaggerate a dispute rather than lead to its resolution. It can engender new disagreements about what the hearing officer actually found and ordered. A clearly structured decision format could help the hearing officer communicate more clearly his/her conclusions and delineate the actions required of both parties, as the hearing officers we interviewed agreed.

A proposed structure for decisions.

The model we developed to rate these decisions seemed adequately to summarize their major dimensions. A finer-grained analysis of a decision's internal logic might have raised many of the substantive issues in special education decision making, but such a project was beyond the resources of this study.

Based on our analysis, we propose the following model for the organization of a decision:

1. *Introduction:* Statement of the law under which the hearing is held; a formal statement of the reason for the hearing; date and place of the hearing; list of the parties present, including their occupations and agencies they represent.

2. *Issues:* Statement of the issues in dispute, as articulated by the parties present. This can be subdivided into main issues and sub-issues, if appropriate, or primary and secondary issues. The issues should reflect the areas of disagreement between the parties and the implications of this disagreement.

3. *Summary of Evidence:* Any written or oral evidence presented before, during, or after the hearing might be included in this section. However, the section should not attempt to summarize all evidence, but only that on which the hearing officer has relied in making the decision and which is therefore pertinent to the subsequent order. Typical relevant evidence includes:

- the educational history of the child;
- a summary of the child evaluation process, and the history of the child's school and independent evaluations, giving dates and results;
- the social history of the child;
- the medical history of the child;
- the psychological history of the child;
- other pertinent evidence presented at the hearing.

4. *Findings of Fact:* A statement of facts which the hearing officer judges to be true and relevant to the subsequent order. These should be accompanied by a statement of the evidence on which each finding of fact is based and by the reasoning behind the finding.
5. *Conclusions and the Actual Order:* The actual order of the hearing officer, clearly stated and accompanied by the reasons for this decision. Any recommendations made by the hearing officer should comprise part of the order.
6. *Formal Compliance Statement:* The courses of action open to each party should there be a failure to comply with the hearing officer's order.

Since the special education reform stresses the importance of informed parent participation, we feel the decision should be written in a non-legalistic format, using non-technical language, so both parents and school officials can understand it. A decision should avoid such legal archaisms as "hereinbefore," "avers," "prayer," and "appellant," which typified one state's published sample decision.

Notes

1. *Statements of Agreement* are made when the dispute is mediated at the hearing and agreement is reached voluntarily. These should eventually be incorporated by the hearing officer into a decision, which has greater legal force. *Preliminary Orders* result from hearings on specific issues, for example, to vacate a summons issued by a school attorney who wished to subpoena certain documents the parents considered irrelevant. A later hearing decides on the educational plan. *Interim Decisions* may be rendered pending further evidence, for example, additional diagnostic testing. *Compliance Hearings* occur when a parent complains that an earlier decision was not implemented. Only one such decision was in this sample, due perhaps to the early stage at which this sample was drawn. Parents also may not have known about this option or have preferred to request a new hearing rather than try to enforce the "outdated" decision.

Section V.

Evaluating the
Due Process Reform

15

Conclusions

Parents' right to participate in the determination of their handicapped child's educational program is a broad-ranging one. As a consumer-advocate based reform, Chapter 766 led parents to expect that they could use the right to appeal an educational plan as a way of expressing dissatisfaction with their child's program. Ideally, parents could use the hearing as a tool to develop appropriate special needs programming for their child.

Our study had two thrusts: to explain the actual functioning of an active special education hearing system, and to understand the consequences of participation in hearings, as viewed by parents, public school administrators, and hearing officers.

Throughout, we were most concerned with whether due process procedural safeguards did in fact involve parents in shared educational decision making for their child. More specifically, we asked whether the appeals option provided a reasonable means for parents to alter their child's program if they felt it was inappropriate. In short, do procedural safeguards—particularly the appeals option—actually produce meaningful parent involvement in their child's special education?

Evaluating the System

Despite the high hopes of those who fought for procedural safeguards, the special education appeals hearing has not functioned as anticipated: it has not achieved its goal of helping parents appeal school programs.

As we have indicated, many parents and schools continued to litigate their disputes long after the initial hearing. This was particularly true for students in out-of-district placements. In these cases, the disputes frequently continued to multiple hearings or to higher-level appeals. Such escalation involved considerable continuing expenses for both parents and school districts, especially when such items as tuition payments and transportation were involved in the dispute.

More distressing is the fact that the schools, in particular, often become obsessed with winning, losing sight of the process's intent: to provide the special needs child with the program most appropriate to his/her needs. School personnel in our study so often became defensive when parents asserted their right to be involved and felt so threatened by the legal proceedings that they frequently personalized the dispute. They failed to remember the purpose of the procedure, losing their professional "cool" and judgment.

The schools' failure to respect parents.

The special education reform was in fact intended to give public schools this comprehensive responsibility by having them coordinate a comprehensive plan of social, psychological, and educational services to handicapped students and their parents with the parents and school staff involved in shared decision making. The predominant impression left by this study is the extreme difficulty school system professionals have in establishing responsive and respectful communication with parents. This is not to absolve parents, some of whom pursue agendas of their own that may not be to the benefit of their handicapped child. There is an abundant literature describing the problems parents have in accepting their handicapped child and cultivating his/her potential for learning and personal growth. It should come as no surprise to teachers and school assessment personnel that parents often have serious difficulties living with their children's handicaps. These difficulties do not excuse professional educators' failure to communicate with parents; rather, professionals must try to help parents address their discomfort while continuing to serve the child. Private schools seemed able to offer such help while public school staff seemed to fail in this area.

The rights accorded to parents under the reform have placed school staff in conflict. On the one hand, they want parents to become involved with their child and to support the school's efforts. Educators decry the detachment of parents who remain uninvolved and do not realistically accept their child's difficulties. On the other hand, when the parents question the thrust or effectiveness of the public school's programs, the same educators tend to resent their intrusiveness, their inquisitiveness, and their assertive concern that their child obtain all possible benefits from the public school. Educators then feel parents should "keep their place," showing proper respect for the school staff's professional judgment.

But professionals know that they do not yet understand all the problems of educating or training special needs children. The most appropriate treatments for many disabilities are not clearly self-evident in this burgeoning area of practice. Given the lack of professional consensus in many instances, parents' insights into their child's behavior become especially valuable. School professionals also tend to forget that parents have to cope with their child day and night outside the cloistered school setting. Parents must deal with their own reactions to having a handicapped child and with their own hopes and aspirations for that child, and school personnel must be oriented to helping them.

Instead, school staff seem so focused on parents' possible assertion of rights and potential resort to appeal, they feel intimidated. They have become so obsessed with the rights granted to parents they ignore the issues which are driving parents' concerns for their child's needs. School personnel have turned parents into fearsome figures rather than viewing them as persons concerned with the progress of their child. Parents who assertively seek the best or most appropriate program for their child are cast in the role of devils, nags, or agitators. Neither the legitimacy of parental concerns nor parents' personal feelings are recognized.

Although they understand in theory that many parents have personal difficulties in accepting their handicapped child, school-based clinicians seem to have considerable difficulty in playing a dual role: to counsel parents while at the same time respecting their concerns. Only when professionals can serve both functions can they build partnerships with parents that will benefit the handicapped child.

The seeds of many disputes, then, are found in the failure of public school staff to listen to and honor parents as partners. Staff tend to become defensive when parents become concerned about their child's lack of progress. Most parents told us they tried to communicate with the school staff but found they could not. They became upset when their evident concern with their child's lack of progress and unhappiness was met with vague or inaccurate assurances ("Your child is making progress") or with accusations that the child's continuing difficulties were caused by "home" or "family" problems. This failure in communication reduced the credibility of the educational plan the parents were offered and seriously impaired the parents' confidence in the staffs' ability to deliver the services described in the plan. Many parents reported it was the alienating contacts with the staff (although usually not the child's actual special education teacher) which turned them toward an appeal or a private school placement.

Poorly managed evaluation and service process.

Poor school-parent communication was not only caused by school staff's lack of respect for parents. The defensive reactions of school staff may also have been due to their sense of having been exposed to criticism because of the way in which their work was structured. For example, in some towns a single staff member was charged with arranging and conducting the evaluations, running the evaluation meetings, writing the educational plan, and negotiating with parents. If the parents contested the proposed plan, this staff member might garner only minimal support from the administration and if a state supervisor reviewed the procedures, the staff member might be singled out for criticism. In other instances, staff members were less aware than parents of special services available in their school system because of poor communication within the system. Sometimes evaluations were conducted by central evaluation teams so overwhelmed by the backlog of work they did not have time to develop working relationships even with the staff members closest to the parents, let alone with the parents themselves.

The significance of the child's progress.

Given these major recurring themes, the "bottom line" for most parents was their child's continued improvement. Parents with children in public special needs programs saw their child become unhappy and resistant to attending school because of frustration in not learning or because of the stigma attached to special education programs. When these parents became concerned, public school personnel tended not to be honestly responsive. When parents talked with independent professionals, they heard about private schools in which children like theirs made considerable academic progress, enjoyed school, and developed more positive self-images. Parents told each other about these private schools. They insisted on public programs that would enable their child to progress in a similar fashion. When these programs failed, were never delivered, or were delivered poorly, parents were drawn to request private school placement. The poor communication and defensive responses of school personnel may have contributed to parents' "radicalization," but their motivating concern was their child's lack of progress, his/her evident academic or psychological deterioration.

Special education appeals will occur, then, even with good parent-school communication, if parents come to feel their child can progress at a better rate elsewhere. Responsive and respectful parent-school communication will minimize appeals, but the overriding consideration for most parents who can afford to appeal is their child's academic and personal growth.

Who Used the Hearings Procedure?

Hearings were disproportionately used by the higher-status parents of learning-disabled children. Only one-quarter of the families in our sample earned less than $20,000 a year, and nearly 40% earned more than $30,000. In our parent sample, 69% of the parents had placed their child in a private school prior to the hearing; 15% were seeking private school placements but kept their child in public school pending outcome of the hearing; and 15% wanted programmatic changes for their child within the public schools. Those who had placed their children in private school before the hearing were generally the most affluent and well-educated.

Among the 49 families with children in private schools at the time the hearing was held, 42 (86%) reported their child was learning-disabled and seven (14%) called their child's primary difficulty "emotional" or "behavioral." Among those who sought private school placements but had retained their child in the public schools, five of the 11 children were said to be learning-disabled, while three were emotionally disturbed. The remaining three children required residential placements. Most of the 11 children whose parents wanted to keep them in public school were mentally retarded or had more traditional physical handicaps addressed by few private programs.

The lower-income nonappellant.

Minority group and low-income families whose children had been evaluated under Chapter 766 were conspiciously absent from the appellant roster of the Bureau of Special Education Appeals (BSEA). To address this issue, we identified parents with special needs children from Boston and three comparable communities who had their children evaluated under Chapter 766 but who did not go to a hearing. One-third of the 57 children in this sample were black and two-thirds white, with one-third from low-income families and the other two-thirds from middle-income families.

In considering the results, we point to two findings of particular interest. First, many of these parents' grievances were not with the inadequacy of the educational plan, nor with the process by which the plan was developed. These seemed abstract concerns to them. Rather, they were unhappy with the inadequate delivery of services to their child. Boston parents in particular were dissatisfied with the quality of services in their children's programs. More than half the Boston parents in this sample felt their child was not making progress, was in the same type of program s/he was in before Chapter 766, and was getting no real education. Parents from the other communities in the sample felt their child was making some progress, but not enough, with some parents saying, "It's too soon to tell."

Second, the parents perceived the exercise of their right to appeal as too difficult. They were too intimidated by the complexities of the educational planning process to further contest the schools' program, even when they believed the school's services were not helping their child. They felt they had neither the psychic nor the economic resources to pursue a formal appeal of their child's educational plan, even when they had the active support of an advocate agency; that the formal appeals system did not provide a timely response, and was relatively ineffective in obtaining the desired changes in their child's program.

Instead, the parents from the smaller communities opted to use political channels of influence within their local school district, or at the local, state, and even federal level. Fifty percent of the parents from these smaller communities who stated their child's needs were being met attributed this progress to their recourse to the Governor's office, the Massachusetts Secretary of Education's office, their superintendent of schools, school committee members, or to the letters they had written to the two Massachusetts senators for assistance.

Many of these parents were upset that the school had not listened to them, making them feel as if they were "a nobody," "a dum-dum," or "stupid." Many, who reported having had their child evaluated several times at their own expense outside the public schools before Chapter 766, also indicated that in every instance the outside evaluator reviewed the findings with them so they might understand them.

Their experience with public school evaluators was very different. They reported the quality of the evaluations to be poor. Evaluators offered little consultation before or after the testing, made few attempts to tell parents what the findings meant; and often failed to include the prior private testing results in their recommendations at the educational planning meeting. In fact, two-thirds of these parents felt the child evaluation team had already drawn up the educational plan prior to the educational planning meeting, regardless of parent feeling or previous private testing. In five of 12 cases in one community, the school ostensibly accepted the evaluation findings and recommendations of the private evaluators, but wrote an educational plan to fit the child into the program the school already had, failing to offer the services the child evaluation team had agreed the child needed.

In sum, working- and middle-class families seemed to have concerns similar to those of upper-middle-class families, but they expressed these concerns differently. Both groups were deeply dissatisfied with the services their child was receiving, and with the school's delivery of those services. But these families seemed more comfortable using familiar political channels for redress, rather than a costly and confusing legal procedure which they found intimidating.

Why Did Parents go to Hearings?

The typical appeal in Massachusetts involved high-status parents with high expectations for their child who had become frustrated by the child's failure to progress in mainstreamed public school programs even with added special education help. They therefore sought private programs that could achieve more effective remediation than the programs their child had already received in the public schools.

Most of these parents had turned to public schools first, but the schools had many new children needing services, as well as some ambivalence about the legitimacy of considering learning disabilities a handicapping condition. They tended to offer these children mainstreamed programs which were less intense and coordinated than the parents felt their child required. Parents became upset over a range of concerns: their perception of their child's continuing difficulties in mainstreamed programs, the frustrations of getting the school to conduct timely and comprehensive evaluations, their perception of school administrators' excessive concern with costs, school personnel's evident resentment of parents and their "demands," and the school staff's inability to communicate with parents in an open and collegial manner.

Although some of these difficulties were undoubtedly due to the rapid expansion of school services, parents interpreted them as reflecting incompetence and a lack of concern. They then looked for other ways to address their child's problems. Independent evaluators often legitimated both their perceptions of their child's needs, and their demands for more intensive and coordinated programming. They found such programs mainly in the private sector.

Higher-income families most readily sought private school placements. By the time a hearing was conducted, 70% of the children from a higher-status family were already attending a private school at the parents' expense. These parents argued that the schools' excessively slow response to their request for an educational plan had forced them to place their children privately, since a new school year was beginning and the child had typically been failing in public school. When these parents won their hearings, the school systems were held liable for the costs of the placement because of the systems' overly slow response. But even if they lost, almost all of these parents kept their children in private schools.

Some states have passed regulations barring a prehearing placement, but this only increases the problem of irresponsibly slow responses to the child's needs by school districts and the appeals system. The state bureaucracy can move at its own speed, with no sense of urgency for the child's situation. It was this situation that resulted in prescribed timelines for local school districts to develop a plan and the state to schedule a hearing and render a decision. But these timelines were often subverted at both local and state levels.

Middle-income families did not have the option of placing their children privately while waiting for a response. With annual incomes of about $20,000, they could not afford private school tuitions without assistance and had to go to a hearing while their children waited in public school. Such children accounted for 15% of our sample.

A two-track system developed. Wealthier parents protected their children from the adverse impact of a hearing by removing them from the public schools, while poorer parents were forced to maintain their children in the public schools during and even after the hearing if they lost.

The parents in our sample found that once they had requested an appeal, the schools did little to negotiate alternative programs. Such behavior was not typical of all school systems; there is considerable evidence that many cases headed for a hearing were settled, frequently at the last minute, after some considerable expenditures of time, money, and worry by the parents. This practice may reflect wide acceptance of the canard that once parents opted for private placements, negotiation was fruitless. In our experience this was frequently not the case. Reasonable bargains can be struck with parents who place their children privately or seek such a placement, but school staff must show sincere interest in parents' concerns and develop responsive programming.

Private Versus Public Schools

The major substantive issues that led parents to appeal were disagreements over the services their children required, the manner in which existing services were offered, and whether these services were effective. Over and above program content, though, parents were upset with the quality of the contacts they had with public school personnel. The schools' failure to negotiate with parents in good faith emerges as a major reason for the parents' alienation from the public schools. Even if public schools were offering learning-disabled children adequate programs, the staffs' frequent assumption of a defensive posture interfered with the development of responsive relationships with parents. Public school staff did not see the parents as clients and resented the parents' attempts to hold them accountable. Administrators were described by parents in particularly harsh terms, while regular "mainstream" teachers were considered unsympathetic. (Special educators were described more positively.) The resulting conflict led inexorably to the adversarial confrontation of a hearing.

This was in marked contrast to parents' generally favorable assessment of private schools. The particular private schools used by most parents in our sample were described as treating the parent respectfully, as a client whose concerns were taken into account. While the focus of the private schools' work was with the child's problems, staffs also worked hard to help parents understand more about their child, shared information with them, and helped parents to address their own feelings about their child's difficulties. Parents who had earlier rejected the public schools' statements of their child's potential lifelong difficulties seemed more accepting of these limitations after they had worked with a private school staff. While such acceptance may have stemmed from the parents' sense of having offered their child the best opportunities to show improved performance, the parents also responded to the staff's attempts to help them understand their child's limitations. An equally responsive attitude to parent concerns by public school staff could have yielded a similarly positive view of public school programs.

Many public school administrators have striven to achieve better communication with parents since these early years, and have expanded their programs for learning-disabled children.

Going to a hearing.

Parents and school personnel entered the appeals hearing with high levels of anger toward each other. Parents typically viewed school personnel as incompetent, insensitive to their child's needs, and manipulatively seeking to subvert their rights as parents. Parents were seen by school staff as illegitimately seeking public special education monies for private schooling. Not surprisingly, the contending parties entered the hearing with a high degree of nervousness about the proceeding. The high costs, the long wait for a hearing, the ceaseless preparation, the anxiety, the adversarial format, the win-lose atmosphere, and the long wait for the decision, all operated to increase alienation and sustain the antagonism.

The need for representation.

While having an attorney or advocate does not necessarily improve one's chances of winning the dispute, most parents in our sample (82%) recommended that other parents should bring an attorney or advocate to a hearing, regardless of whether they themselves had been represented. Parents felt they needed this assistance to manage the emotional strain of the proceeding, to organize their presentation, and to cope with the formality of the proceeding and its emphasis on rules of law. Many parents reported being overwhelmed by the schools' ability to bring many witnesses, the unexpected belligerence and apparent untruthfulness of the schools' presentation, and the sense they were being personally attacked.

Parents said that lawyers acted "as a mediator between us and the school" and "as a counter force to the school counsel." Almost half the represented parents reported that an attorney or advocate "added a feeling of authority to the evidence."

There was considerable variation in the tasks actually performed by advocates and lawyers. Some advocates went so far as to prepare dossiers of testing materials and other documents to present at the hearing, even recommending to parents that additional evaluations be obtained or arranging for such evaluations. Other advocates and lawyers expected the materials to be compiled by parents. Most lawyers made an initial presentation to the hearing officer, though some had parents make such a presentation. Most lawyers and advocates cross-examined witnesses; a few had parents do this. Some lawyers restricted their participation to points in the hearing when matters of law or procedure were in dispute. Despite the high rate of representation in our sample, parents invested considerable energy and effort in assembling the materials required and often in presenting their own cases.

On a very practical note, an attorney who represents parents informed us that in 1981 he represented only one of three parents who solicited his services for an appeal; the others could not meet his fee of $2,000, plus the fees for expert witnesses, added evaluations, etc., required to present a case adequately.

The role of witnesses.
Many parents reported themselves to be at a disadvantage at hearings because they could bring few witnesses while the schools brought many witnesses. Almost 35% of the parents, versus only 7% of schools, brought no witnesses at all to the hearings. Parents tended to rely on the written reports of independent evaluators while school systems brought a broad range of personnel to hearings: special education teachers, diagnostic teachers, psychologists, social workers, and such administrators as special education directors and principals. School administrators, however, complained that the evidence given by the parents' evaluators, who tended to be from prominent local hospitals, clinics, universities, or private schools, was given greater credence by hearing officers than the evidence of school personnel.

The schools' testimony.
Parents were upset by what they felt was the unexpected and dishonest quality of the schools' presentation. For example, one-fifth of our parents claimed that the educational plan presented at the hearing had been changed without notice from the plan they had previously rejected, changes which might have resulted in a prehearing settlement had the parents been informed of it. Some parents noted that the school kept adding elements to their proposed program

as the hearing progressed. One-fifth of our parent sample claimed that schools had falsified the progress of their children. Fifteen percent reported that schools claimed to have lost evidence; whereas parents believed that, in fact, the schools had suppressed documents which might have supported the parents' case.

Parents were particularly distressed over allegedly dishonest testimony on the quality of the school's programming. Many parents had lost faith in the schools, saying that the programs promised in their educational plans had been promised—and not delivered—before. School staff tended to deny this failure of delivery at the hearing, a practice which seemed dishonest to parents already cynical about the schools' promises.

That so many parents interpreted the schools' testimony as dishonest is an indication that the adversarial process had widened the gulf betweeen parents and and schools. This is distressing since it makes future educational planning for the child very difficult.

Results of a Hearing

Appeals hearings often seemed to fail in resolving parent-school disputes. In 13 of 16 cases in which children remained in public schools after a hearing, parents reported continuing conflicts over their child's program. Some complained that the schools did not implement the hearing officers' written decisions, particularly when unusual services were required, for example, physical therapy. As changes in a child's program became necessary, the worsened relationship generated by the hearing process precluded easy consultation. In six of 16 cases these continuing conflicts resulted in additional hearings or court appearances. In other cases parents were dissatisfied with their children's program but felt the appeals process was too costly, too slow, and too traumatic to use again.

For the more affluent families with learning-disabled children, the decision to appeal and go to a hearing also led to continued conflicts. Even when parents won private school cases, more than half of these 34 cases were involved in subsequent conflicts. For example, at the end of each school year, each child must be re-evaluated. If a public school program is proposed again and if parents again reject this proposal, another hearing must be scheduled. For some cases, this occurred for several years. Faced with this situation, some parents chose to pay the tuition themselves; others capitulated and returned the child to the public schools to avoid the continuing controversy and costs. Some school districts failed to pay the required tuition. Others sued to overturn the decision in court, allowing them to withhold tuition payments pending resolution.

The initial hearing, which had been costly in time, expense, and emotional energy, often required substantial additional monies to pay withheld tuitions and continuing legal fees, and might be followed by an annual hearing. Negative feelings between parents and school personnel often escalated over these payment issues. Parents vividly recounted these continuing disputes and their negative impact on themselves, their marriage, work, and family.

Parents who lost their appeal had to confront similar options. They could choose to pay the tuition and other costs themselves, return the child to the public school program, or continue to argue their case annually before a hearing officer. In addition, either party could, and often did, appeal the hearing officer's decision to higher levels: the State Advisory Commission for parents, or the state or federal courts. For many parents, their first hearing was only one step in a long-term battle with the schools.

The Schools View the Hearings Procedure

When we conducted interviews with special education directors we found that many of the administrators who had managed our parents' cases were no longer working in the same school district within one year following the hearing—a 50% turnover rate! The interviews that we did conduct indicated administrators' recognition that the process was traumatic, confusing and demoralizing to school personnel and parents. These administrators often felt their professional judgment had been questioned and their relationships with the parents were severely impaired. Uniformly, school personnel viewed hearings as proceedings to avoid because of their negative impact on staff morale, their drain on productive time as staff prepared for the hearing, the trauma of going to a hearing and having one's testimony and professional competence questioned, and the actual costs in time and legal fees for the hearing.

The Results of the System

In sum, the experiences of the initial users of the hearing process in Massachusetts indicate a profound disillusionment with hearings, even though the participants believed the hearings had been conducted fairly. The adversarial hearing process seemed to inflame rather than reduce the antagonism and led to alienation of the contending parties. The contending parties often returned to their home community to continue their dispute over an ambiguously worded decision that served to stoke rather than extinguish the flames of the dispute.

An average of four years after their initial hearing, about 40% of the children who had attended private special needs schools had eventually returned to public school programs (18 of 44), while 30% had transferred to other private day schools (10) or residential schools (3), either regular or special needs. When the children remained in private schools, some parents chose to opt out of the public system and pay the costs themselves. These children often remained in nonpublic schools for the course of their subsequent educational career.

Given this situation, it is not surprising that some parents were found who, having despaired of the hearing process, took actions that seem to be detrimental to their child. One child was removed from school for one and one-half years while awaiting court review. The parents of a severely language-impaired, nearly autistic high school student removed him from all special services because of the bitter feelings engendered by the dispute. It is easy to criticize parents for such actions, but the fault should more properly be assigned to an appeals process that the parents tried and found wanting.

When children returned to the public schools, it was usually because the child wanted to be reunited with friends, the special education administrator involved in the case had been replaced, the child had improved substantially, or because suitable nonpublic-sector programs were no longer available.

Many poorer parents in the sample, especially those whose children had serious physical and mental handicaps, expressed a low degree of satisfaction with the results of the appeals process, even when they won, because the schools did not seem to be making the changes mandated by the hearing officer and there were continuing conflicts over the program. These parents could not afford either to withdraw their children or to reopen an appeal.

Following up the decision.
A major structural deficiency was the failure to include mechanisms to insure that decisions would be implemented. There was no routine follow-up contact by the hearing officer familiar with the case, nor by any other agent of the state education agency, to assure the school district's compliance with the decision. If the decision was not implemented, the parents had to file a complaint charging noncompliance or institute another appeal, requiring another burdensome and costly initiative.

The Appeals System as an Agent of Change

We have spent much time discussing how the hearing system is not truly accessible to working-class and moderate-income families and how it has often failed to resolve individual grievances. However, the very existence of a hearing system has legitimated parents' rights directly and indirectly benefited many special needs children. Access to appeals and judicial review lends credence to the parents' right to question the programs offered their children, even if few parents actually make successful use of the appeal. An active hearings system pressures bureaucratic/political organizations such as school systems to become more responsive to children's needs. A district's loss of several hearings, especially when high tuitions are incurred, seems to hasten the development of programs to serve many more handicapped children.

Private schools spur change both as immediate costly alternatives to public programs, and as possible models for new public program development. The threat of hearings may be most effective when alternative placements are available in the surrounding area.

The administrative hearing serves as an agent of change. By requiring particular services to meet the needs of an individual child, the appeals system often provides programs and services to other children with similar needs in the community. For example, to avoid a private school placement for one mentally retarded adolescent, vocational training was instituted for that child. That child's classmates also benefited from the program. Likewise, in larger school districts, special needs students in many schools may eventually benefit from the upgrading of services for a single child, as the changes result in improved practices more generally.

This situation was most clearly evident in providing services for learning-disabled children. Our parents reported many school systems did not accept a learning-disability definition of the problems that some children were experiencing, preferring to see these children as emotionally troubled, immature, or simply recalcitrant learners. In early cases, private placements were awarded to parents because of the schools' inadequate evaluations. In some later cases, parents complained that the same diagnoses had been used at the child evaluation meeting, but by the time of the hearing, the school claimed to be offering learning-disability programming. Despite parents' continuing frustration, this represented a considerable progress, as it indicated the schools were developing learning-disability programming to avoid the economic consequences of a private school placement. School personnel felt considerable ambivalence about the concept of "learning disabilities." That population was markedly underserved before the reform. But when hearing officers accepted the claims of these children's needs, including requests for private schools, special classes and new resource room arrangements, schools had to comply. We know of school systems that went so far as to hire private school staff to set up programs in order to satisfy parents and prevent future appeals.

There can be little doubt, for example, that at least partially because of the pressures of having lost a few appeals, school systems in Massachusetts quickly learned to write more specific educational plans for all children. In many of the earliest hearings, private placements were awarded to parents because they were offered insufficiently specific educational plans which failed to state clear objectives for the child or to specify precisely the services to be provided. Schools burdened by private placements quickly learned to write better plans. Later, in fact, we found parents complaining that the educational plan was indeed well written, but the school system had no mechanism for delivering the promised program.

The appeals system further led some school systems to reconsider their entire mode of operation. Following losses at early hearings, some special education directors used these losses to argue for improved local programming and for more effective communication with parents. A lost hearing not only involves an economic loss for the school. The self-image of the school staff and the community image of the school system are at stake, especially in communities which pride themselves on their schools.

However, while the appeals system has had a significant impact on Massachusetts school districts, consumer groups must find a way to broaden this impact. To focus this impact, advocacy groups must learn to use hearings to clarify or expand policy in reference to special education practices. If advocacy groups targeted particular issues in defining service needs, the hearing system could be used as courts are, to define standards by setting precedents for acceptable educational practices.

Insuring Access to the Appeals System

We have seen that poor and working-class parents initiated few appeals. In part, this may indicate their lower educational aspirations: although these parents would like their special needs children to do well in school, poor performance may be more acceptable since other children in the family, and perhaps the parents themselves, may have done poorly at academic work. However, before we accept this type of explanation, we must recognize the extent to which both the educational planning process and the appeals process are biased against working-class families.

Biases in the system.
The evaluation process pits a generally isolated parent against a variety of school specialists, who often attend the child evaluation meeting en masse. This situation can easily be manipulated by school personnel, so that parents feel pressured to sign the educational plan, no matter how faulty. Upper-middle-class parents have the great advantage that their own occupational

and educational status may outrank that of local educators. They may also have the resources and know-how to secure outside consultants to help them face the school system. Working-class parents cannot as easily build the type of support system middle-class parents can construct. Working-class parents who did not use the appeals system would not request a hearing because of the implicit intimidation of the educational planning process, the cost of going to a hearing, and the lack of a support system, as well as the availability of more familiar informal political channels. A public school evaluation process that does not provide support to the parent will be biased against less affluent parents.

The appeals process contains other built-in biases. The affluent parent who places her child in a private program pending the hearing is in a very different position from a parent whose child must continue to attend a local school while awaiting the outcome of the dispute. This second parent often fears that if the child remains in the school, s/he may draw the resentment of school personnel. Further, the parents of children attending a private school have access to the private school's resources in preparing their testimony, and can present a stronger case if private school personnel can report the child is progressing at their school.

The social class bias that is intrinsic to the appeals process is extremely difficult to overcome. Minimally, access to free and experienced legal counsel or educational advocates would provide some equalizing potential for this imbalance of resources. Other necessary support would include free access to school records, funds for independent evaluations, and access to affordable expert witnesses.

Independent evaluations.

Parents of all classes must have access to professionals who can make truly independent recommendations. There may be fewer independent professionals than it might appear. Professional judgments offered by private clinics, practitioners, and schools may in fact be colored by "business considerations." A recommendation to return the child from a private school made by a private clinic or practitioner may be made in response to the public school's request rather than for the child's benefit, though it may not be so stated in the report to the parents or in testimony. Without the services of independent professionals, parents come to perceive the system as rigged against them.

The dollar costs.

Preparing for and attending a hearing is costly in both dollars and emotion. Parents' reports indicate the considerable emotional distress they experienced trying to communicate with school officials, and when this communication failed, having to confront them in an adversarial hearing. There are considerable frustrations involved in negotiating the complex bureaucracy of the schools, a bureaucracy that becomes increasingly antagonistic as the hearing preparations progress.

Out-of-pocket expenses include legal counsel/advocates, expert witnesses, independent evaluations, copying records, and so on. In the group we sampled from 1975 to 1977, the costs of unreimbursed evaluations, lawyers' or advocates' fees, and expert witnesses averaged $381. This figure is too low, however, since over one-third of the families (37%) were represented by free advocates supplied by a private learning-disability school. Another one-third of the families sampled said their costs were about $500, and the remaining third spent more than $500. Lost work time is a hidden addition to these costs.

By 1981, costs were considerably higher. Attorneys who specialize in this area of law charge a usual minimum fee of $2,000, not including such additional costs as additional evaluations, expert witnesses, etc. Schools now prepare more carefully for hearings, requiring in turn more costly preparation by the parents. Parents must substantively document not only the child's lack of progress in the public school program but also the child's potential for improvement in other programs. This requires considerable expert testimony. In effect, the burden of proving the inadequacy of the public school's program has shifted to the parents.

16

Suggestions for the Design of an Appeals System

The System Requires Speedy Hearings and Decisions

An important factor increasing a hearing's emotional cost to families is the long waiting periods between the rejection of an educational plan and a hearing, and again between the hearing and the written decision. In our sample, the wait for a hearing averaged 18 weeks; the wait for a decision averaged 10 more weeks.

The slowness with which the hearing process moved during this period was particularly frustrating to parents whose children were still enrolled in public school programs that parents considered inappropriate. Having decided to appeal the educational plan, these parents experienced difficulty interacting with program personnel and sometimes reported continuing unpleasant contacts. They had to cope with behaviors of school personnel they felt were unreasonable. For example, sometimes school staff sought to test a child further, which parents saw as designed to provide evidence for a hearing rather than to serve any currently useful purpose. In three cases in our sample, parents reported incidents they interpreted as deliberate coaching of their child to report favorably on the program to assessment personnel. Those parents who wanted to place their child in private school sometimes severed all ties with the public school their child was still attending. In other cases, however, parents were anxious about the impact of the dispute on their child's current experiences, a significant concern when the average case took nearly a full school year to be processed.

The speed with which a hearing is scheduled and a decision rendered is especially crucial when the child is in an emergency state, for example, out of school. In these cases, the wait for a hearing results in long absences from any schooling or, at most, minimal home tutoring. At the very least, administrators of a hearing system should be able to set priorities among cases based on the child's current situation, and the system should provide mechanisms geared to a quick response to crisis.

Although long delays have particularly serious consequences when the child is doing poorly in a public school program or is out of school, these delays also hurt families whose children are in private school. For example, some parents have had to finance a second year of private schooling out of their own pockets before a hearing officer ruled on their case. More often, decisions come so late in the school year that the child's annual review of progress and planning for the next year, which comes at about the same time, often rekindles the dispute, regardless of the original decision. Parents will seek to maintain their child in the private placement if the child has been progressing, whereas the school generally wants to recapture the child for a public school program. This generally results either in a subsequent hearing in which the parents try to retain the tuition payments or in parents opting out of the system and paying the tuition themselves.

The Need for a Prehearing Conference

Hearings occur because of disagreements which arise between the parents and the schools. In many instances, these conflicts become exaggerated and could be resolved, or at least clarified, if the parties met with a disinterested third party. When such meetings have occurred in Massachusetts, they have been run by a state-employed mediator. But the hearing officer might also assume this role under the guise of seeking to understand the outstanding issues that will be addressed at the hearing. A prehearing conference would serve several purposes:

1. It could clarify for both parties and the hearing officer the outstanding issues. These may not be evident to the disputing parties since their communication has likely been very distorted, if not outright hostile, for some period of time.

2. The process of focusing the issues might lead each party to a better understanding of the other's position, so that agreements could be negotiated.

3. If not able to complete negotiation at the prehearing meeting, the parties might continue discussion, in the hope of settling their differences informally before the hearing. We have frequently observed this outcome.

4. If the parties wish to take the case to a hearing anyway, the hearing procedures can be explained.

5. An important though little recognized benefit of such conferences would be that hearing officers themselves would come away with a better understanding of the issues in the case, which in turn would help to structure their approach to the hearing. Officers would also come to appreciate the facts that they would be required to judge, and might tell parties beforehand what types of information would be useful to present at the hearing.

The Appeals System Should Take the Responsibility for More Active Advocacy on Behalf of the Handicapped Child

An important function of the hearing officer is to focus testimony at the hearing, making clear to the parties what information is required to decide what the child needs. Officers must learn to depend not only on the information presented by the parents and schools but also on their own efforts to elicit relevant material, based on their prior active identification of the central issues in a case. Such identification in turn requires officers to preview the case records before the hearing, so they can relate issues cited in the prehearing conference to the facts documented in the records. They could then query witnesses to obtain missing information. In many hearings, a complete sense of the child's needs, abilities, problems, and educational situation did not readily emerge from testimony and cross-questioning; the hearing officer should have been able to identify the lacking information and elicit it.

This practice is in fact already required by the agency's guidelines. But many hearing officers eschewed this active role, feeling it would impair their impartiality. While hearing officers should be impartial, we nevertheless believe they must be able to act actively on behalf of the child. The hearing officer must assume an active role in seeking to resolve the dispute, whether by negotiation before the hearing or by actively seeking information during the hearing; it is not enough for an officer simply to judge passively the cases presented at a hearing.

For either a hearing or a mediation, the system's major concern should be with maintaining fairness. We think "fairness" must be defined as the kinds of procedures that would facilitate the hearing officer's understanding so that the decision or agreement can lead to maximum realization of the child's potential. The judicial model, with its impartial—read inactive—hearing officer, is not appropriate for making decisions in a field where there is no general agreement on what programs are best and in an area where each case is so different. Rather than attempting a chimerical "impartiality," the hearing officer must be an active advocate for the handicapped child.

The State Must Follow-up Cases to Assure Implementation of the Decisions

Since parent-school disputes almost always continue even after the hearing, the state must routinely follow up decisions to assure they have been implemented as ordered. Currently, the appeals system depends on parental initiative to assure compliance, placing an undue burden on the parents. The appeals system must be supplemented by an active administrative oversight mechanism that routinely follows up the implementation of the decision. This follow-up might be the hearing officers' responsibility, since they are most conversant with the case.

States should consider the effects of training and background in their selection of hearing officers.

The education, training, and experience of the hearing officer will have much to do with how a hearing system actually operates. Some states use professionals in special education and psychology as hearing officers; others use lawyers. Little is known about the relative merits of each profession. The lawyer who serves as a hearing officer must make substantive judgments not of law (there is little relevant law in this area) but of special educational practices, many of which are ill-defined even for the practicing professional, whereas the professional educator or psychologist has probably had less experience managing a legal proceeding. The two types of officers probably render different types of decisions, but the proportion of parent vs. school wins does not seem to be affected in the two states we examined, Pennsylvania and Massachusetts. We suspect that lawyers may be less able to make specific program-relevant suggestions than a psychologist or educator, while the latter's management of hearings may be more variable than that of a lawyer.

Out-of-district school administrators utilized as hearing officers seem to operate on still different grounds since they are most likely to identify with the viewpoint of the school. Whereas school administrators tended to favor schools, university-affiliated educators and psychologists favored parents in their decisions in one year's tally in Pennsylvania. The Massachusetts experience suggests that a lawyer may be more suited to the hearing officer role, while a social worker-psychologist-educator may operate more effectively as a mediator. Such a role assignment has been established in other states, including New Jersey and Connecticut.

Locus of initiation of the appeal.
States vary in the manner in which the first level of a hearing is initiated and the person by whom it is conducted. An appreciable number of states delegate this to the local school district. There is no data on the differences in effect of local district and state level appeals.

Decisions should be clearly written.
The findings, conclusions, and actions required by the hearing decision must be explicitly understood by both parties. Ambiguously stated conclusions and orders have often inflamed the disputes and required further hearings for clarifications.

The Need for Alternative Dispute Resolution Procedures

The adversarial character of the administrative hearing dictates a conflict stance, a win/lose orientation, that may not be in the best interest of the child. Although hearings must be available to parents who do not feel they can negotiate with the schools any further, negotiation-based procedures seem a more appropriate way to resolve parent-school disputes since they encourage the parties to reach an agreement, rather than to compete for a "victory."

Negotiation is desirable for a number of reasons. First, most children will probably continue their school careers with the staff of the same public school system for some years. For the sake of the child, school and parents should not become locked in adversarial relationships, creating a substrate of mutual dislike and bitterness that might harm the child by impeding constructive parent-school dialogues.

Second, although a hearing officer can help fit a plan to a child's needs at the time of the hearing, those needs may change rapidly and unpredictably. In the absence of comfortable communication between the parents and the schools, future adjustments in the plan may be difficult to effect, again to the potential detriment of the child. Because the disputants must work together on behalf of the child over an extended period of time, procedural options should minimize long-term conflict, whereas hearings seem to inflame it.

In a general discussion of the assumptions underlying negotiating procedures, Fuller (1971) suggests that these are most appropriate when rules of law cannot specify all the answers to a multi-faceted problem. The role of a judge—or hearing officer—is to order parties to conform to rules. A negotiator, on the other hand, tries to persuade parties to agree to an ongoing plan whose rules and content they determine between them. Whereas law operates as a judgment upon acts, the negotiation process is directed toward helping persons with ongoing relationships meet contingencies for which rules may not provide explicit solutions. The central quality of the negotiation is its capacity to reorient parties toward each other by helping them to achieve a new shared perception of their interaction and by assisting in the development of a program acceptable to both sides. If an agreement is reached, it becomes a written document signed by the parties and is presumably implemented by the schools, with parents still having recourse to a hearing or other legal action should the schools renege.

Mediation was recommended by the P.L. 94-142 regulations. In Massachusetts, mediation sessions are available at the request of parents. They are scheduled by a specially trained staff working out of the regional education offices of the state. The mediators contact parents and schools to schedule the sessions within the first week following registration of the parents' rejection of the educational plan. The mediation session generally takes about three hours, as opposed to the more usual six to seven hours for the hearing, which is often continued over more than one day. Mediation involves a minimum of formal exhibits, few or no witnesses, and no cross-examination, although either party may bring counsel or experts to aid in support of their argument. Occasionally mediation will continue for a second or third session, usually allowing the parties to think about the progress that has been made, to obtain additional evaluations, or to visit possible program sites. It may also allow the school to prepare a new educational plan that reflects an attained agreement.

Mediation, like any negotiation-based procedure, involves bargaining, and parents have reported they are uncomfortable about bargaining for services they feel their child has to have. The usual procedure at mediation is for neither side to be accompanied by counsel. Some parents report feeling intimidated by the imbalance of power when they confront school staff alone; the setting of a mediation makes them feel they are supposed to be accommodating when the schools offer alternatives that seem responsive. If the parents are not willing to take their grievances to a hearing, they feel intimidated because they realize they must accept what the schools offer during mediation as the best their child can get. Some parents have criticized this perceived implicit pressure to settle their dispute.

Although active negotiation rather than an adversarial hearing appears to be the procedure of choice, negotiation must therefore be carefully structured to ensure that parents are not manipulated or pressured. The procedure must enhance the reform's intent to guarantee parents' rights, and to develop collegial parent-school relationships.

The key concept in all special education reform should be the developing of alliances between school personnel and parents. Chapter 766 has begun to restructure the relationship between parents and schools, but to realize the reform's latent intent more work must be done. The appeals hearing provides one avenue for parents to exert their power legitimately. The hearings are necessarily an option more easily available to wealthier parents or those with considerable outside support, although their effects extend to children whose parents could not go to appeal. Since many parents may not be able to use the hearings system, alternative systems must be considered—less than ideal, perhaps, but potentially accessible to larger numbers of parents. In a world of continuing pressures on allocating increasingly limited resources, the option to appeal continues to represent an important potential avenue for parents to maintain their status as partners in their child's education.

17

Tips for Schools to Minimize Hearings

The consequences of involvement in a hearing are extremely costly to parents and school personnel, both in economic terms and in intangibles such as family strain and staff morale. Although parents should have access to an appeal if their child's needs are not being met, both parties to a dispute should be urged to pursue a settlement by informal means before turning to a hearing.

In this report, we have shown how parents experience the school's evaluation process and the events that led to appeals. While the reports of parents who have entered appeals may not accurately reflect school practice, they do point out three problem areas.

First, a high proportion of parents said evaluation meetings seemed coercive. They felt that the educational plan had been decided on prior to the meeting, that they were not being listened to, and that they were not accorded a meaningful role in the planning process. Instead, they were being "sold" a plan. Evaluation team members may wish to deny this characterization, but they must still work with parents who have this perception, a perception which is supported by studies in other states.

Second, parents reported few attempts to negotiate with them after a planning meeting. Some were simply not contacted to see if they were satisfied; others wanted to deal with a school official who seemed impartial and could provide a fresh perspective but felt no such person was available to them.

Finally, parents told us that school systems were extremely disorganized as they began to implement Chapter 766. For example, we were told regular and special education personnel rarely communicated with one another and, therefore, produced fragmented programs for children. Also, as the educational plan was being developed, parents were frequently given contradictory information by classroom teachers and evaluation personnel, by administrators and evaluators, or by principals and district-level administrators. These reports indicate that school systems have experienced severe difficulties in developing a coordinated work pattern among the different kinds of school personnel who have traditionally worked in isolation.

Partnerships with Parents

Clearly, schools need help in developing structures that can effectively individualize programming for handicapped children. School personnel should work to establish relationships with parents, trying to understand their grievances and helping them to deal with their anger toward the school's prior programming. Positive relationships with the parents should be cultivated not only to avoid the acrimony of a hearing, but also to develop arrangements for school staff and parents to work in concert, supporting each other's efforts. Schools must recognize that input from parents can be vital in creating an effective program for the child. They need to work more effectively to elicit parent concerns about their child early in the evaluation process, when assessments are being decided upon.

1) One critical recommendation of this report is that schools develop *inservice training programs* to help their staff learn to work more effectively with parents. School staff must become less defensive in responding to parental inquiries and complaints and more skilled in viewing the parents as both partners and clients. They must learn to respect parents' opinions while helping them to cope with the frustration and confusion inherent in living with a handicapped child. Parents can offer unique insight into the nature and character of their child's problems, insights which must not be dismissed out of hand.

2) School administrators should develop *early warning systems* to flag parents who have special grievances or anger toward the schools or difficulty in accepting their child's handicapping condition. Evaluation team leaders must be able to identify early on cases in which the relationship with parents is not proceeding amicably and should have

formal mechanisms by which to alert others in the system to potential problems. These difficulties may stem from parents' bitter memories of poor prior relationships with a particular school staff member or from a variety of other causes, for example, parental anger about having a child with a handicapping condition, initial miscommunication with the school, etc. School staff should not take these difficulties personally, but should simply attempt to solve them. Staff should recognize that sometimes another professional needs to talk with parents to understand their unhappiness with the evaluation team proceedings. This person may be from the school department's staff or from outside it but should be far enough removed from the dispute that parents can trust him/her. Staff's intent at all times should be to improve the parent-school relationship, using professional restraint to avoid becoming personally involved in bitter disagreements.

3) School staff need to *spend more time with parents* before educational planning meetings *to explain test results* so that parents are prepared for the meeting. In one community, parents are mailed assessment information a week prior to the meeting; the special education director told us this allows parents to be more comfortable at meetings and to participate more fully. They may also call school staff for explanations in the interim. These local innovations should be offered as models to other school systems that are trying to improve their practices.

4) *Parent visits to the program proposed for the child* make good sense since parents can then see more concretely what is being offered. But frequently, a program will be serving children with an array of problems, and parents may be disturbed by having their child associate with some children included in the program. *School staff must accompany parents* on program visits to help parents understand what they see.

5) School systems must develop *quality control systems* to ensure that written educational plans include the necessary information and conform to what parents were told at the meetings, that the programs described are appropriate for the child, and that they are implemented.

6) *Schools must follow up families* that do not return signed educational plans, and find out why the plan was not returned. If parents are unhappy with the proposed plan, school staff should be ready to discuss the reasons for what was proposed and, if necessary, negotiate other solutions. In short, they must understand the role of and the need for a positive parent alliance and learn how to cultivate it.

7) Schools that are frequent participants at hearings must *develop data* on the effectiveness of different programming options for children with specific types of special needs, and these schools should be encouraged

to institute *ongoing assessments* of the effectiveness of their programs. Otherwise, schools have no objective data either to reassure parents or to present with their case at hearings. Self-assessment procedures are available or are easily devised. Such evidence will become more important as hearings increasingly focus on the quality of programming and less on procedural errors.

8) Schools, as well as parents, need to learn to *control their resentment* more effectively at hearings and present an organized and coherent account of their case. Experienced lawyers and advocates seem to help schools and parents to organize and manage a coherent presentation at hearings.

Serving the Learning Disabled

In addition to the problems of organizational change, important questions are raised by this study concerning school services for learning-disabled children. We found that the parents who appealed were rejecting mainstreamed, resource-room programs and selecting full time programs. (See Chapter 9.) School personnel have been given little guidance as to when such segregated placements are appropriate and for what types of children.

Given the high levels of satisfaction expressed by parents with segregated, full-time learning-disabilty programs, educators must begin research to describe these programs and evaluate their effectiveness. Only three private schools were used by most parents in our sample, and these schools do share a particular viewpoint on the treatment of learning disabilities. They also have a local reputation of great success with these children. Although little or no data are available to support parents' claims of their children's success in these schools, parents dissatisfied with public programming did express strong satisfaction with their child's progress there. In addition, many prestigious clinical professionals have a low regard for much public school programming for handicapped children, especially in areas of learning disability and for severe or multiple handicaps requiring specialized staff or facilities.

If these private schools are as effective as the parents in our sample claim, researchers must examine their practices to see what can be used in a public school program. Such research would include attention to the characteristics of the children who have been helped most successfully and would be designed to help public school staff make more informed programming choices for the learning disabled. It could also help educate hearing officers about the types of children likely to be helped by particular options.

18

Tips for Parents
Who Go to Hearings

This report should provide encouragement to parents and consumer groups. There can be little doubt that an active appeals system is a new and powerful resource that can be used to promote educational change, particularly when there are alternative techniques and institutions that hearing officers can select to serve children.

Special education reform places heavy demands on parent and consumer groups. We have seen that parents need help at child evaluation meetings to understand what is being presented, to ensure that their views are made known, and to withstand the social pressures inherent in the situation. In Massachusetts, some more affluent families routinely employ lawyers to deal with the schools. The State Office for Children has offered limited advocacy support to poorer families, as do various advocate agencies. Comprehensive advocacy services, offering experienced help to families at all stages of the planning and appeals process, must be available if working-class and even middle-class families are to have access to the system. Presumably, such services must be state-supported. Working-class communities are especially unlikely to use the special education reform to protect their handicapped children unless advocacy support is available.

This study has investigated the outcomes of specific appeals cases. However, our data suggest that the appeals process has broader effects: it is an important quality control mechanism; it judges the adequacy of school programming and then imposes meaningful negative sanctions for poor performance. Our impression is that this function of the appeals system has had considerable impact on learning-disability programs in public schools. When hearing officers can mandate costly private tuitions, public schools become motivated to change their practices and prevent appeals. In disputes where children remain in public programs after a hearing, the decisions probably have less effect on the system, since there are no mechanisms to insure implementation of the decision. Our policy recommendations earlier in this chapter would move the appeals system towards greater involvement in school decision making and, we hope, would strengthen the impact of the appeals system on the quality of services for all handicapped children.

We offer parents the same advice we have offered the schools: try to avoid an appeals hearing! The costs, in money and emotional distress are high all the way through the process. In too many of our cases, hearings created more acrimony than resolutions. Negotiate the dispute, if at all possible. In many difficult cases in our sample, a history of poor relationships between parents and the school district exaggerated the substantive issues. A reasonable negotiator listening to both sides, who tries to minimize the highly charged feelings involved, can be useful in clearing the air and helping the parties find solutions to the outstanding issues. Hence we have suggested that the schools develop early warning flagging procedures to identify parents who are unhappy with the schools' activities, and that the schools provide some disinterested third party to talk with the parents, whether this party is from inside or outside the schools.

Parents must be ready to negotiate program and service issues, though they must be careful that the compromises they make will not prejudice the progress of their child. They will need advice and help, in an uncertain area, about what they feel they can concede. In discussing mediation, parents have told us they felt uncomfortable during these negotiations. They felt they were being asked to compromise to reach an agreement, without feeling the school was equally willing to compromise. Given the imbalance of power and resources to pursue an appeal, they felt keenly the implicit pressure to settle the dispute at the cost of their child's best interests.

Parents must be prepared for the complexities of the child evaluation process; throughout they will face numerous decisions, often with too little information. Given the state of the art of special education knowledge, there is no guarantee that the program selected by the school will in fact be the most appropriate for their child. One is always in a best-guess situation, where "success" is governed mainly by the child's sense of satisfaction and progress. There is one caution that parents can appreciate: for some children progress can be exceedingly slow.

The parents' responsibility begins with following their child's progress, by reading his or her schoolwork, attending teacher conferences, and monitoring reactions to and progress in school. If the parents perceive a problem, they should discuss it with the classroom teacher, looking for evidence that the teacher has some grasp of it and is seeking a means to address it. Explanations of the child's behavior using concepts such as laziness, daydreaming, tiredness, or immaturity are not helpful in formulating a specific remediation program. When the teacher's explanation is vague, the parent should ask for specific illustrations. If a teacher offers an educationally specific diagnosis and suggests what might be done in the classroom and school to help the child cope with the identified problem, parents should initially support these efforts. The evaluation process for services under the special education act is cumbersome and time-consuming, but the teacher suggestions that we have described can be implemented relatively quickly and are often all that is needed. Also, it is our impression that there often is a stigma attached to special education instruction, particularly at middle and upper grade levels, among both peers and staff. If well thought out modifications in programming at the local school level are sufficient, these are preferable. Unfortunately, school staff are not always willing to consider options flexibly; often they see their major option to be referring the child for special services, rather than trying out modifications.

When teachers cannot specify the problem, parents can suggest to the teacher or principal that a school specialist observe the child and offer programming suggestions. This observation can be done informally, and need not be part of the formal child evaluation process.

If the teacher indicates a more formal child evaluation is necessary, s/he probably feels that the child needs some special services. At this point, we suggest that parents thoroughly read the laws of their state, the administrative regulations of their state department of education, and any information provided by the school system. Know the process you are getting into, from the very start.

If the teacher does not suggest an evaluation and, over time, the child seems not to be progressing, parents can request an evaluation. Parents should already have begun to collect examples of the child's work assignments, notes of previous teacher conferences, and any other material which illustrates the child's problem. Just as laws for handicapped children require the school to keep extensive records, so should parents learn to keep these records: detailed notes of every meeting, conversation, and evaluation throughout the pre-evaluation, evaluation, and educational planning process.

Parents must agree, in writing, to have their child evaluated. Before giving their approval, parents should insist on meeting the chairperson of their child's evaluation team. Ask what problems are suspected, what information the proposed evaluation procedure will add to the school staff's understanding about these problems, who will be doing the evaluations, and when. School systems tend to provide a standard assortment of evaluations to all children, regardless of the child's suspected needs; for example, intelligence tests seem to be routinely offered even when evidence of adequate intelligence is available. Parents should agree only to evaluations geared specifically to their child's suspected problem. During the evaluation process and before a formal educational planning meeting, the parents should also have the opportunity or ask for the opportunity to discuss in detail their perceptions of the child's needs, either with a social worker or the chairperson of the evaluation team.

To prepare for the child evaluation meeting, parents should request that the results of all evaluations be sent to them in advance, so they are not surprised by the findings and are able to respond to them in a meaningful way at the educational planning meeting. This is a good educational practice that most schools neglect. If the evaluation results are confusing or disturbing, parents can return to the schools for clarification before the formal meeting or can attempt to get help from outside professionals.

Do not attend an educational planning meeting alone. At the very least, both parents should attend, so that a clear recollection can be developed after the meeting as to what occurred. You may also want another parent who has already been through the process to attend the meeting with you. A friend or neighbor or someone recommended by a local association for special needs children may be available. A professional child advocate can be a knowledgeable and useful support, if a good one is available.

The educational planning meeting is an opportunity to discuss fully and frankly your child's difficulties and how they can be constructively addressed. It is not an appropriate forum for expressing any grievance toward the schools you might hold, for attacking the concern or competence of school personnel, or for developing an adversarial stance toward the school system. Parents should be there to focus on the child's needs and on the services that will help the child. It may be difficult not to express disappointment with the school's earlier programming for your child, but it is not constructive to dwell on prior failures unless you feel the school, based on your past experiences, is not capable of fulfilling its promises. Take a person to the meeting who can listen with you, who can help you express your views, who can help you ask the questions you wish addressed, and who can help develop a cordial atmosphere rather than a confrontation.

At the educational planning meeting, school personnel should be able to offer specific detailed characterizations of your child's problems in lay person's language so you can understand them. They should discuss with you what specific services and programs they are recommending to address those needs, again, in language you can understand. If the language is loaded with jargon and you can not follow their presentation or the subsequent discussion, you should feel free to ask questions and try to have the school staff explain their findings and program ideas so you can understand them. A good test of a child evaluation meeting is whether the child they are talking about sounds like your child. If not, it is time to begin asking questions.

Ask the staff with what degree of certainty they understand your child's needs and difficulties, whether other kinds of tests are available to clarify their understanding, and whether these should be given at the present time. Ask how staff plans to determine whether the remediation is effective, and at what intervals, so you can know that changes in the program will be made as they seem necessary and that some person is charged with monitoring the appropriateness of the program for your child.

When a program is recommended, parents should ask what the school's experience has been with children with similar problems in the same program. How successful have the teacher and the program been and for what types of special needs? Schools have considerable difficulty addressing this issue systematically. They are often so unwilling to collect information about children's performance, even if such information has only to be compiled from existing files, that they cannot provide support for their claims for the program. Nor can they indicate the probable course of the child's subsequent school career. Nonetheless, parents should be able to ask if, in the staff's experience, other children with these needs continued to require ever more intensive services. How long, on the average, did such children stay in the program being recommended? What was the usual course of their activity? Do children with these problems usually return to regular education programs? Do they later require no, or reduced, special help? How do they fare in subsequent years? What continuing difficulties do they struggle with?

When parents assert at hearings that their child cannot succeed in the program the school is offering, the schools cannot address these statements with data because they have not compiled the data already in their files. Yet, in Massachusetts at least, the regulations for Chapter 766 require each district to "establish a system of evaluating the [effectiveness annually of] special education programs it provides or arranges to have provided ... [including] a method for determining which programs are successful and which are unsuccessful in helping the children . . . achieve the goals set . . . in their [individual] education plans"."Whenever more than ten percent of the children . . . assigned to a particular program do not achieve . . . those educational goals for which the program is responsible," a district must make the necessary corrections in the program.

We have found that school systems faced with a child experiencing moderate to severe difficulties tend to load the child with extensive specialized services, thereby isolating him/her in special settings, rather than trying to modify the regular classroom to accomodate his/her needs. No firm evidence has yet established whether services delivered in special education settings are more effective than services delivered in regular classroom situations. Therefore, parents must look for evidence in the plan of close coordination among the specialists, the special educators, and the regular class teachers, regardless of where services are delivered. "We all get along fine together" is not a sufficient response. Lack of coordinated and mutually supported delivery of services is probably one of the weakest aspects of public school programming.

After the planning meeting, parents should expect a detailed educational plan in the mail which reflects the joint discussions. If parents have any questions, they should feel free to contact the evaluation team chairperson for further discussion. It is also good practice to visit the proposed program, insisting that a member of the child evaluation team accompany you on the visit to explain why the program is suitable for your child. Parents should meet the specialists who will work with their child.

After amicable meetings with the chairperson of the evaluation team to discuss any difficulties with the educational plan, parents can suggest that a further evaluation is required, if necessary. The laws make the schools responsible for payment, although parents should check on the exact procedures the school requires to arrange for the independent evaluation. An independent evaluation means the professional does not work for the schools and maintains an independent stance toward the child and family situation. If possible, avoid professionals who have frequently been involved in adversarial situations with school personnel, so that he or she is not seen by the school as "pleading the parent's case." The purpose of an independent evaluation should be to get more useful information on the child's needs, not to "build a case." Our advice would be to select a leading hospital, clinic or institution in your community, if possible.

In some instances, legitimate disputes about a child's programming will arise, no matter how careful parents have been to maintain a cordial tone nor how honest the school staff's communication process. To the extent possible, such disputes should be mediated. A state-employed mediator (in some jurisdictions) or an independent professional who attends a meeting with you and the school staff may facilitate negotiation of the outstanding issues.

When You Do Choose to Go to a Hearing

When the dispute cannot be mediated or negotiated informally, parents have the obvious option of formally rejecting the educational plan and requesting a hearing. Some tips for parents are:

1) Keep notes on statements and agreements made in your contacts with school personnel, whether teachers, psychologists, special educators, guidance counselors, social workers, or others.

2) Obtain and keep copies of all reports that were made on the child, whether they were done by school staff, private professionals, or clinics. You are entitled to copies of all reports and records from school staff, free of charge or at a minimal cost upon request.

3) If you are seriously preparing for a hearing, you will probably want a lawyer experienced in this area or an advocate trained to work with parents in special education cases. As we have indicated, an experienced lawyer or advocate will help you first to evaluate the strengths and weaknesses of your case. S/he should be able to help you estimate your chances of winning the case, given your child's situation and the outstanding issues. If there seems to be some reasonable chance to win, and you choose to proceed, counsel will help you to organize the materials you have accumulated, help you obtain the records you may be missing, and be able to recommend experts who can help you evaluate the elements of the case you must present to maximize your chances to win at the hearing. The attorney should also be able to help you control displays of emotion in the face of what may seem like bitter personal attack from the schools.

4) The case you present at the hearing must be well organized: you must know what arguments you wish to make to substantiate why the program you are requesting will be more appropriate for the child than the program proposed by the school. The information presented should be focused to substantiate the argument you are making. As a general rule, a dispassionate, organized presentation is more desirable than emotional outbursts, though as we have indicated in Chapter 12, some types of "emotionalized" testimony have been effective in strengthening the argument. For example, some children's testimony can be extremely effective in portraying their experience in a particular program. Lawyers and advocates serve their most important function in organizing the presentation, and orchestrating it at the hearing.

Once they are committed to the adversarial system, parents may wish to have independent evaluations and expert witnesses to testify on particular aspects of the case. Experts may be available from clinics or appropriate university departments, although potential conflicts of interest from their various past and future relationships with the schools must be kept in mind when the parents solicit their help.

More specific tips are available in Bateman's "So You're Going to Hearing" (1980). Though written most clearly for the school administrator planning to respond to an appeals hearing, it is a simply and clearly written guidebook, which can be useful to parents and school administrators alike.

Developing an educational plan can allow parents and school personnel to develop mutually supporting relationships to the benefit of both—and of the special needs child. But the planning process must be a cooperative sharing of information about the child, not a confrontation between opposing forces. As the material in this book documents, confrontation almost invariably works to the detriment of all parties, whereas negotiation permits parents and schools to cooperate in the best interests of the child.

19

Special Education Appeals: The Last Three Years in Massachusetts

by Carol Kervick
Director, Bureau of Special Education Appeals Massachusetts Department of Education

Introduction

The appeals process is the most visible, controversial, and negatively perceived aspect of Chapter 766. Although fewer than 1% of the parents of handicapped children reject individual education plans and fewer than .3% pursue a hearing in any year, this is the forum in which the tensions of implementing the law surface most visibly. From my vantage point as director of the Bureau of Special Education Appeals in Massachusetts, I have seen played out in the cases many of the tugs of war that prevail today for special and regular education. Sometimes the tensions produce creative solutions and positive change results. In other cases roadblocks unanticipated by the framers of the law arise and are found impenetrable. Such cases tend to juxtapose social, political, and fiscal issues that are in fact insoluble within the hearing forum.

That the intended benefits of social reform do not always reach the beneficiary is nothing new to social science policy or research. Nor should we be surprised that Budoff and others (Daynard, 1980; Yurchack, Bryk & DeSanctis, 1982) who have focused their microscopes on due process in special education have found discomfort, disenchantment, and disillusionment among all participants, including the decision makers. Citizens have mythic, as well as realistic, expectations of the appeals process, which embodies some of the central tensions in special education. For example:

- fiscal vs. humanitarian concerns;
- the perceived superiority of private over public education;
- parent participation weighted against professional judgment;
- "more is better" services as opposed to "least restrictive" placement;
- the expanding role of schools in treating the broad array of social problems that affect children and families;
- the lawyer/educator miscommunication;
- the abdication of other human service systems, or their inability to respond as resources dwindle;
- the differences among experts about what special education is, what it can do, and what it can only guess at;
- the role of the courts as the ultimate arbiters of these many different issues.

To address these issues, I offer an impressionistic update of the due process system in 1982, in light of the latent tensions inherent within such a system, and the efforts of hearing officers and mediators to cope with them.

One must say at the outset that the appeals process is perceived as a more monstrous *bete noir* than it really is. The visible controversy of hearings tend to allow its critics a larger audience than they would otherwise merit. And those who complain the loudest, even the best and brightest, may have ceased thinking about the question.

The participants in special education disputes tend to have unreal expectations of vindication. To some degree, these disputes are nurtured by abstract societal notions of "justice" or naive perceptions of "the law" as viewed on television. What the "due process" system actually offers—a forum which compels a fair decision based on the facts—most participants are unable to comprehend or accept. Most parents and school staff are unaccustomed to the confrontational approach of a hearing. And most are unprepared to buttress their opinions with facts. No matter how justified one's cause it must be supported by "substantial" evidence or "a preponderance of" the evidence. The forum that seeks to resolve these disputes is a legal one, and the decision will be based on the facts elicited. The issues to be resolved were those not susceptible to "good faith," "cooperation," "understanding," and "flexibility." Now "facts," organization, and argument must prevail. Magic is not part of the process.

A cursory look at the statistics reveals that the vast majority of Massachusetts cases are resolved through voluntary mediation to a degree similar to most civil suits, through the services of a trained mediator provided by the Bureau of Special Education Appeals since 1976. Over 95% of the parents rejecting an individual education plan avail themselves of this service. Despite these rather dramatic figures, there has been, until recently, little interest at the federal or state level in studying the benefits of a process less threatening, less costly, less adversarial, and more effective than an adversarial hearing. Organized groups of both parents and educators have resisted mediation, fearful of being "pressured" into compromises they would not otherwise make.

The myth that a court or a hearing officer will magically arrive at "the truth" or the "right" decision persists. In fact, a court or a hearing officer faces stringent limitations. Many of these limits are inherent in any formal legal process; some are peculiar to special education disputes. My own experience leads me to highlight a few:

- A hearing officer cannot change attitudes.
- A hearing officer cannot resolve the theoretical or methodological disputes rampant among special education experts.
- A hearing officer will usually find for the party who presents the most cogent, factually based case. But because the quality of representation may be as influential as the case's actual merits, hearing officers will take an active role in pursuit of all the pertinent facts.
- A hearing officer generally will not deal with hidden agendas and motivational issues.
- A hearing officer cannot resolve social policy issues that are not within his/her authority.
- A hearing officer is only human and cannot perform "Solomon-like" tasks.

To recognize these limitations, however, does not call into question the validity of the process. Hearing officers have broad authority to improve the quality of special education for handicapped children. Perhaps more than others, they have an overview of the state of the art in Massachusetts and as a result have an ability to measure "quality" issues. Because Massachusetts employs full-time hearing officers, they hear expert testimony two or three times a week. They become adept at identifying the less credible opinions and able to perceive the gaps and weaknesses of a case. Some of the strengths of the process are:

- Hearings do bring finality to disputes when all other efforts have failed.
- Hearings refine and clarify legal issues that are unresolved by regulation.
- Hearings give parties their "day in court," which allows them some catharsis.
- Parties are more able to accept a decision if the process is fair and the hearing officer impartial.
- Hearing officers, because of legal training and immersion in the area, are skilled at resolving extremely complex and difficult issues.
- Hearing officers will actively pursue the best evidence regarding the child's needs. This is particularly important when there is an inability on one or both sides to adequately present their case.

Courts must ultimately deal with constitutional, statutory, or regulatory issues raised by radical changes sought by new legislation, such as special education. In my view, the most positive benefit of the hearing system is that it makes educational decisions subject to question, that the public role in education is open to some degree of accountability and that decisions are available for close scrutiny.

The role of legal counsel.

Massachusetts brings at least as much legal sophistication to special education disputes as other states. Because of the nature of the process, most parents and school districts in 1982 feel they need legal representation at the hearing. Parents who cannot afford attorneys' fees may seek legal assistance from a trained group of attorneys or advocates in this state whose services are free or at low cost.

Some 30 to 40 Massachusetts attorneys can reasonably hold themselves out as experts in special education law. This cadre of expertise weeds out cases less likely to win and those mainly driven by hidden agendas and personality conflicts. Administrators and parents are apt to be well informed of the risks and expense of an appeal and are more likely to base a decision to appeal on the value of a case as novel or as precedent. Even though administrative decisions technically do not create legal precedent, the perceived reality in the community is otherwise. If a parent of a severely handicapped child is successful in an appeal for a 12-month program, the next day 20 other parents are likely to be on the doorstep of the special education administrator demanding the same.

The 1982 Prototypical Cases

Simple straightforward cases are a distant memory. Some of the themes are the same but the stakes are higher and the cases developed with more complexity. Between 1974 and 1982 the various forces were successful in improving public special education programs. The mediation process has successfully dealt with miscommunication, hidden agendas, and non-compliance, resolving 65% of the rejected independent education plans in this forum, thereby weeding out the less complex cases. Those cases which do surface at a hearing present more unique handicaps, raise subtle legal and factual questions, and involve major battles over fiscal versus humanitarian concerns.

A Current Easy Case: The Climate and the Participants

An observation of a recent hearing:

> The witness testifying is the tutor for a 15-year-old adopted Vietnamese-American boy who is identified as having moderate to severe learning disabilities and emotional problems. When the court stenographer interrupts the testimony to clarify a point, the witness says that his heart is beating very fast. Although his demeanor is confident and "relaxed," it is clear that he feels very nervous. His responses to questions are definite. He seems direct and honest, yet one cannot help but wonder if the situation is as black and white as he paints it.[6]

> As the witness continues, I observe the mother's expression change from sadness—hearing about the boy's degree of disability—to consternation to confusion to anger, as the two attorneys battle over procedure. There are 17 people in the room. The hearing officer and a court stenographer are at the head of the table; the parents, their attorney and five of the seven witnesses they will call to testify are on my right. To my left are seated the attorney for the school and six of the seven school witnesses.

The school system has a national reputation for excellence. The private placement preferred by the parents is also well regarded. Both sides offer expert witnesses; for the parent, a psychiatrist and various private school teachers testify. Dr. P.'s manner is assured, low key, and reasonably vague. The younger teachers, by contrast, are intense, sensitive, and articulate, but often irrelevant. Some are clearly enjoying the experience, once over their initial anxiety.

The public school administrator is knowledgeable, competent, direct, and somewhat brusque. He evokes open hostility and anger from the parents. The mother, who has a doctorate in psychology, suddenly interrupts the testimony, stating accusingly, "You never told us that, Dr. S." She is taken aside by her attorney and reminded that she will have a chance later to rebut whatever is said. Only this once during the hearing does the undercurrent of hostility rise to the surface. At all other moments in this two-day hearing the persons present are controlled and low key—except for the attorneys, who engage in jousting from time to time. This behavior seems as much for show as to make a legal point, and occasionally so exaggerated as to provoke laughter.

A witness testifies about an appealing aspect of the child's personality and everyone smiles. But much of the testimony is repetitive and boring. One witness knits. Other school witnesses pass notes to each other and to the school's attorney. The parents are suspicious and concerned about the note passing but say nothing.

Today's cases are marked by a far higher level of sophistication on the part of attorneys, witnesses, and hearing officers. Levels of hostility and lack of trust have become even more intense. Court stenographers are sometimes hired by both parties, on the apparent assumption that the case will go to court no matter what the outcome. Tension is high, in part because of the fiscal impact of a decision in a community that may already have laid off many teachers and other municipal employees. The number of witnesses has increased, as has the quality of their testimony. Both parents and schools call primarily experts as witnesses, and both sides have had independent experts evaluate the child.

Fiscal Costs and Interagency Collaboration Cases

Although fiscal issues have always been the hidden motivation of some appeals cases, in the past there was little or no attempt to present arguments or introduce evidence of budgetary problems. Not so today. The passage in 1980 of a referendum question (Proposition 2 1/2) severely restricting the taxing powers of local communities and also removing budget-setting authority from the school boards has had a moderate to severe impact on school financing. Concurrently, the abdication by human service agencies of any role in the provision of related services (psychotherapy, residential placements, care for the severely retarded) escalates as state and federal cuts impact on all agencies. Clearly, the framers of state and federal law did not foresee this fiscal belt-tightening. An illustrative case:

> *Interagency Cooperation: Chrissy's Case.* All six experts called by the various parties (school system, state departments of Mental Health, Education, and Welfare, and the parent) agree that Chrissy, 14, is a legally blind, at least partially deaf, multi-handicapped young woman whose autistic-like behavior accompanied by seizures and violent episodes dictates a 24-hour, highly structured residential placement where intense behavior modification can be implemented. At issue are the extent to which the various agencies are fiscally responsiblee for the program and the inability of the agencies to place Chrissy, in part because there is no guaranteed source of funding. Legal and political issues dominate this hearing. Although interagency cooperation is exhorted in statutory rhetoric, little cooperation exists in reality.
>
> Chrissy is currently not receiving any services. She is housed in an adult ward of a state mental hospital.
>
> The attorney for the school committee speaks first: "What Chrissy needs goes far beyond current or traditional notions of 'education.' Clearly, the legislative intent was not to make schools the health, education and welfare agency for all persons 21 and under. There are limits to education and the hearing officer must draw them in this case."
>
> The other attorneys argue that the schools are required under the law to produce the range of services demanded for Chrissy by the parent. The hearing officer must offer a decision that no statute, regulation, policy or interagency agreement addresses.

Clearly, neither Chapter 766 nor P.L. 94-142 intended to shift the responsibility for providing *all* children's services to school districts. Both statutes recognize that handicapped children are likely to require assistance from a variety of public agencies. In fact, the concept of shared responsibility, shared funding, and shared service delivery is a theme that permeates all legislation dealing with the rights of handicapped persons. The dilemma that manifested itself in many 1980-82 hearings is the discrepancy between the ideal "concept" and the reality. Handicapped children are *entitled* to special education and related services from the state or local education agency, whereas they are only *eligible* for services from other agencies. As a result, Chrissy's parents are forced to argue that the school district is responsible for all of the services required by their daughter. What the school committee has not yet been able to achieve through negotiation—a cost-sharing arrangement (where they would pay the day costs and the Department of Mental Health would pay the rest)—they ask the hearing officer to order. However, the hearing officer's authority extends only to the local and state education agencies, regardless of how sympathetic he or she may be to the fiscal, humanitarian, and policy issues in the case. The agonizing process of analysis begins and the hearing officer strains to categorize the services as "education" or "habilitation." She writes, in an attempt to deal with the dilemma:

> The needs of Chrissy are of a severe and chronic nature, are complex, are demanding and dependent on the expertise of professionals in mental health, education and medicine, among others. To attempt to classify the service requirements as all mental health, all education or all medicine is to ignore the needs of the individual and the expertise that must be brought to free her from isolation and imprisonment. To pretend that such complex problems can be facilely resolved leads to bureaucratic decisions that allocate responsibility in an arbitrary and simplistic manner. Such decisions perpetuate the limbo of environmental deprivation and seclusion where Chrissy and other similar children now deteriorate.

The hearing officer's conclusion holds the local school district responsible for only the day educational program, but the officer thinks the decision will be overturned on appeal because Chrissy so clearly needs the residential service. The school's dilemma is that under the statute's broad definition of special education almost any service required by a severely handicapped person can be labeled "education."

Social workers representing human service agencies have recently become more active participants in the appeals process. These cases demonstrate the continuing effort to shift responsibility for the provision of all necessary services for the 3 to 22 age group to the school districts. Some cases pose legitimate claims. Many reflect the current fiscal crunch and the lack of substantive interagency commitments that bind all agencies to participate in the provisions of a free appropriate public education. Children subject to interagency "turf battles" still tend to fall through the cracks or wait lengthy periods of time for the education or care that will assist them. They can least afford to wait, for they tend to be severely emotionally disturbed or profoundly multihandicapped, the children whose needs are most immediate. Because, as with Chrissy, there is no guaranteed funding for the totality of their program, a residential facility may refuse to accept them and they may remain inappropriately placed in the adult ward of the state hospital.

Other "New Cases"

In the early years of Chapter 766 all of the requests for hearing were filed by parents. Now school systems and human service agencies with legal custody of children are requesting hearings, largely to return to public school programs children who had earlier been placed in expensive private schools. The schools argue they have now developed a "less restrictive" public school placement. The parent is reluctant to return the child and customarily has expert witnesses articulate a "more is better" argument and an argument in favor of a "less stigmatizing" private environment. Public schools often win these cases, as the options they now offer are far superior to the programs they offered earlier. Even though they persuade a hearing officer that they have an appropriate program, they may be forced to continue paying for the private placement if the parent appeals the case to a higher court. The federal law provides that the child remain in the last agreed upon placement pending resolution of all administrative *and* judicial appeals, another unanticipated roadblock in the provisions of free appropriate public education.

Discipline cases.
Disputes concerning discipline problems surface more frequently in 1982, perhaps reflecting society's increasing "get tough" attitude toward deviant behavior. Perhaps because of Massachusetts' long history of local control of education, schools continue to resent intrusions by the parent, the student, and/or the state represented by administrative decisions. In any event, discipline cases evoke the local autonomy issue in its most dramatic form, leading to the closest scrutiny of administrative judgment.

The Law in Evolution

Although the hearing officer typically reviews at least a hundred documents and hears one or two days of testimony, many disputes will ultimately be resolved by a state or federal court. After the decision, the losing party will decide whether or not to file in state or federal court. The choice of forum may well determine the outcome of the case, since different standards of review apply: in state court "substantial evidence" is enough to support a hearing officer's decision, while in federal court there must be a "preponderance of the evidence." A federal court is also required to "allow additional evidence at the request of either party," while state courts, except in rare cases, base their decision solely on the administrative record. Case law is also different. In Massachusetts state court the judge follows the Supreme Judicial Court's decision on retroactive reimbursement,[1] that is, s/he must offer parents retroactive payment for a voluntary private placement when a school's individual educational plan has been found inappropriate and the private placement found appropriate by the hearing officer. The U.S. District Court, on the other hand, has issued inconsistent decisions on this issue.[2]

The federal courts across the country are in the early stages of interpreting the scope of the statute, much as the Bureau was in 1975-76. Not surprisingly, federal decisions are often inconsistent. Most of the cases decided by federal courts have been brought on behalf of individuals. The decisions have been narrowly drawn and the relief tailored to the individual's special education needs. But even where the court has strained to caution future litigants against a general interpretation, the temptation to deal with handicapped children as "classes" remains.

As a seasoned participant in this process, I can easily recognize the simplistic approach to complex issues that some courts are seduced into taking. And however complex the issue may be in its educational, social, political, and fiscal ramifications, some aspects of the law encourage simplistic solutions. For example, the overly broad definition of special education and related services allows one to successfully argue that practically every service a multihandicapped child needs, except for clearly medical ones, is the responsibility of an education agency. Five recent cases involving residential placements essentially reach this conclusion. The children in these cases presented severe handicapping conditions that required education and care in a setting other than the home. In four cases, the court required the school district to provide 24-hour schools. In the fifth case,[3] however, the court found that a community-based "group home" and a school-based program would satisfy the child's educational needs. To my knowledge, this is the only case where the court has treaded ever so gently into the controversy regarding "least restrictive environment" and interagency responsibility. Was it the intent of the proponents of deinstitutionalization that the handicapped child continue to be isolated in 24-hour institutions labeled "schools"? Is the educational establishment willing or able to set up group homes for children who need care in an environment that cannot be provided by their families?

What this federal confusion means for litigants is unpredictability and discomfort at this time. Any attempt to make broad and sweeping generalizations from the existing body of decisions is to my mind premature. And total reliance on the "arbiters," be they hearing officers or federal or state courts, is unfounded. The lack of unanimity will continue until there is a sufficient body of case law that presents precedents so clearly indistinguishable (or clearly distinguishable) as to compel "standard" conclusions. But we cannot expect a solid body of case precedent in the near future. In addition to the conflicting definitions of special education that currently exist even among professionals, lawyers and hearing officers must face conflicting court decisions. To add to the confusion, the Reagan Administration now proposes radically to amend the special education statute, its regulations and the funding formula.

The Hearing Officers

The hearing officer is the most visible actor on the scene of hope, blame, and discomfort that accompanies this particular attempt at educational change. S/he tends to be the spokesperson, the "voice of authority" for a bureaucracy unaccustomed to asserting itself other than in an advisory capacity. The intrusion of courts into the domain of professional educators has forced a somewhat reluctant public agency to realign its priorities and take seriously its rhetoric about "equal education opportunity."

The change in focus will be long debated and largely unresolved. To expect miracles of legal intervention is naive. To expect institutions to change without crisis and chaos is equally naive. The hearing officer has the unique and lonely role of orchestrating the positive and negative aspects of this change: unlike the earlier class action cases, there is no court monitor, no consent decree, no consultant for the otherwise insoluble cases. The hearing officer is armed only with statute, regulations, basic principles of administrative law, fundamental fairness, and one or two decisions that offer precedent. The state education agency contracting for their services offers little or no support. Rather, many educators and the state education agency would like to see all hearings disappear. But the hearings continue, allowing parents and taxpayers to point accusatory fingers at state and local inadequacies, as well as at the general inadequacy of public education.

If any characteristics are common to the 12 current hearing officers, they are an ability to deal with complexity and uncertainty without panic, an excitement about being on the cutting edge of a new law, an ability to empathize with all the participants and the real pressures they are under, and a sincere belief in public education and its promise to benefit all children.

In 1975 a decision was made by the Bureau of Special Education Appeals to hire attorneys as hearing officers. This decision was partly based on a very limited experience with special educators as hearing officers. In hindsight, we can see the original hearing officers began work without sufficient training or supervision. Not surprisingly, their decisions were legally insufficient. My own preference is to hire individuals offering a combination of legal acumen and education expertise. In 1982, such people are not difficult to find in Boston and they are willing to work hard for inadequate compensation.

As in any similar group of individuals, hearing officers have variations in personal style, political alliances, past achievements, and future goals. Some are parents, others are not. Some have taught in public schools, others have only their own brief public education to refer to. Many officers have no pretensions to being perfect or always right. They are aware of the important role they play but also of its intrinsic limitations. They are serious and reflective, with an abundant appreciation of the often tragicomic quality of the dramas which they direct.

They share the tensions and uncertainty of many in this special education arena. At times they demand and do not receive black and white rules of procedure. At times they write six different decisions before they come up with one that "feels right." Parties at hearings probably assume that decision-making is easy for the hearing officers. It is not. More than anyone else, hearing officers are painfully aware of the strengths and limitations of the system, and of the possible ramifications of any one decision.

Hearing officers are not as isolated, immune from pressures, or enamored with their adversarial role as some imagine them to be. Most of them will make all reasonable efforts to resolve a case without a hearing and most will aggressively attempt to leave black and white behind to get at the gray areas in the case. In this pursuit, many of the recent cases have resulted in a compromise type of order. And in some cases hearing officers have conditioned approval of an individual education plan on the willingness of a local school system to conform to modifications and accept technical assistance in program development and monitoring.

The decision to hire attorneys or individuals with legal training was a sound one, I think, despite the controversy that still surrounds the issue. I don't question the ability of educators to make sound educational decisions. But they have not been trained to apply law in a forum that demands a detailed written exposition of one's analysis. The forum also frequently demands an ability to research and analyze increasingly complex legal issues that go far beyond special education law. Consider, for example, a recent case where the issue of retroactive reimbursement for costs of a private placement was raised by a trustee on behalf of a trust fund of which the child was one of the beneficiaries. Or the case where the validity of a waiver of the psychiatrist-client privilege was at issue.

The Decisions

Since 1974, over 150 of the Bureau's 1,000 decisions have been appealed to court. Only five cases have been reversed or modified. The rest have been upheld, dismissed by stipulation or are pending. One reason the rate of reversal is so low is that decisions are well written. As I look back, I can identify three phases in the evolution of decision writing. In the first phase, decisions tended to be brief, related certain facts, exposed little analysis and reached somewhat vague conclusions. As hearing officers realized the inadequacy of this approach, phase two decisions tended towards overkill. Almost anything even remotely relevant was discussed by the hearing officer and s/he took great pains to discuss all the facts and to explain why certain testimony was or was not credible. The conclusions and orders were clear and specific. No longer did we get requests for clarification or accusations that we had failed to consider Dr. X's point of view, but decisions were often overly long and difficult to read. During this phase the attorneys representing parties tended to use the "kitchen sink" approach to evidence.

Phase three decisions are more precise and concise. As the hearing officers became more sophisticated craftsmen, they were able to narrow the issues and weed out irrelevant information. Representation also became more skilled and better prepared. Most decisions now give a brief statement of the history, a precise statement of the issues in dispute, a summary of each party's position, the salient facts, and conclusions that squarely expose the hearing officer's analysis of the law as applied to the facts.

A sense of confidence in methodology, however, does not make its application simple. In 1977-78, reaching the conclusion was generally easy for the hearing officer. At the close of the hearing one generally knew which party had presented the more persuasive case. Now most cases are toss-ups on the facts. The legal argument may predominate. Hearing officers may now waver, trying to balance the interests of the individual against broader concerns: "If I order the school to develop a program for deaf high school students, then 6 to 10 children may benefit. On the other hand, Jenny is doing well where she is. If I move her she may quit school." This balancing act is increasingly common and, one hopes, cases are resolved in such a way that both interests are respected. Although the hearing officer's role is clearly to decide individual cases, it is impossible, and perhaps irresponsible, to close one's eyes to issues of allocation of resources as they become more and more scarce.

Unfortunately for lawyers, then, most decisions now issued offer no valid legal precedent because of the unique facts of each case. However, if decisions fail to create legal precedent, they do succeed in forcing educators to address certain trends that may be guidelines for future practice. Sometimes a decision has spill-over effects—with varying degrees of benefit, depending on one's point of view. For example, one local community expressed reluctance to create any self-contained classes or separate programs for children with learning disabilities. After three or four parents successfully sought private placements for their learning-disabled children, the school changed its position and organized a very successful separate program in collaboration with a neighboring community. The appeals abruptly stopped. In another case, a decision mandating a program for one particular child led to the district identifying 41 other children who could benefit from such a program.

But to pretend that such spill-over is always positive would be wrong. A decision upholding a school's individual education plan for a particular child may be used to deter parents of apparently similar children from pressing their claim. A close decision offering one set of parents private placement may pressure school systems to give in on other cases, when in fact they truly believe that they could serve another child. But these judgment calls are not the Bureau's to make. These are the province of parents, school committees, and their attorneys.

If the participants in the appeals process have learned anything meaningful in these eight years of experience, it is that the adversary hearing need not be the only forum for the resolution of most educational disputes. The lesson is one that most lawyers grasp eventually, as they usually resolve most civil cases out of court. Parties in special education cases have even more incentives than ordinary disputants to resolve cases informally and amicably. The most obvious incentive is the need for parent and school to have an ongoing positive relationship, as they will both ultimately be involved with the child over an extended period of time. Special educators are better at diagnoses than remedies. Programming for particular children depends on trial and error by experimentation, with expectations raised or lowered as the knowledge about the child increases. This trial and error cannot take place without parent-school cooperation.

Although an adversarial process must be available as a means of redressing grievances, bringing finality to disputes, and untangling certain legal knots, mediation is clearly a better way of settling cases. Voluntary agreements are far more likely to be implemented graciously than fiats, and mediation can also be more responsive than hearings to hidden agendas and idiosyncratic concerns.

The Mediation Process

To reduce the adversarial nature of the process, the Bureau of Special Education Appeals developed a pre-hearing stage of mediation. Mediation is used either to prevent the escalation of a dispute or to facilitate its resolution. The state mediator opens lines of communication, clarifies facts, eliminates misconceptions, and proposes compromise solutions. If no resolution is achieved, the mediator prepares the parties for the more formal structure of the hearing by informing them of the appropriate information to submit, clarifying rights and procedures, and answering questions from both parties. One full-time regional mediator is located in each of the Education Department's regional offices. A mediator is assigned to every case where a parent has requested a hearing. These moderators are impartial in the sense that they have no vested interest in either the parents' or the school's position. However, they are not neutral in that they do represent certain interests: those of the child. They are committed to the placement of the child in an appropriate program and ensuring compliance with the law. The Bureau of Special Education Appeals has adopted the position that its mediators cannot reach an agreement for a clearly inappropriate program or for a program which the mediator knows cannot be implemented.

Mediation can achieve the following goals:

- It allows the disputed areas of a child's educational future to be discussed in an informal non-adversarial situation.
- It facilitates speedy delivery of services to the child if the dispute should be resolved at this time.
- Because discussion is informal, several alternative plans for the child may be considered, as opposed to the more structured hearing forum. Under the regulations for the implementation for Chapter 766, the hearing officer has only three choices: to order the placement recommended by the administrator of special education, to order the placement requested by the parents, or to order a third alternative placement which schools and parents will not have been able to discuss.
- Parties who have reached agreement through mediation have generally worked together better and more often on behalf of the child than they did prior to the mediation session, and agreements reached through mediation are implemented more quickly than decisions rendered by the full hearing process.
- The financial and emotional costs of mediation to all parties are far less than those of a hearing procedure. The Bureau saves too, as a mediator can handle roughly twice the caseload of a hearing officer.
- The addition of a mediation step has not increased the length of time involved in the Massachusetts system. This is due to strict adherence by the Bureau to statutory time-lines on the scheduling of a hearing date. The parties have on occasion, however, agreed to postpone a pending hearing in order to continue their mediation efforts.
- Public schools view mediation as an effort by the state not only to resolve the problem but also to give technical assistance to the school. For

example, a hearing officer cannot take the school offical aside to point out problem areas in the child's educational plan, while a mediator can and does. The mediator can also suggest to the school how they may better come into compliance with the law. The hearing officer of course can do this in his decision, but it is usually after the fact.

How Mediation is Begun

When he/she receives an individual education plan, the regional mediator contacts the parties involved to explain mediation and determine whether or not the parties will agree to attempt it. If the parties agree, the representative explains the mediation procedures.

The following people are recommended to be present at the session: the parent(s) and if they so choose, their advocate, attorney and/or specialist; the person(s) from the public school with the authority to agree to alternatives in the educational plan, who can also provide information on the proposed program and its alternatives. The fewer people present, the more effective communication will occur. Although neither party is being asked to abandon their basic beliefs about the child's capabilities and needs, both parties are asked to (a) consider alternatives which could be incorporated into the proposed plan; (b) be aware of the other party's concerns; and (c) be realistic concerning the speed with which programs can and should be implemented.

Function of the Mediator

The mediator does not render a decision on the appropriate program for the child but assists the parties in the development of an acceptable program. If an agreement is reached, it becomes a written document signed by all parties; if no resolution is possible, the mediator will prepare parties for the hearing.

The initial step in a mediation session is to establish procedure, the role of the mediator and the tone and purpose of the session. Next the mediator will conduct a round table discussion to acquaint him/herself with the child's situation and the positions of the parties, and also to acquaint the parties with their respective perceptions of each other. The second phase is one of agreement building. An observant mediator will note points of commonality and areas of flexibility of the parties during the meeting and later will question the parties further on these points.

Conditions for mediation.
Mediation requires an environment where free communication is possible. Parties must be assured that they may exchange information and explore

alternatives without feeling they will be bound at a hearing by what was stated at the session. Accordingly, no verbatim record is made of the mediation session. If memoranda, agreements, or other documents result from the session, they will be retained in a separate file to which the hearing officer will not have access. Communication between mediators and parties will be privileged and not admissible. If any party chooses to have such information presented to the hearing officer, they may do so by offering it in evidence at the hearing.

Mediation techniques.

The mediator will use some of the following techniques in mediation:

1. *Caucus.* This is a meeting with one party alone in order to clarify issues and discuss alternatives in a confidential setting. The mediator will not reveal anything discussed in caucus unless given permission by the party concerned to do so.
2. *Floating Alternatives.* Although both parties are expected to come to a mediation session ready to present alternatives to the proposed plan, the mediator must sometimes suggest alternative courses of action after becoming more familiar with the case.
3. *Technical Assistance.* The mediator will provide information to both parties about the appeals process, Chapter 766 regulations, Bureau policies, advocacy groups, education plan writing, program development, and any other areas which need clarification.

I believe that this area of informal dispute resolution is Massachusetts' greatest contribution to the resolution of disputes in special education and represents an approach that needs to be implemented broadly, but with appropriate care and concern for the needs of the parents and child.

Notes

1. *Amherst-Pelham Regional School District* v. *Massachusetts Department of Education*, 367-Mass. 480.
2. *Blomstrom* v. *Massachusetts Department of Education*, C.A. 80-2577-MA.
3. *Daniel Abrahamson, et al.* v. *Corrine V. Hershman, et al.*, C.A. 80-251B-K (Mass.).

Epilogue

Chapter 766, like P.L. 94-142, the Federal statute, has many radical features. Among them is the requirement that parents be intrinsic to the processes of evaluation, program planning and service delivery for their special needs child. Providing the right to appeal the school's proposed program to an administrative hearing and, ultimately, to the courts, legitimates these rights.

This report has shown that resort to the appeals option has many unanticipated consequences. It quickly becomes legalistic, in part because the hearing proceedings and the decision are subject to judicial review. It is expensive, in money and emotionally, making the participation of even middle income persons difficult. Hence the bias among participants toward wealthier families. But to denigrate its effectiveness because of these unanticipated effects is to ignore the fact that the legal system is largely used for civil cases by well heeled clients using (usually) expensive lawyers. These consequences, then, are unanticipated because they are intrinsic to the American legal system.

The Massachusetts appeals system has become increasingly sophisticated over the eight years since Chapter 766 became operative law. Schools and parents have become more aware of the realities of the law. Hearing officers have become more sophisticated in the nuances of issues, and the lawyers and advocates understand better the issues that lend themselves to clarification through hearings. The hearing has become recognized for what it is: an adversarial confrontation within the context of a legal proceeding, however flexibly it may be conducted. Problems must be phrased in terms of facts, and hearing officers must make difficult decisions between compelling sets of realities.

In Massachusetts in 1982 the realities of the tax revolt may mean increasingly a confrontation between a special needs child's service requirements balanced against the nonhandicapped children's programs in the school system. This has been a continuing concern since Chapter 766, fortunately never realized. The realities of largely fixed local tax bases for the school budget forces reliance on increased state aid for schools in a state that has classically relied heavily on local property taxes for support of schools. This, in turn, will require increased state taxes, an unpopular option. The conflicts surrounding resource allocations have become more severe, and may become more so as inflation drives up the cost of services. The challenge of meeting the needs of handicapped children in the eighties will become ever more challenging.

The cases appearing at appeals hearings often reveal the difficulties of dealing with the ambiguities of requirements in the reform. An example:

The requirement for placement of a special needs child in the least restrictive environment initially led many schools to recommend programs within mainstreamed settings. Thus, learning disabled children would be offered programs divided between regular classes and a resource room. Parents felt these programs confused their children and resulted in relatively little progress. (See Chapter 9.) They saw their child change when placed in a substantially separate program only with other learning disabled children. Hearing officers, on comparing the child's progress in the two settings, soon began to order the segregated placement, arguing this was consistent with the appropriateness standard and thus was the least restrictive option for the child at that time. This position significantly influenced placement practices, increasing the number of substantially separate programs, since these could be implemented by schools with their own resources.

When the child's and family's needs fall within the province of several state agencies, coordinated programs are very difficult to order by special education based hearing officers. Mental health and vocational rehabilitation agencies used the mandate of Chapter 766 to withdraw 100% state and federally funded services from children under 22 years of age, though they had been served prior to the reform, because the schools had been assigned responsibility for assuring provision of these services. Blue Shield, as a major third party insurer, has taken a similar position that services required by the child's educational plan are not reimbursable to schools or through private practitioners. They have lobbied successfully against legislative measures that would alter this interpretation.

It seems hard to imagine it was the intent of the Congress or the Massachusetts legislature to have local schools assume the costs of providing services already funded through state and federally funded agencies resulted in this shift of responsibility onto primarily locally funded schools.

The appeals system in Massachusetts now has to face very difficult issues, such as "ordering" the Department of Mental Health to share costs for residential placements when severely emotionally disturbed children, such as Chrissy (see Chapter 19), require appropriate residential treatment outside an adult psychiatric ward which has no educational services. The result is no action, since one bureaucracy cannot effectively order another bureaucracy to provide funds or services. This pooling of resources can only occur through cooperative arrangements, unless the courts or the legislature choose to interpret the parameters of responsibility of the specialized agencies. Lodged within the Division of Special Education, hearing officers cannot even marshall the resources of the other perograms in the Department of Education. Yet they are charged with defining the program appropriate to a child, and especially in the areas of non-instructional services, such as residential care, physical or occupational therapy or psychotherapy. They must order services to be provided, and these must be paid by the schools. The effect of this comprehensive mandate is to force schools to duplicate services available elsewhere, at high costs.

It is no wonder that an active appeals system such as that available in Massachusetts is least popular among local school district staffs, or even within the state bureaucracy. As a highly visible bureau, forced to make difficult decisions about appropriate school practices, they antagonize the local districts, which are the natural constituency of this bureaucracy. Willynilly, they also force a greater measure of visibility and accountability onto the state bureaucracy and can alter its views of and enforcement of acceptable practices.

Judicial review of decisions provides opportunities for the court system to clarify ambiguities in the special education reform, the rights of children and their parents to services, and most particularly, the role(s) of agencies which deliver services to these children and their families. Decisions from the Federal appeals courts and the Supreme Court will guide schools, parents, and hearing officers, and define our society's responsibilities to handicapped children.

Advocacy groups have failed to consider the possibilities of altering school practices by using the administrative hearing to clarify knotty issues. This strategy requires a careful and judicious selection of cases. Issues such as eligibility for 12 month programming or an in-class interpreter could be addressed by hearings. The resulting decisions could be used to influence the stated development of guidelines for practice by local districts at a considerably faster rate than waiting for the courts' decisions.

While one may argue that the hearings system may not be effective since it has largely served wealthier parents seeking private school placements, this argument fails to understand the ripple effects of the decisions on school practices, a process which requires more thorough documentation.

The appeals hearing also seems to be an agent for changing school systems' practices, directly when cases are lost, and indirectly when schools view their own practices in the light of decisions in particular cases. The classmates of a seriously mentally retarded adolescent who is awarded vocational training will also benefit from this program. Hopefully, once implemented within the system, they become institutionalized. Although no one has yet documented whether changes required by a decision for a particular child persist beyond the needs of that decision or that particular child.

School systems, viewing the large number of decisions that ordered private special needs placements for learning disabled children, instituted substantially segregated classes for these children to forestall appeals based on the presumed inadequacies of resource room mainstreamed programs. Some systems consciously copied the content of the programs of the particular private schools.

The appeals option, then, is an instrument for ensuring the accountable behavior of a social institution. The limitations we have cited are mainly indicative of the difficulties of dealing with our legal system and bureaucratized schools. Recognizing these limitations, we have argued that the states and local school districts must cultivate more informal negotiation-based procedures for resolving these disputes as they develop. A mediation option in Massachusetts has successfully reduced the number of potential hearings. Clearer recognition is required by professional organizations and local and state education bureaucracies that informal negotiation, instituted early, when dissatisfaction seems to be surfacing, would help parents and school staff learn to talk more effectively with each other. Although active negotiation rather than an adversarial hearing appears to be the procedure of choice, it must be structured carefully to ensure the parents are not manipulated or pressured. The procedure must enhance the intent of the parents' rights provisions.

Parents now have a right to participate. School staff must learn to honor that right, and more importantly, learn to develop collegial relationships of mutual support so the joint efforts can enhance the child's optimal use of his or her available talents, and so benefit the person each is seeking to help—the special needs child.

Glossary

appeal. One of several recourses open to parents who are not satisfied with the educational plan provided by their school district and reject it. If parents choose to appeal the plan, an administrative hearing must be offered. Alternatives to resolve the dispute include mediation, informal negotiation, or providing the child with private services at the parents' expense.

Bureau of Special Education Appeals. The Bureau in the Division of Special Education of the Massachusetts Department of Education responsible for resolution of disputes between schools and parents. Under Chapter 766, the Bureau is responsible for providing parents and schools with information on the appeals process, for notifying parties of their rights under the law, for attempting to mediate the disputes, and for scheduling a hearing if either party wishes it. The Bureau receives pertinent materials on the case from both parties, which it passes on to a state employed hearing officer to conduct the hearing and write the decision. The Bureau has a representative in each educational region of the state charged with conducting mediations as a first step toward resolution of the dispute.

CET. See Core Evaluation Team.

Chapter 766. The Massachusetts law, passed in 1972 and implemented in 1974, reformed the rights of special needs children for a free, appropriate public education. This law identifies special needs children, ages 3-21 years, on the basis of their poor school performance and need for special services, rather than through diagnostic labels. It requires parent participation in all phases of referral, evaluation, and program planning for a special needs child, and offers the hearing system as a means for parents to appeal programs with which they are dissatisfied. It makes the school district responsible to assure the delivery of the services required by the child, and to purchase them if appropriate public services are not available. Similar federal legislation, The Education of All Handicapped Children Act, or P.L. 94-142, was passed in 1975.

compliance hearing. If, after a hearing, the parents feel the school is not complying with the hearing officer's order, they may request a compliance hearing. If a Bureau investigation substantiates a parent's complaint of noncompliance, it will schedule a compliance hearing to review the complaint, and seek procedures to ensure compliance with the decision's order.

consent decree. When a party to a civil court case concedes the issue(s) without trial, coming instead to a negotiated agreement. A consent decree legally binds both parties to the agreement. The consent decrees in the Pennsylvania (*PARC*) and Washington, D.C. (*Mills*) court cases were the basis for extending due process specifically to handicapped children excluded from school, and laid the groundwork for the legislative reform of special education practices.

core. See: Core Evaluation Meeting; Core Evaluation Team.

Core Evaluation Meeting. Also known as "core." When a child has been referred for special services under Chapter 766, s/he is evaluated over a 30-day period by a multi-discipline team, which examines the child's current educational, psychological, physical, social and emotional status. Parents are invited to a Core Evaluation Meeting with members of that team to review the findings and sketch out the essentials of an individual educational plan appropriate to meet the child's special needs. See also: Core Evaluation Team; Evaluation; Individual Educational Plan.

Core Evaluation Team. Also known as "CET." The members of the team charged with evaluating a child's need for special services, and for specifying those services in the form of an individual educational plan. This team includes a chairperson, designated by the school district's Director of Special Education; a "registered nurse, or social worker with a Master's degree in social work, or a certified guidance or adjustment counselor"; a "certified psychologist or one licensed to practice in Massachusetts"; "a physician who is licensed to practice in Massachusetts" or in another state with comparable requirements; a teacher who has recently had the child in his/her class; the child's parent; and the "primary person, if any, who will be assisting the teacher in implementing the educational plan," for example, a resource room teacher or tutor. Parents may also bring outside professionals to the conference at their own expense, and a child over age 14 may be invited to attend. School staff converted this underlying concept of a core of required disciplines on the assessment team to a verb, "coring" a child; the child was "cored," etc. See also: Core Evaluation Meeting; Evaluation; Individual Educational Plan.

decision. The written and legally binding outcome of a hearing. The Massachusetts Administrative Procedures Act requires some written record of every hearing, to include the hearing's outcome and the hearing officer's "statement of reasons." The hearing also contains the order, which specifies what each party is legally bound to do.

The Education of All Handicapped Children Act. Also known as (Federal) P.L. 94-142. Passed by Congress in 1975, this law mandates rights for handicapped students and their parents similar to those specified by Massachusetts' Chapter 766, assuring each handicapped student access to a free, publicly supported education appropriate to their needs, and guaranteeing their parents the right to participate in the development of such programs, with recourse to a state hearing.

educational plan. See: Individual Educational Plan.

evaluation. The determination of whether or not a child requires special education services. A multi-discipline team has 30 working school days to develop a complete evaluation, to include: an assessment of the child's educational status; a statement by a teacher who has recently taught the child; a health assessment; a psychological assessment; and the parents' choice of either a home visit or an interview at the school. Evaluations must also include statements of how these assessments were performed, and the diagnostic significance of the findings for the particular child. Once the evaluation is completed, the evaluation team plus the child's parents and outside professionals invited by the parents form the "Core Evaluation Team," which writes the individual educational plan, specifying the services to be provided to the child at a core evaluation meeting. See also: Core Evaluation Meeting; Core Evaluation Team; Individual Educational Plan.

expert witness. An independent professional expert who testifies on the parents' or school's behalf. Expert witnesses might include private practice psychologists, psychiatrists, physicians, or staff members of a special needs school or a clinic. They might testify specifically about the child's medical, psychiatric, or educational history; offer specialized knowledge of the child's particular learning or emotional problem(s); or present the results of sophisticated tests or evaluations conducted privately. See: Independent Assessment.

50% random decisions sample. A sample of half the decisions written between the implementation of the hearing system in September, 1974, and March 1, 1977, selected at random, i.e., every other decision was included in the study sample. This sample included 161 decisions in this study.

grandfathered children. Children who had already been placed in programs outside the public schools by state agencies (e.g., Department of Education, Department of Public Welfare) at the time of the effective date of Chapter 766.

hearing. A formal administrative procedure whereby an impartial, state-appointed hearing officer hears presentations from parents and school district representatives regarding the appropriateness of the child's educational plan. See: Appeal; Chapter 766.

hearing officer. The impartial person appointed by the state to hear the presentations of both parties to an educational dispute and render a judgment legally binding on both parties. Massachusetts hearing officers are usually full-time state employees attached to the Bureau of Special Education Appeals in the Division of Special Education, and are usually either lawyers or have some legal training/experience. Special education knowledge is not required for this position, though most officers in Massachusetts are familiar with the field.

home problem. A term used by the schools to designate problem(s) of the child they consider primarily emotional, caused by the parents or the home environment, hence not their programmatic responsibility. Parents occasionally accused schools of failing to provide adequate educational services by claiming that the child's problems in school were due to "home problems," thereby seeking to justify why there was no valid *educational* reason to offer a child, say, a residential placement.

IEP. See: Individual Educational Plan.

independent assessment or **independent evaluation.** Evaluation of a child's special needs by an "independent" professional hired by the parents to check the findings of the public school. These were from clinics or were private practitioners.

Individual Educational Plan. Also known as "IEP." The plan prepared by the parents and the (Core) Evaluation Team at the Core Evaluation Meeting, specifying the special needs of the child, short- and long-term goals appropriate to meet these needs, and the services required to be provided. The goals must be specified in measurable objectives, stated in behavioral terms, so the child's progress can be evaluated. A plan includes instructional services and such related services as counselling, physical, speech or occupational therapy. See also: Core Evaluation; Core Evaluation Team; Evaluation.

Leaving School Cases. A case in which a parent wishes his/her child to leave public school and enter a private program, but retains the child in public school until the hearing's decision has been reached. Leaving School cases accounted for about one-sixth of the cases in this study sample.

mainstreaming. Also known as "integration" of the child with non-special needs children, or placement in the least restrictive alternative. The theory is that a special needs child should have as much contact with non-special needs children as possible.

mediation. A first level informal process conducted with the agreement of the parents and schools by a regionally deployed state education mediator who initiates the contact upon being informed the parent rejected the educational plan. The parties meet together to clarify the issues in dispute and settle issues when possible. If the dispute cannot be resolved, the mediator prepares the parties for the procedures involved in the hearing. The state claims 90% of the disputes are resolved at this informal proceeding.

P.L. 94-142. See: The Education for All Handicapped Children Act.

Private School Cases. Cases in which the parents placed their child in a private special needs school prior to the hearing in which they were requesting this placement.

program prototype. Chapter 766 eliminated the use of diagnostic labels and sorted children by the proportion of weekly time they spent in special education services. The range was from less than 10% to more than 60% time in special education services. The latter prototype (more than 60%) were considered substantially separate programs or special classes, in traditional terms. They were defined as follows:

502.1 A program prototype in which the child spends less than 10% of his/her school time in special education services.

502.2 A state designation for a child spending less than 25% of his/her school time receiving special services.

502.3 A state designation for a child spending more than 25% but less than 60% of his/her school time receiving special services.

502.4 A state designation for a child spending more than 60% of his/her school time receiving special services; also considered a substantially separate program; a special class.

502.5 A state designation for children placed in out-of-district, day-school programs for special needs children.

502.6 A state designation for children placed in residential (24 hour care) programs.

State Advisory Commission (SAC). A group constituted equally of education professionals and concerned citizens, with representation from the six education regions of the state. Parents could appeal an adverse decision to this body.

Staying-in-School Cases. Cases in which the parents sought alterations in their child's public school program.

substantially separate program. A program prototype in which children spent more than 60% of their time in school each week in special education programs. More usually, this meant the child was in a special class.

References

Abeson, A., Bolick, N., & Hass, W. *A Primer on Due Process*. Reston, Va.: Council for Exceptional Children, 1975.

Appeals News. 1977-78, #1. Boston: Massachusetts Department of Education, Bureau of Special Education Appeals.

Appeals News. 1978, #3. Boston: Massachusetts Department of Education, Bureau of Special Education Appeals.

Bateman, B. *So You're Going to a Hearing*. Chicago: Hubbard, 1980.

Brown v. *Board of Education*, 347 U.S. 483 (1954).

Budoff, M. Engendering change in special education practices. *Harvard Educational Review*, 1975, *45*, 507-526.

Budoff, M. Implementing due process safeguards: From the user's viewpoint. *Criteria Study 4: Developing Criteria for Evaluating the Due Process Procedural Safeguards Provisions of Public Law 94-142*. The United States Office of Education, Bureau of Education of the Handicapped, 1978.

Budoff, M., and Orenstein, A. *Human Response to Involvement in Due Process Proceedings*. Cambridge, Mass.: Research Institute for Educational Problems. Reprint No. 115, 1979.

Budoff, M., and Orenstein, A. Special education appeals hearings: Are they fair and are they helping? *Exceptional Education Quarterly*, 1981, *1*, 37-46.

Budoff, M., Orenstein, A., & Abramson, J. Due process hearings: Appeals for appropriate public school programs. *Exceptional Children*, 1981, *48*.

Budoff, M., and Weissboch, S. Responses of parents to mediation in the due process system. Cambridge, Mass.: Research Institute for Educational Problems. Reprint No. 122, 1979.

Daynard, C. *Due Process: The Appeals Hearing Under Chapter 766*. Unpublished dissertation, Boston Univiversity, 1980.

Fuller, L. Mediation - Its forms and functions. *Southern California Law Review*, 1971, *44*, 305.

Goss v. *Lopez*, 419 U.S. 565 (1975).

In re Gault, 387 U.S. 1 (1967).

Kirp, D., Buss, W., and Kuriloff, P. Legal reform of special education: Empirical studies and procedural proposals. *California Law Review*, 1974, *62*, 40-155.

Kotin, L., and Eager, N.B. *Due Process in Special Education: A Legal Analysis*. Cambridge, Mass.: Research Institute for Educational Problems, 1977.

Kuriloff, P., Kirp, D., & Buss, W. *When Handicapped Children Go to Court: Assessing the Impact of the Legal Reform of Special Education in Pennsylvania.* National Institute of Education, 1979.

Merton, R.K., Fiske, M., & Kendall, P. L. *The Focussed Interview.* Glencoe, Ill.: The Free Press, 1956.

Mills v. *District of Columbia Board of Education,* 348 F. Supp. 866 (D.D.C., 1972).

Mintzer, B. The role of the lawyer in special education appeals hearings. In: *Appeal News,* Fall, 1978, #3. Boston: Massachusetts Department of Education.

Mitchell, S. *Mediation in Due Process: The Connecticut Experience in Special Education.* Unpublished manuscript prepared for the Connecticut State Department of Education, 1977.

Orenstein, A. *Chapter 766: Implementation in Two Communities.* Final report to CERI/OECD, Paris, 1976.

Pennsylvania Association of Retarded Children v. *Commonwealth of Pennsylvania,* 343 F. Supp. 279 (E.D. Pa., 1972).

Tinker v. *Des Moines Independent School District,* 393 U.S. 503 (1969).

Turnbull, H.R., and Turnbull, A.P. *Free Appropriate Public Education: Law and Implementation.* Denver: Love Publishing Company, 1978.

Weatherley, R. *Reforming Special Education: Policy Implementation from State Level to Street Level.* Cambridge, Mass.: MIT Press, 1979.

Weatherley, R., & Lipsky, M. Street-level bureaucrats and institutional innovation: Implementing special education reform. *Harvard Educational Review,* 1977, *47,* 171-197.

West Virginia State Board of Education v. *Barnette,* 319 U.S. 624 (1943).

Yoshida, R. Developing assistance linkages for parents of handicapped children. Xerox, Office of Special Education Programs, U.S. Department of Education, 1979.

Yurchack, M., Bryk, A., & DeSanctis, J. *Chapter 766: Coordinated Case Studies.* Cambridge, Mass.: Huron Institute, 1982.

DATE DUE

DEMCO 38-297